WordPress® 24-Hour Trainer

Continues

WordPress® 24-Hour Trainer

WordPress® 24-Hour Trainer

George Plumley

Wiley Publishing, Inc.

WordPress® 24-Hour Trainer

Published by
Wiley Publishing, Inc.
10475 Crosspoint Boulevard
Indianapolis, IN 46256
www.wiley.com

Copyright © 2010 by Wiley Publishing, Inc., Indianapolis, Indiana

ISBN: 978-0-470-55458-6

Manufactured in the United States of America

10 9 8 7 6 5 4 3

Library of Congress Control Number: 2009937281

This book is dedicated to my family: to my wife Kim and daughters Grace and Ella (thanks for being so patient the whole summer of 2009), and to my parents, Adelaide and Stan and my sister Patricia.

Credits

Executive Editor
Carol Long

Project Editor
Ed Connor

Technical Editor
Mike Little

Production Editor
Daniel Scribner

Copy Editor
Kim Cofer

Editorial Director
Robyn B. Siesky

Editorial Manager
Mary Beth Wakefield

Marketing Manager
David Mayhew

Production Manager
Tim Tate

Vice President and Executive Group Publisher
Richard Swadley

Vice President and Executive Publisher
Barry Pruett

Associate Publisher
Jim Minatel

Project Coordinator, Cover
Lynsey Stanford

Compositor
James D. Kramer, Happenstance Type-O-Rama

Proofreader
Nancy C. Hanger, Windhaven

Indexer
Robert Swanson

Cover Image
© istockphoto/Daft_Lion_Studio

About the Author

Acknowledgments

George Plumley is a web developer living on Vancouver Island, Canada. After doing graduate work in philosophy at York University, Washington University in St. Louis, and Rutgers he went on to web development in 1993. He's been working with various content management systems ever since, and then in 2006 discovered the joys of WordPress. He also runs the WordPress help site www.seehowtwo.com.

Acknowledgments

I want to thank Carol Long for sending the tweet that got this all started and for being a great Acquisitions Editor/hockey mom through the entire process; the whole Wiley team, in particular the editorial staff headed by Ed Connor, Kim Cofer who made sure my that's and which's were right way round and my voice was active, and Mike Little for his indispensable technical editing; Doris Michaels for pointing me to my wonderful agent, Carole Jelen, who's been so supportive; friends like Karen Hollowell who got me addicted to 3x5 note cards and was my Canadian/American cultural attaché, Ann Douglas for running the mother of all author support lines, Peggy Richardson for her insights into the art of writing books and for doing some research, and Angela Crocker for all her support; the programmers who make WordPress possible, and the WordPress community, from whom I've learned and continue to learn so much; and finally I want to thank all my clients over the years who, by asking great questions, have helped me learn to explain things more clearly.

Contents

Contents

Contents

Contents

Contents

Contents

Contents

Contents

Introduction

While WordPress is currently the world's number one blogging software, **this is not a book about blogging**. In *WordPress 24-Hour Trainer,* you learn how to use this open-source software to build and maintain a website, whether it's a blog, has a blogging section, or has nothing at all to do with blogging. I treat WordPress as a content management system — a system you can customize in a number of ways to make it do exactly what you need.

Whether you're building a website for yourself or for someone else, you need to be concerned about two things: the ease of setting up the site and of maintaining it. This book will show you how WordPress offers both.

Website owners also face two growing challenges: the demand for ever-changing features and for ever-growing content. Both require a framework that makes the expansion of content fast and easy, and accommodates technological change quickly and easily. WordPress is well-positioned to meet these challenges and that, combined with its increasing popularity, makes it software well worth learning.

Since I began building websites exclusively with WordPress, I've noticed an important change in my clients: they look forward to updating and expanding their sites. When changing some text, let alone adding a new page, is like pulling teeth, you're less likely to do it. With WordPress, not only are my clients making their own changes, but they're excited about it and that's also made them more involved in their sites. Instead of having a site built and then sitting back, my clients are actively thinking about what they can change or add to make their sites better because they can go in and do it themselves when the thought strikes them.

That's the real power of WordPress: putting more control in the hands of the website owner.

Who This Book Is For

This book is for beginners at two levels: those who've never built a website and those who've never built a WordPress website.

This book also assumes that you're using what's sometimes called the self-hosted version of WordPress, which means that you or someone else has installed WordPress on your hosting provider's server. The self-hosted version is not to be confused with the free, hosted blogs you can sign up for at WordPress.com. While much of *WordPress 24-Hour Trainer* applies to the hosted version (how to enter content, how to upload photos and documents, how to layout content, and so on) the important difference is that you have very limited choices to customize blogs on WordPress.com.

What This Book Covers

As of the writing of this book, the most recent version of WordPress is 2.8 and I cover the latest features available in it. However, anyone running 2.7 (apart from being strongly advised to upgrade) will find only small differences with the interface and most of the features are the same as well. Users of 2.6 (you should upgrade too) will still get a lot of out of the book, though visually the interface is different and not all of the features will be available. Still, the basics of organizing and entering content are all there.

You'll learn how to set up a WordPress website from scratch, using the default features of the software. Each lesson covers a specific set of topics, so you can follow the lessons in order but you can easily dip into any one of them to refresh your memory. Later in the book I cover some customization of the look of the site as well as the addition of plugins, which are bits of code that add extra features to WordPress.

Keep in mind, this book is not what I call an extended manual. It does not aim to cover every feature of WordPress. Instead you'll learn how to make the software work for you in real-world situations, and we do that through showing you not just the basics, but the tips and tricks that make things as simple as possible. We do that both in print and on video; because seeing something done in real-time makes things clearer and helps reinforce the concept.

How This Book Is Structured

This book consists of short lessons covering tasks you'll typically need when building and maintaining a website with WordPress. This means that not every feature of WordPress is covered — I'll provide links to places on the Web where you can get that kind of detailed reference material. The goal here is to show you the key skills you'll use every day.

The 37 lessons are grouped into themed sections:

❑ **Section 1: Before You Start** — Get to know how WordPress thinks about content and what planning you need to do before starting your site.

❑ **Section 2: Firing Up WordPress** — Instructions for installing the software, an overview of the administration interface, and the basic settings you'll need to get going.

❑ **Section 3: Working with Written Content** — Entering your content and publishing it.

❑ **Section 4: Working with Media Content** — The ins and outs of uploading images, video, documents, etc. and using them on your site.

❑ **Section 5: Managing Your Content** — Navigating through various types of content, editing it, moving it around.

❑ **Section 6: Making Your Site Social** — Dealing with links, comments, RSS feeds, social networking, and multiple users.

❑ **Section 7: Customizing the Look of Your Site** — Some basics for making the site look exactly the way you want using CSS style sheets.

❑ **Section 8: Becoming Search Engine Friendly** — Basic techniques for optimizing your site so that you get indexed in the best possible way.

❑ **Section 9: Housekeeping Chores** — Keeping an eye on your site statistics, making sure your software is up to date, and getting into good backup habits.

❑ **Section 10: Extending WordPress** — Extending the power and possibilities of WordPress using these addon bits of software.

When you're finished reading the book and watching the DVD, you'll find lots of support in the p2p forums, as you'll see in a moment, but there's also the WordPress community on the Web. Hundreds of thousands of people around the world are using this software and a lot of them give back in so many ways. It's a spirit that's reflected in the quality of WordPress and its continued improvement.

From the people who created and maintain WordPress, to the people who make plugins and themes, to the people who write about WordPress on their blogs or contribute to the official and unofficial forums, there are thousands of bright minds giving back to the community with code, ideas, fixes, and more. You never have to feel you're alone when you're using WordPress. I like to think of it as a world-wide 24-hour help line. Whether you need help or can offer help, you're welcome any time.

Instructional Videos On DVD

As I mentioned earlier, learning is often enhanced by seeing in real-time what's being taught, which is why most lessons in the book have a corresponding video tutorial on the accompanying DVD. And of course it's vital that you play along at home — fire up WordPress and try out what you read in the book and watch on the videos.

Conventions

To help you get the most from the text and keep track of what's happening, we've used a number of conventions throughout the book.

> **Boxes like this one hold important, not-to-be forgotten information that is directly relevant to the surrounding text.**

Notes, tips, hints, tricks, and asides to the current discussion are offset and placed in italics like this.

 References like this one point you to the DVD to watch the instructional video that accompanies a given lesson.

As for styles in the text:

❑ We *highlight* new terms and important words when we introduce them.

❑ We show URLs and code within the text like so: `persistence.properties`.

❑ We present code in the following way:

```
We use a monofont type for code examples.
```

Errata

We make every effort to ensure that there are no errors in the text or in the code. However, no one is perfect, and mistakes do occur. If you find an error in one of our books, like a spelling mistake or faulty piece of code, we would be very grateful for your feedback. By sending in errata you may save another reader hours of frustration and at the same time you will be helping us provide even higher quality information.

To find the errata page for this book, go to www.wrox.com and locate the title using the Search box or one of the title lists. Then, on the Book Search Results page, click the Errata link. On this page you can view all errata that has been submitted for this book and posted by Wrox editors.

> *A complete book list including links to errata is also available at* www.wrox.com/misc-pages/ booklist.shtml.

If you don't spot "your" error on the Errata page, click the Errata Form link and complete the form to send us the error you have found. We'll check the information and, if appropriate, post a message to the book's errata page and fix the problem in subsequent editions of the book.

p2p.wrox.com

For author and peer discussion, join the P2P forums at p2p.wrox.com. The forums are a web-based system for you to post messages relating to Wrox books and related technologies and interact with other readers and technology users. The forums offer a subscription feature to e-mail you topics of interest of your choosing when new posts are made to the forums. Wrox authors, editors, other industry experts, and your fellow readers are present on these forums.

At http://p2p.wrox.com you will find a number of different forums that will help you not only as you read this book, but also as you develop your own applications. To join the forums, just follow these steps:

1. Go to p2p.wrox.com and click the Register link.

2. Read the terms of use and click Agree.

3. Complete the required information to join as well as any optional information you wish to provide and click Submit.

4. You will receive an e-mail with information describing how to verify your account and complete the joining process.

> *You can read messages in the forums without joining P2P, but in order to post your own messages, you must join.*

Once you join, you can post new messages and respond to messages other users post. You can read messages at any time on the Web. If you would like to have new messages from a particular forum e-mailed to you, click the Subscribe to this Forum icon by the forum name in the forum listing.

For more information about how to use the Wrox P2P, be sure to read the P2P FAQs for answers to questions about how the forum software works as well as many common questions specific to P2P and Wrox books. To read the FAQs, click the FAQ link on any P2P page.

Part I: Before You Start

1

Thinking Like WordPress

WordPress provides you with the tools to organize your website content, but those tools function in specific ways, just as one type of word processing software has its specific buttons for creating, say, lists. But there's a difference between knowing which button to press to create a list and thinking about ways you can use lists in your documents. That's what this chapter is about: learning to think like WordPress so that you can organize your content in an efficient and flexible manner right from the start, and be able to use it in new and useful ways later.

Dynamic vs. Static Websites

When you open a website in your browser, you see a single page filled with text and media (graphics, photos, video, and so on) like the page in a magazine or newspaper is a single entity made up of text and images. But what you see in a browser window is created from a series of instructions: the HTML code. So ultimately the HTML is the single entity behind what you see onscreen; the equivalent of the printed page.

However, there's an important difference between an HTML page and a printed page. The HTML that's fed to your browser may be a single entity when it arrives at the browser, but it may or may not be a single entity sitting on the server waiting for browsers to retrieve it, like a magazine on a newsstand waiting to be purchased. The HTML may be made up of chunks of code that get assembled into a whole in that split second when the browser pulls it off the shelf.

That's the difference between dynamic and static web pages. Static pages are complete sets of HTML waiting to be retrieved, whereas dynamic pages are chunks of HTML that are assembled at the moment of retrieval into a single entity that's displayed in your browser (some systems store the most recent static version of a dynamically created page to keep the server from being overworked, but ultimately the browser pages were created dynamically).

What I want you to take away from this lesson in particular, but the book in general, is to reject static thinking in favor of dynamic. You might have a vision right now for the content of a particular page on your website, but if you learn to view the content in chunks, there may be ways to use part of that content on another page as well. *Dynamic thinking* means you want to keep that chunk of content separate and reusable, not welded to the other content.

Content Management Systems

Creating HTML pages dynamically is one half of what a content management system (CMS) does: it takes chunks of code (your content) and pieces them together into a single HTML page. The other function of a CMS is to provide an easy way for you, the user, to manage all those chunks of content.

Managing content does not just mean allowing you to enter text or upload images; it also means making it easy for you to determine the relationships between chunks of content. Selecting a category for the article you're working on, for example, tells the CMS to assemble that chunk in a particular way when someone on the Internet requests a page on your website.

Everybody understands the role of a CMS when it comes to managing content: it saves having to know HTML coding. But why not just have the CMS manage the content of individual HTML pages? All this assembling business seems like a lot of extra work. If you had a five-page website that never changed, that might be true. But suppose, even on a five-page website, that you decided you didn't like the top section or header that appears on all the pages of your site. Although a CMS for static pages would make it easy to change, you'd still need to change the graphics on all five pages separately, because they're all individual, physical pieces of coding. Now imagine that task on a site with five hundred pages or five thousand! Even with search-and-replace capabilities you would need to upload all five thousand pages back onto the server to replace the old version, then do it all again for the next change. Ouch!

By separating the content of individual HTML pages into chunks, a CMS offers tremendous flexibility. Say you wanted three thousand of your pages to have a different kind of header than the other two thousand. Easy, with a CMS. What if your business partner decides that your line of five hundred different wuzzbuzzes should be categorized under buzz instead of wuzz? Easy, with a CMS.

We're always being told to embrace change, and one of the advantages of a website over print is that it allows you to change things as much as you want, as often as you want. The advantage of using a CMS instead of manually creating manual or dynamic web pages is that the managing of change is much easier and more flexible, which is exactly what WordPress does.

WordPress as a CMS

Even if you get the bit about dynamic thinking and managing chunks of content, you might still be asking yourself: isn't WordPress blogging software? Yes, and blogging software is nothing more than a CMS that's geared toward a type of website structure—the blog. Real estate CMSs, for example, are set up to manage the kind of structure and content that you typically see on a real estate site. Online stores are managed by CMSs that organize content into catalogues or what we call shopping carts.

But I don't want a blog, you say, so why would I use WordPress for my website? Fair question. Part of the answer is that you could use any CMS to build any website; it's a matter of how much work it would take to do it, how much customization, how much training to use the interface in a way it was not intended, and so on. The rest of the answer is that WordPress's design — the simplicity and the flexibility — make it an ideal CMS for a huge variety of uses. Yes, there will need to be creative thinking, sometimes add-on software, sometimes customization of the coding, but if that weren't needed, we'd be talking about a custom CMS for every website.

The point is that all websites have a lot of common elements that may have different names and different functions, but from the standpoint of HTML coding they operate in basically the same way. For instance, I need a page full of testimonials whereas you need a page of all your current specials. If a testimonial and a special are the chunks of content, all we need the CMS to do is assemble our chunks into whole pages. Your header and footer may be very different in look and content from mine, but we both need a header and a footer. A good CMS could care less which is which—it just assembles and manages, easily and efficiently. Like WordPress does.

How WordPress Assembles Pages

Three basic structures in WordPress interact to create HTML pages: the *engine*, the *theme*, and the *database* (where content is stored). What I call the engine is the set of files that perform the tasks of storing, retrieving, and assembling content. The database is where the content is stored and the theme is made up of template files that provide instructions to the engine about what to retrieve and how to assemble it, as I've tried to illustrate in Figure 1-1.

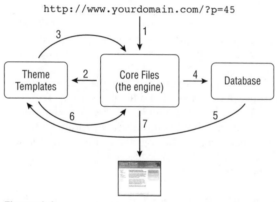

Figure 1-1

The web address you type into a browser window goes to the WordPress engine and tells it which template file to look for in the theme. The engine then reads the template file and follows the instructions about what chunks of content to retrieve. Depending on the complexity of the template, there may be dozens of chunks to be located in the database where they're stored (technically, not all chunks are physically stored in the database, but at least the information on how to find them is stored there). Having found the content, the engine then assembles the chunks according to the template's instructions and you see the result as the HTML page in your browser. And of course all of this has happened in a split second (or two).

Why Separate Is Good

You saw earlier why it's important that a CMS keep form (design and structure) and content (text and media files) separate, and now you're seeing the particular power of the way WordPress achieves this. Remember that earlier example of wanting three thousand pages to have one header and two thousand pages a different header? Depending on exactly how WordPress generates those pages, you might have to add only one template file to your theme to accomplish the change.

If you want to see a dramatic example of how the separation of form and content works on the Web, visit a site called CSS Zen Garden (`www.csszengarden.com`). You can instantly switch between dozens of incredibly different looks, all presenting exactly the same content.

But separating form and content isn't the only useful kind of separation that WordPress employs. It also separates the form from what I've called the WordPress engine — the set of files that do the actual assembling and managing. That engine is completely separate from the theme and the content, which is a good thing from a number of standpoints, the most important of which is the ability to easily update the engine.

Software of any kind is constantly being given new features, strengthened for security, made more efficient, and so on. If you had to completely redo your theme every time the engine needed an update, it would be very inefficient, just as having to redo your website content because of a new structure or look would be inefficient. As I said earlier, WordPress at its heart is a set of three separate structures — the engine, the theme, and the content (in a database) — each of which can be tweaked, updated, or completely replaced, all independently.

There's a fourth separate structure to WordPress that is entirely optional: plugins. These are bits of extra code that you literally plug into the WordPress system and they provide additional functionality, from letting people rate the content on your site to automatically creating tweets on Twitter.

Sometimes people ask why they don't just incorporate the plugins into the engine, but that would be defeating the whole purpose of this elegant and flexible system. To begin with, plugins are meant to address specific needs. Why clutter the engine with features that not everyone uses? Sometimes a plugin is so useful to everyone that it is eventually incorporated into the engine, but most plugins aren't like that. Also, the more complex the engine, the better the chance things will break down. Keep the engine simple and add on extras as you need them. I have some WordPress sites with only two plugins, and others have dozens.

Another reason for keeping extra features as plugins is that there can be many variations of a plugin, each one serving the needs of a group of users. A good example would be plugins for photos — some are very simple, some are very complex, some work better than others. Having a choice of those plugins, rather than being stuck with only one, is another important advantage.

How WordPress Manages Content

Very easily, thank you. Like any CMS, WordPress stores the chunks of content it uses to assemble HTML pages in a database. Getting that content into the database, letting you edit that content, and then storing instructions about how that content relates to other content is really what managing the content means. All databases work pretty much the same way, and though part of WordPress's simplicity and flexibility stems from the way its creators built the database and the files to run it, what ultimately matters to users is the interface that's used to do the managing. It's this administrative interface (a sample screen is shown in Figure 1-2) that my clients and hundreds of thousands of users around the world find so easy to use — for them, it *is* WordPress.

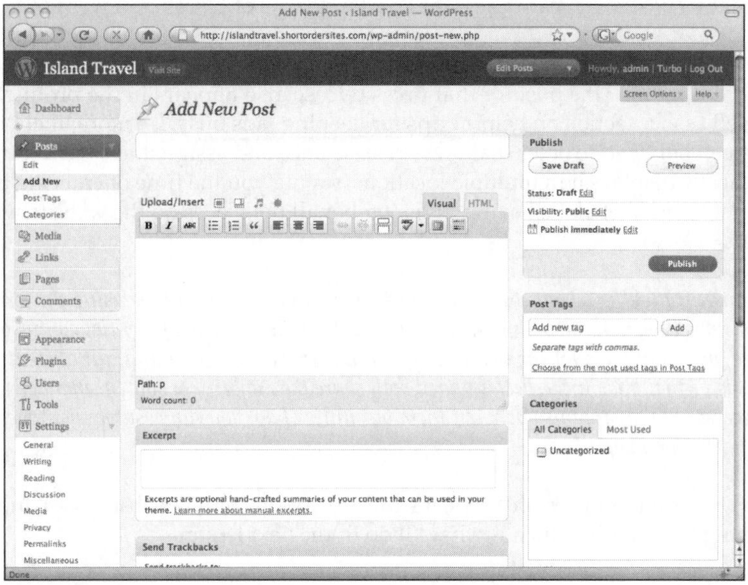

Figure 1-2

Every CMS has its particular way of dealing with content and though WordPress is extremely easy to use, you still need to understand how it refers to content and the methods it uses to organize content. Take *posts* for example. In the world of blogging, people refer to the act of creating a new blog entry as posting. So it's not surprising that the primary kind of content chunk in WordPress is called a post, but that doesn't mean we have to use WordPress posts exclusively for a blog. A post is just a block of text and some instructions stored in a database. They could just as well have called them *chunks*. We don't want to get tied to how we use posts simply because they were originally intended for and named after an element within blogs.

WordPress has another type of content chunk called a *page*, but not the HTML pages you see in your browser. Like posts, WordPress pages are essentially blocks of text and accompanying instructions stored in a database. They're different from posts, though, in several ways. For a start, you can put only one WordPress page at a time into the final assembled HTML page. On the other hand, you can have dozens or even hundreds of posts displayed on a single assembled HTML page.

Suppose you set up WordPress so that each press release for your company is entered as an individual post. Then, you tell WordPress to show the five most recent press release posts. Whenever you add a new press release, it goes to the top of the list. On the other hand, the content describing your company's mission statement doesn't change that often — it's static in comparison to press releases — so you set up a WordPress page for that content. That's how you'll hear people describe the difference between posts and pages: one is for dynamic content and the other is for static content. *The main thing is not to confuse a WordPress page with the final HTML page that gets generated and viewed by the public.* WordPress pages and posts are both chunks of content that just get utilized in different ways.

There's another important difference between posts and pages: posts can be categorized whereas pages cannot. Pages can be a sub-page of another page, but it's a very limited relationship. There's a lot you can do with categories as you see later, but I'll mention one here: a post can be placed in multiple categories at the same time. That has enormous consequences for how you use posts. It makes it very simple for the content of a post to appear in several or even dozens of places on a website.

For instance, if I don't go to the press release area of your site I won't see your announcement of a new wuzzbuzz for kids. But if the post for that press release also appears in the products section of the website, as well as in a section on helpful tips for keeping kids busy, it's more likely I'll notice this new product. Yet, you only had to enter that press release once and assign it to several categories. WordPress then automatically displays it in multiple locations, saving you the time of entering the same information two or more times, let alone having to remember all the places on the website where that information is needed.

Okay, having just told you how posts and pages differ in WordPress, I'll be using the term posts *throughout this book to mean both posts and pages. Partly it's to avoid potential confusion over the term* page, *but mainly it's for the sake of simplicity. The way you enter and edit content for posts and pages is virtually identical, because they both share the majority of content management features. Where necessary I'll distinguish between them but unless I do, you can assume that when I say* posts *I mean both posts and pages.*

Now that you're thinking like WordPress, it's time to take an actual website plan and see how it can be organized using WordPress, which is what I'll do in the next lesson.

Try It

There isn't anything specific to try based on the material in this lesson, but one thing you could do is examine your favorite news website and count how many different chunks of content are on one page. Then go to another page on the site and think about what's common with the previous page and try to imagine how the builders have divided up the structure of the page — map it out on paper.

 There is no video to accompany this lesson.

Planning Your Site
for WordPress

It's beyond the scope of this book to go into the entire planning process for a website; rather, the goal is to take a plan for a website and make it work using WordPress. If you're setting up a blog and nothing more, WordPress has done much of the structuring for you and you can skip to the next chapter. For everyone else, this is a very important step because with the right kind of planning up front, you'll not only save yourself lots of time and energy down the road, but it will help you think about ways to make your website even more useful and easier to navigate. To build a site in WordPress you have three key things to consider:

❑   How are various kinds of content going to be entered in WordPress?

❑   What categories are needed to organize that content?

❑   What do the layout and design roughly look like?

The sample site you'll be working on is for a company called Island Travel, a small travel agency with two locations that specializes in vacations to the Caribbean. Its primary goal is to have a website that provides a very personal touch, with information largely written by its staff, and of course the company wants it to be as easy as possible to update and expand.

What I've learned over the years from my clients is that "easy" doesn't just mean having a WYSIWYG (what you see is what you get) text editor. It also means being able to clearly understand how what they see on the administrative side fits with what's seen on the site — how the various parts of the site fit together.

How Content Will Be Entered

I've talked about how WordPress assembles chunks of content into HTML pages, and one of the most important tasks of the planning process is to develop a useful and straightforward organization for those chunks. Another important task is to decide how to break down the content into the smallest logical chunks. It's easy to assemble those chunks in different ways later on (perhaps in ways you can't even envision at the moment); it's costly to break apart chunks later when you figure out that they're too large. As a simple example, it's better to have each testimonial as a separate chunk than to have one single chunk of all testimonials. With that in mind, look at a basic site map for Island Travel shown in Figure 2-1.

Figure 2-1

You can see the sub-pages for each of the vacation companies Island Travel deals with and sub-pages for the various destinations for which they book vacations. Then the rest of the site is a series of individual HTML pages, all linked, of course, through a common menu, and there would be various links between them within the content of the pages.

Now, keep in mind that this is a plan for how the site will be organized when you view it, but as you saw in the previous lesson, that's not the same as how it might be organized in a content management system like WordPress. Of course, you could build the exact structure shown in the plan using WordPress pages and sub-pages. But remember that example about testimonials? If you just create a single WordPress page and keep adding testimonials to it, you can't do anything more with the individual testimonials. You can't reuse them in any way. But if you enter each one as a post in WordPress, the sky's the limit.

For example, you could create a category called Testimonials, and then a series of subcategories corresponding to each of your vacation destinations. When a new testimonial is added, it would be assigned to the subcategory for the destination the testimonial is about. Now if you want to show all testimonials at one time, it doesn't matter how many subcategories there are; they're all under the parent category, so you could show all testimonials as a group. At the same time, on the Jamaica destination page, for example, you could have a link saying Read Testimonials About Jamaican Vacations and it would connect to all the testimonials in the Jamaica Testimonials subcategory.

Suppose the testimonial concerns Jamaica and The Dominican Republic. Simply categorize it under both destinations and the same testimonial will show up in three places automatically — the Testimonials page, the Jamaica page, and the Dominican Republic page. That's the power of keeping your content in the smallest chunks possible.

It's really the same thinking that led to the original site map showing suppliers and destinations as sub-pages. You could put all the suppliers on a single page, but not only might that make for a very large page (not very friendly for visitors), it just wouldn't be as flexible, such as having a link to a specific supplier. So, suppliers were broken down into their smallest possible chunks — same with the vacation destinations. You're applying that principle even further when you're thinking about how to use WordPress.

Another way to think of this process is to look at content and ask whether it can be used in multiple ways across the site. If it can be or even if you think it might be in the future, it's better to enter the content as a post now.

Coming at it from yet another direction, enter your base products or services as WordPress pages and supporting information as posts. That's not a hard and fast rule by any means, but it's a starting point. For example, Island Travel has vacation suppliers, each of which has many products, has ever-changing company news, has customers giving testimonials about them, and so on. The supplier's basic information (logo and so on) does not belong anywhere else, whereas its products could be listed in several places on the site, as could its company news, testimonials, and so on. So keep the supplier as a WordPress page, the rest of the information as individual posts, and then just link those posts to the page through categories.

Going back to the site map, then, here's a list of how you're going to enter various types of content into WordPress:

> Suppliers — individual sub-pages
>
> Destinations — individual sub-pages
>
> Specials — individual posts
>
> Staff Picks — individual posts
>
> Travel News — individual posts
>
> Testimonials — individual posts
>
> Staff — single page
>
> About — single page
>
> Contact — single page
>
> Customer Deals — password-protected single page

You could of course deal with the content in other ways, but I think this is a logical approach and leaves a lot of room to get even more creative later on.

How Categories Will Be Organized

Now it's time to give some thought to the category structure for posts and how that structure will relate to your primary types of content chunks: suppliers and destinations. Consider two approaches you could take:

Two Approaches to Categorizing

Subject-based	Type-based
Jamaica	Testimonials
Jamaica Specials	Jamaica Testimonials
Jamaica Testimonials	Sun Worship Testimonials
Jamaica Travel News	Cancun Testimonials

Continued

Two Approaches to Categorizing *(continued)*

Subject-based	Type-based
Sun Worship Holidays	**Travel News**
Sun Worship Specials	Jamaica Travel News
Sun Worship Testimonials	Sun Worship Travel News
Sun Worship Travel News	Cancun Travel News

At first glance, it might look as if the Subject approach is nicely geared to your primary content chunks. The parent categories — Jamaica and Sun Worship Holidays are the examples shown — correspond to sub-pages on the site. The problem is, other than linking the Sun Worship Holidays category to the Sun Worship Holidays page, how would you easily use the posts in that category?

Let's go back to the example of testimonials for a moment. If you choose the Subject approach, it wouldn't be easy to have a single testimonials page displaying all testimonials at one time. You'd need to figure out some way to gather together the various testimonials categories rather than letting WordPress's parent-child category structure do the work for you. Same problem if you want to have a random testimonial from the list of all testimonials appear on the site's sidebar; unless they're all under one parent category, there'd be some customization work needed.

But with the Type approach, not only can you easily have an "all testimonials" page, but you simply link the Sun Worship Holidays testimonials category to the Sun Worship Holidays page. Keep it simple; keep it flexible; that's the motto in this planning process. So let's go with a category structure based on content type and not on the destination or supplier.

How the Site Should Look

Part of the planning process for any site is to determine the layout of the pages and the way they'll look. As you saw in Lesson 1, WordPress assembles and delivers HTML pages through a group of template files called a theme, so all you need to do is choose a theme that will give you the look you want, or at least something very close to it. You can of course get a customized theme created for you, but there's very likely an existing free theme that will give you something close to what you want.

The best place to look for a theme is the WordPress.org theme directory http://wordpress.org/extend/themes/ (Starting with WordPress version 2.8 you can do this directly from the administration screen, which I cover in Lesson 33). Not only are the themes in this directory free, but more importantly they've been checked to make sure they function properly. Right now, however, you're simply planning what you want in a theme.

A word of warning as you browse through the themes: don't get caught up in what I call the *magpie effect* and be dazzled by all the bright shining objects. That directory contains a lot of very nice looking designs, but you need to follow some guidelines. As I say, it's highly unlikely that any theme in the WordPress directory is going to be exactly right for your travel site or any particular site — at the very least you're going to want to add your own logo — but the better idea you have of the layout and the look, the less you're going to have to do to make that theme work for you and the less likely you are to be a magpie.

Site Layout

When it comes to the overall site layout, conventional and safe is not only good, it's essential. People have come to expect certain things in certain places — why mess with their minds? Besides, you want them to focus on your content, not on the fact that your main menu sits sideways on the right-hand side of the screen and does a cool slide out when you mouse over it. You want people to find things easily, and the best way to do that is to follow conventions. Let your individuality come out in the header and the content, but for the basic layout, follow the path well-worn for a small business site, as Figure 2-2 illustrates.

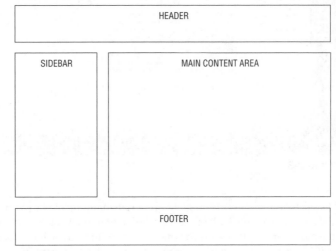

Figure 2-2

You start with a header area across the top, including the menu of all your pages. On the left-hand side you have any secondary navigation plus additional information such as random testimonials, important specials, and so on. Your content will fill the rest of the page and then at the bottom you have your footer, including a reduced menu with just key pages listed. Simple, easy to follow, and no surprises. Now you know what you're looking for in a theme's layout.

Site Design

This is a far more individual issue than site layout, but you still need to think of your visitors, and from that standpoint simplicity of design is always better. It's just easier to find your way around a simple design because it's less cluttered and visitors are more likely to focus on the content. Of course, if the point of your site is to show off design skills, that's another matter. For the Island Travel site, you're concerned about creating the right mood (fun, relaxation, sunshine, and so on) but at the same time making it clutter-free and easy to see content on the page.

To capture the right mood, I think something light — no thick lines, fancy graphics, or strong areas of color — with light browns and sky blues could be one way to go. If you have a graphics program, even a basic one, it's worth creating a simple mockup of your site design, like the one in Figure 2-3 for Island Travel, or simply sketch out a design on paper, making notes about colors.

Figure 2-3

This mockup will be useful for whoever is going to do the customizing of your WordPress theme — the topic of Lessons 27–29. I'm leaving the look of the site until later in the book because getting content entered and organized is the most important task and as that process unfolds, new ideas for the design may come to mind. But at least for the moment, you have a good idea of where you want that design to go.

If you need design inspiration, the official WordPress theme directory I mentioned earlier is a great place to start. If you find something very close to what you want, all the better because it will be simpler to modify and get exactly the look you want. For the purposes of this book, you're going to work with the Default theme that's automatically installed with WordPress. And speaking of installing, that's the subject of the next lesson.

Try It

This lesson does not have a step-by-step instruction you can follow, but it would be good for you to create the kinds of planning documents discussed in the lesson for your own site:

- ❑ A site map
- ❑ A list of types of content and whether they will be pages or posts
- ❑ A category structure you think you'll want for posts
- ❑ A site mockup

 There is no video to accompany this lesson.

Part II: Firing Up WordPress

3

Installing WordPress

The WordPress website talks about its famous five-minute install. It's no idle boast — everything in this lesson can be done in five minutes, but it took me a few WordPress sites to get it down to that time. If it's your first install, and you're handy with an FTP program, familiar with database installs using a hosting panel like Parallels/Plesk or cPanel, and at ease with editing files in a text editor, I would count on about 10 to 15 minutes. If you're relying completely on this lesson to lead you through the steps, it could be 30 minutes or more.

What the five-minute install really refers to is the fact that once you have files in place and a database created, clicking the Install button has you up and running in less than five minutes. This lesson is mostly about what comes before clicking the Install button.

Because this book covers the self-hosted version of WordPress, I'm assuming that you have a hosting account on a web server. This is different from having a domain name. Domain names point to servers where the files for a website are stored and having a place to put your web site files is what I mean by a hosting account.

> **Some hosts offer auto-installation of WordPress, so check for that, but be sure they're using the latest version.**

There are very few requirements for WordPress, and most hosting packages these days — even the most basic — should meet them. Still it's best to double-check the host you're planning to use or your existing account for the following:

- ❏ MySQL database version 4.0 or greater
- ❏ PHP version 4.3 or greater

> If you're not sure how to word your question to your hosting company, the WordPress site provides you with the text for an e-mail you can send: `http://wordpress.org/about/requirements/`. You'll notice that the letter adds a third item to the list: The mod_rewrite Apache module. This module is needed for the custom permalinks feature in WordPress and while there is a way to use custom permalinks without it, it just makes life a bit easier. Most Linux servers have the module installed.

Once you've confirmed that these requirements are met, you're ready to begin the installation process.

Uploading the WordPress Files

The first thing you're going to need is a copy of the latest version of WordPress, and you can easily get that from the official WordPress website at `http://wordpress.org` where you'll see a big orange button at the top right called Download. That takes you to a page where the latest release is always available. Click Download WordPress 2.8.4 (or whatever the current version is).

If you have your browser set to ask you where you want to save downloaded files, find your My Downloads (Windows) or Downloads (Mac) folder and create a new folder called WordPress, then save the `.zip` file there.

If your browser just starts downloading the file you may need to do some hunting around to locate it (hopefully it's just on your Desktop). Create a folder called WordPress in your My Downloads or Downloads folder and drop the `.zip` file there.

All the WordPress files are zipped up or packed into a single file, so you'll need to "unpack" it. If you right-click the `.zip` file you should see an option in the popup window to open the file. If you don't, it means your computer does not have a program capable of unzipping the file; for Windows try 7-Zip at `http://www.7-zip.org`; for Mac try Stuffit Expander at `http://my.smithmicro.com/mac/stuffit/expander.html`.

The unpacking process will leave you with a new folder containing all of the WordPress files, which now need to be uploaded to your server. For that, you'll need an FTP program and the following information: hostname, user/login name, and password. You would have received a username and password from your hosting company or the person who set up the account for you. The hostname is usually just `ftp.yourdomain.com`, but you'll need to check that's the case. If you don't have an FTP program, lots of choices are available for Windows and Mac. An excellent free FTP program for both platforms is FileZilla at `http://filezilla-project.org` or you can go to `www.downloads.com` and search for FTP.

In your FTP program you create a new connection and enter the hostname, user/login, and password. When you click the Connect button, the program logs in to your server. Virtually every FTP program operates by showing you a screen like Figure 3-1, which is split between your computer on the left and the server on the right.

You can see the WordPress files you downloaded over on the left. They all have wp- at the beginning, which is very useful because it makes it extremely unlikely that they'll have the same name as existing files on your server, so there's no chance of overwriting something you shouldn't (except for index.php).

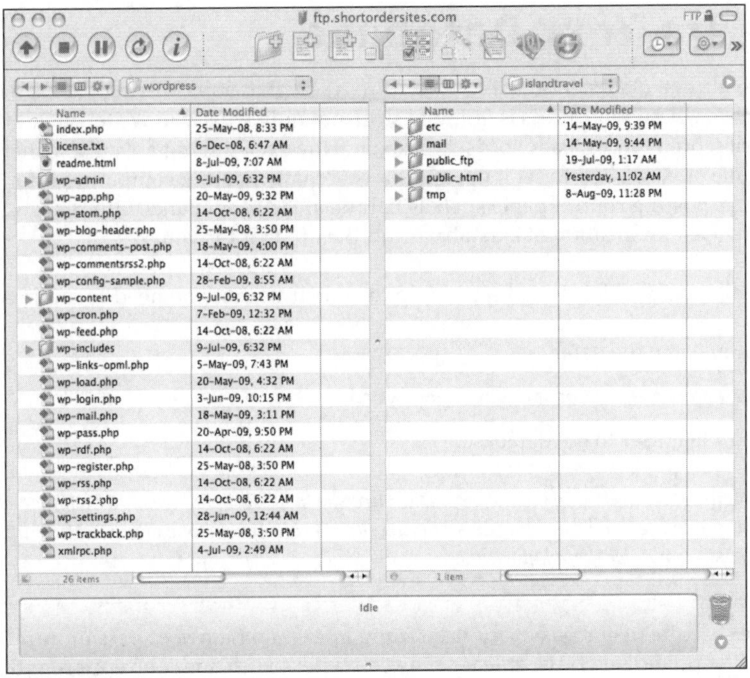

Figure 3-1

The decision you need to make now is exactly where you want to put WordPress on your server. If WordPress is going to run your entire website, the decision is simple — it goes in the root folder of whatever is the web directory on your server. This directory will have different names depending on your server — like public_html or httpdocs or www — you'll need to check that out with your hosting company. In Figure 3-1, the web directory is public_html, so you would open that and put your WordPress files in there.

If you have an existing website and you're going to be using WordPress as an add-on, you could still put it in the root directory; as I mentioned, the naming convention likely wouldn't overwrite any of your existing files, but you should always double-check of course, especially with index.php, which may already be the homepage of your site. Or if you have a particularly crowded root directory you might want to create a folder called "wp" and put the files in there, just to make it easy to find things.

Once you've decided where to put WordPress and you're in that directory on the right side of the FTP screen, you simply highlight all the files on the left side and click the button that goes the direction you want. Typically FTP programs use arrow buttons, and as you cans see in Figure 3-1 it's an up arrow button (top left of the screen), indicating that you're uploading to the server. Other programs use left and right arrows to indicate you're transferring from one side to the other.

In a short time you'll see all of the files on the left copied over to the right. You're one third of the way to completing your installation. Now you'll just need to set up a database and configure one file before you're ready for the Install button.

Setting Up Your Database

One of the requirements I mentioned for WordPress was that your hosting package include a MySQL database. That's where WordPress is going to store not only what you write, but all the details about your categories, preferences, passwords, and so on. However, having a database included with your hosting still means you need to set it up, and for that many hosting companies offer an interface, usually as part of a hosting control panel such as Parallels/Plesk or cPanel. Other hosts may require you to submit a request for creation of a database and they'll do it for you.

I can't cover all the possible ways of setting up the database, but you need to do three things:

1. Create/name the database.

2. Create a user — a username and password.

3. Assign that user to the database.

When assigning the user to the database, make sure she has "all privileges," which means the user can read and write to the database, alter its structure, and so on. If someone else is setting up the database for you, make sure to let them know this.

Make sure the user's password is a strong one — no names of pets or numbers based on birthdays. Have at least nine characters with a mix of upper- and lower-case letters and numbers in it.

For the installation of WordPress you'll need the following information (keep track of it as you set up the database or make sure you get it from whoever does the install):

1. The full name of the database.

2. The username.

3. The user password.

4. The host or server name for the database (usually it's "localhost").

Most of you will be hosted on what's called a shared environment, which simply means a whole lot of websites on a single server. Typically in a shared environment, the name you enter for the database is combined in some way with your username to make sure the database's name is unique.

So if you call your database "mydb" the actual name could be "mydb-myhostlog-inname." At the end of the database creation process, hosting panels like Parallels/Plesk and cPanel will display these complete names, so be sure to write them down and not just the name you entered when you created the database.

Doing the Installation

With all the WordPress files uploaded to your site, your database set up, and your database details by your side, it's time to do the installation.

In your browser window, enter the address **www.yourdomain.com/wp-admin/install.php** (if you uploaded the files to a subdirectory, you'll need that in there as well) and hit Enter.

The resulting screen tells you that WordPress can't find the configuration file, but that's ok because there isn't one included in the files you downloaded from WordPress.org — it has to be created. You have two options at this point:

1. Continue and let WordPress try to create the file for you.

2. Manually edit the sample configuration file included with the WordPress files you downloaded.

Option 1 is the simplest way to go, so I'll be demonstrating the automated creation of the configuration file. Sometimes, a server won't allow WordPress to create the file and you'll need to use Option 2. I cover the manual creation of the configuration in this lesson's video.

After clicking Create a Configuration File you'll see a screen like the one in Figure 3-2 outlining the information that you'll need to proceed (the four items I told you to write down when you created your database).

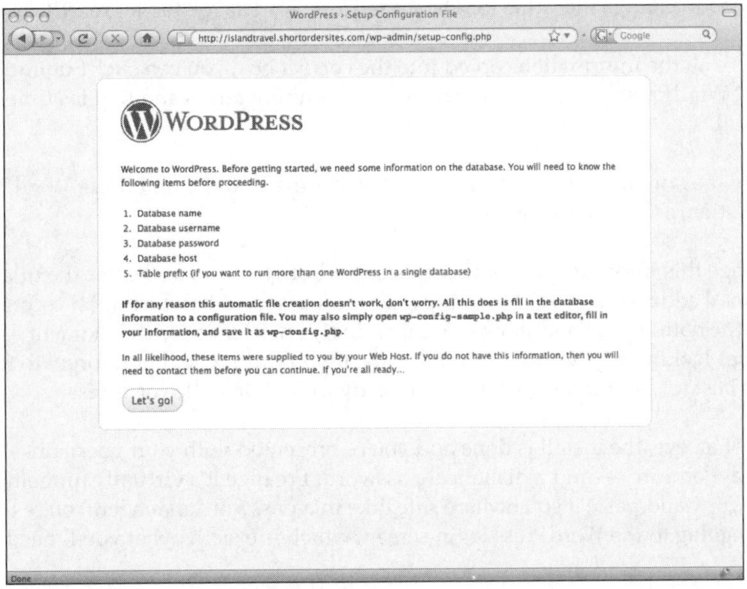

Figure 3-2

The screen in Figure 3-2 also explains about manually creating the configuration file if the automated process doesn't work. When you click Let's Go, you're taken to the screen shown in Figure 3-3.

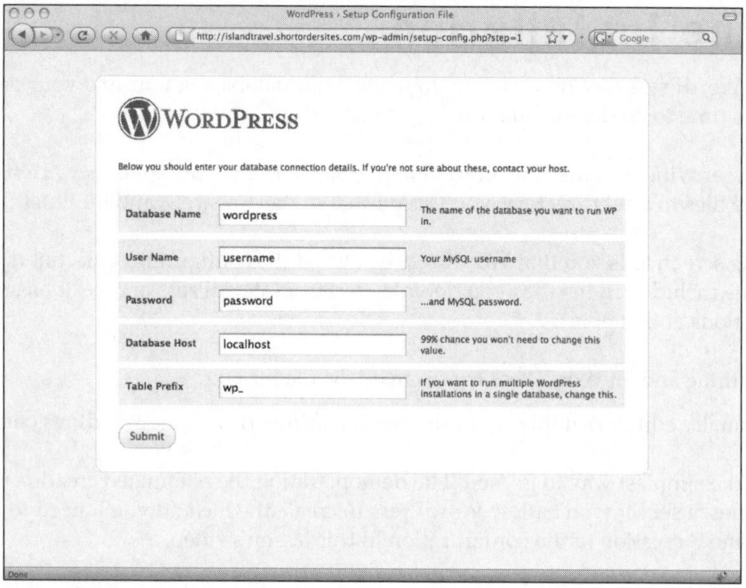

Figure 3-3

This is where you'll enter the information about your database. As the screen says, it's extremely rare that you'll need to change the value for Database Host. And as for Table Prefix, leave it as you see it.

Once you have all the information copied into the correct box, you can click Submit. The next screen tells you that WordPress and your database are on speaking terms and that it's time to install, so click Run the Install.

This is where the famous five-minute install really begins, and the first thing WordPress wants is a bit more information, as shown in Figure 3-4.

You can change this information later if you need to, but go ahead and enter the title of the website and your e-mail address (that's where a copy of your password will be sent). I recommend leaving the checkbox at the bottom (the one about search engines) unchecked for the moment — you don't want search engines looking at your site until it's ready. If you think you might forget to turn this on later, however, it's best to check it now. Then you're ready to click Install WordPress.

In the blink of an eye, the install is done and you're presented with your username — no offense, they call everybody "admin" — and a diabolical password. I realize it's virtually unmemorizable, but that's a good thing. Copy and paste it somewhere safe, like in a password manager. You're then presented with the option of going to the WordPress login screen, which is exactly what you'll need to do for the next lesson.

Figure 3-4

Try It

There's nothing additional to try in this lesson — hopefully you completed the installation using these instructions. If you don't plan on doing the installation right now, you could always set up an FTP program if you don't have one or download WordPress for use later.

You can see more details, such as creating a configuration file by hand, under Lesson 3 on the enclosed DVD.

4

Admin Area Overview

One of WordPress's greatest strengths is the user-friendliness of its administration interface. Both from an organizational and a design standpoint it's laid out in a way that's pretty intuitive. Like any system, of course, you need to take some time and learn how it works, where things are, and so on, and that's what this lesson is about: helping you familiarize yourself with the WordPress administration area.

Logging In

The moment you install WordPress, your website is up and running with a home page and an about page — you'll see the home page by entering your domain name in your browser. Now you need to set up the structure of the site and enter content, which is done through the administration interface, and to get there, you have to log in. On the default theme, there's a Log In link over on the lower right hand side.

> Most WordPress themes include a login link, usually on the sidebar or in the footer, but if not, you can get to the login screen using the address www.yourdomain.com/wp-admin. If you installed WordPress in a subdirectory you would need to add that before /wp-admin, of course.

Clicking the Log In link takes you to the login screen shown in Figure 4-1, which asks for your username and password.

Figure 4-1

If you ever lose your password, WordPress can reset it for you, but that only works if the e-mail address in your profile is up to date (I show you how to do that in Lesson 5).

The first time you log in to WordPress 2.8 you'll see a warning message in red, asking whether you want to keep the diabolical password automatically generated for you or change it to something more memorable. Say No to changing that password. "Memorable" makes it sound like the name of your dog is okay as a password.

If you absolutely want something memorable, at the very least make it a bit diabolical and certainly long. For example, the street address of your first home + your dog's name backwards with a mix of lower- and uppercase + your aunt's birth month and day + the first four letters of your favorite movie. And remember to replace the original password from your installation, wherever you kept it safe.

The warning message at the top of the administration area will disappear once you answer yes or no.

> When you log in a cookie is created in your browser that tells WordPress you're logged in. If you close your browser or the tab where you were working on the admin screen, and then come back in a few hours, you'll find that you're still logged in. More commonly, people return to their WordPress site and notice Edit links everywhere and think that the world can get into their site and access the admin screen. What's happened is that you never logged out and the cookie is still active — that's why it's important to log out, especially if you're working on a public terminal or your roommate or your children get a hold of your computer!

The Dashboard

When you log in to WordPress, the first screen you get is called the Dashboard, which is the home page for the administration area. The top half of the Island Travel dashboard is shown in Figure 4-2.

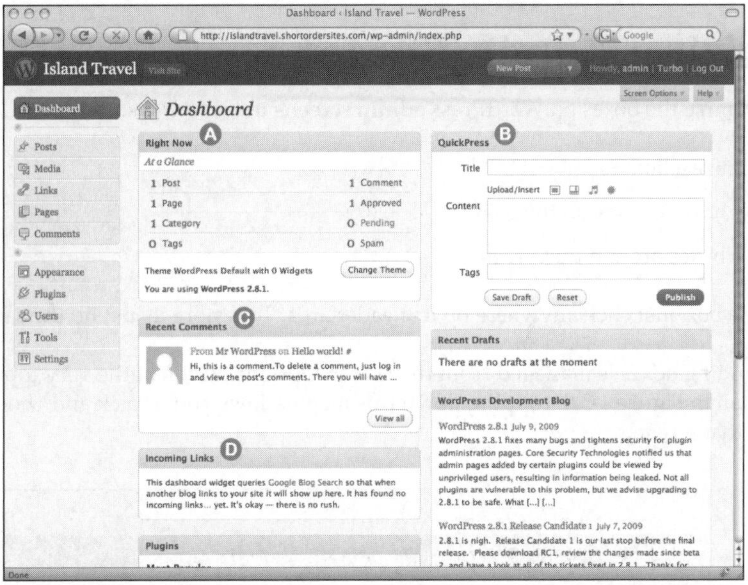

Figure 4-2

There's a lot going on in the Dashboard, so I'll only cover the main functions here.

Item A is the Right Now box, where you'll find a quick overview of your WordPress installation: how many posts, pages, drafts, and comments you have, with links directly to each of those areas of the admin section. You'll also see what version of WordPress you're running, and if you don't have the latest version an Update button automatically appears (or if you're not an administrator, a warning to contact your administrator).

Item B is QuickPress, which can be a handy little tool for quickly posting new items to your website. However, an important limitation of QuickPress is that you cannot choose the category to which the post is assigned — it automatically goes into your default category.

Item C is Recent Comments and it displays a couple of lines and the author from the five most recent comments on your site. The View All button takes you to the Comments screen of the admin area.

Item D is Incoming Links. It shows you what blogs are linking to your site. The default feed comes from Google Blog Search, but you can customize this and I show you how in Lesson 32.

The rest of the Dashboard contains the latest news about WordPress, the latest plugins available, and your recent drafts.

I must admit, I don't make a lot of use of the Dashboard in day-to-day maintenance of sites, except in the case of blogs, where knowing at a glance where comments stand and what incoming links there are can be very useful. Still, it's good to be able to have your finger on the pulse of your website and the WordPress community whenever you log in.

Customizing Admin Screens

You can customize the boxes on WordPress admin screens in three ways:

❑   Minimize a box

❑   Show or hide a box on the page

❑   Move boxes around the screen

To minimize a box, just click anywhere on its header area. To restore it, just do the same.

Showing or hiding boxes is managed from the Screen Options button at the very top right of the screen, shown in detail in Figure 4-3. Dropping down this menu allows you to pick and choose from the boxes available for that screen.

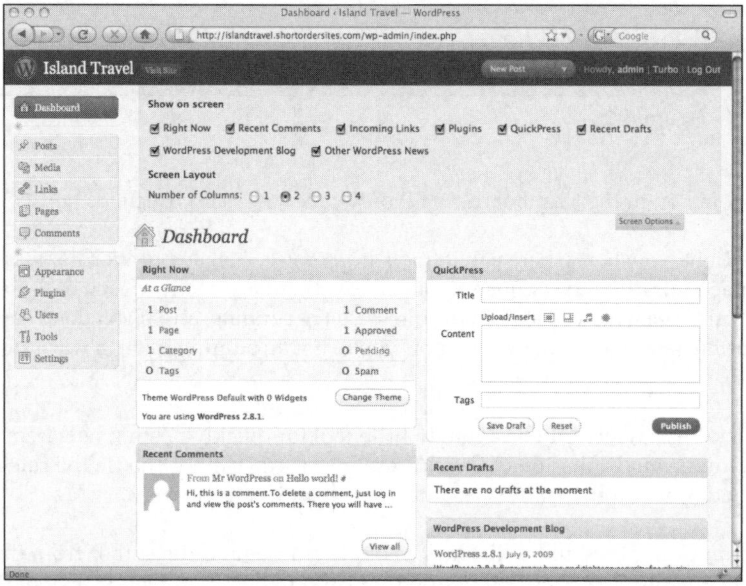

Figure 4-3

Checking a box makes the element appear and unchecking it makes it disappear. What's nice is that this happens in real time so you can see what the change looks like before closing Screen Options.

In addition to deciding what's shown, as of WordPress 2.8, you can choose how many columns wide the screen will be. The default is two, but for the increasingly wider screens of today's monitors it can be helpful to expand that up to four columns wide.

The third way to customize the display of boxes is to physically move them around the page. For example, if I don't use the QuickPress feature so much, but I do read the development blog info, I can switch places by moving them around.

All you do is place your mouse over the dark gray header bar of the box and you'll see it change to the hand cursor. At that point you can click and drag. As the box moves it disappears from its original location, and a blank box inserts itself between existing boxes wherever you point the mouse, as shown in Figure 4-4.

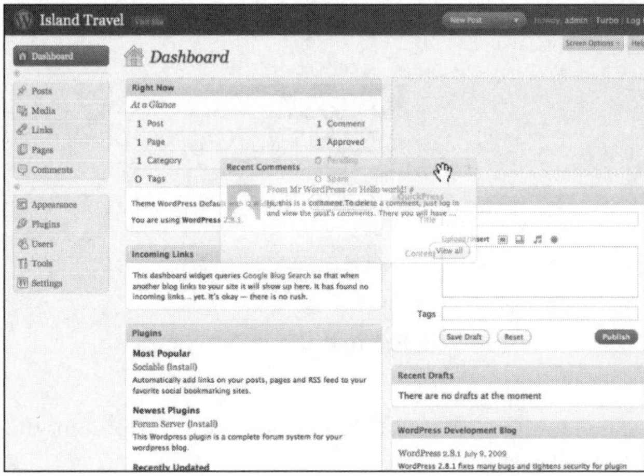

Figure 4-4

When you see that blank box in the spot you want, you just release the mouse button and the screen has been rearranged.

> **With larger boxes, it can be easier to collapse them first and then move them around.**

Getting Around the Admin Area

Your primary way of navigating the admin area is with the menu over on the left-hand side of the screen. The default setting for the menu, with all submenus collapsed, is shown in Figure 4-5A. When you click one of the main links, you're taken to that admin section and the submenu items are shown, as in Figure 4-5B.

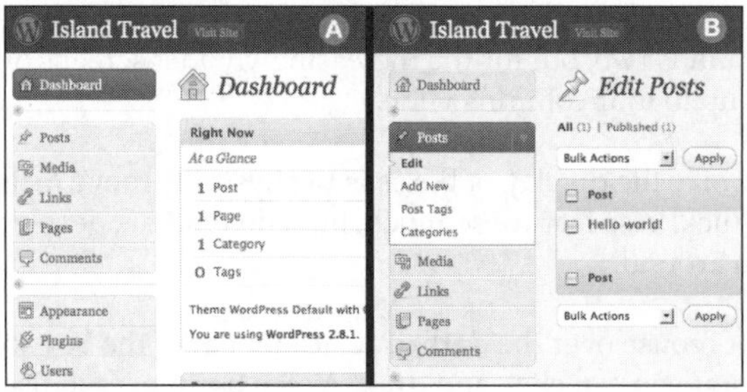

Figure 4-5

You can force a submenu to stay open all the time by mousing over the right edge of a menu header and clicking the little down arrow shown in Figure 4-6.

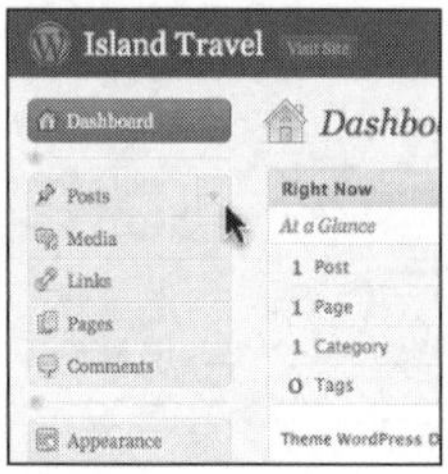

Figure 4-6

The menu stays expanded until you close it again, which is very helpful for those submenus you access all the time, like Posts and Pages.

The entire side menu can be collapsed to icons-only mode and that can help save space. You just need to click one of the two lines circled in Figure 4-7A. Once the menu has collapsed, to view the submenus simply mouseover an icon as shown in Figure 4-7B.

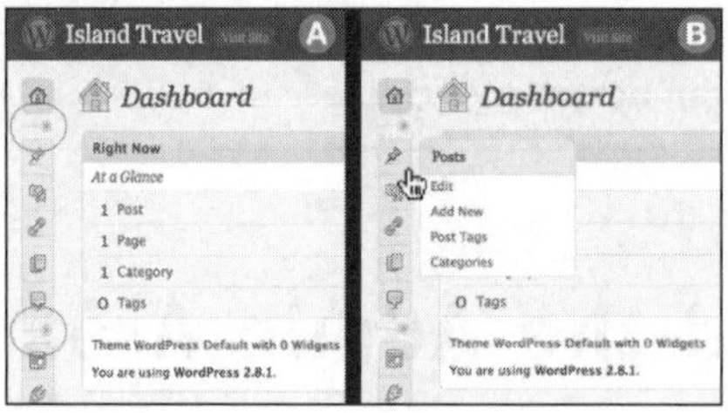

Figure 4-7

The other way of navigating around the admin area is with the drop-down menu at the top right of the dark header bar, as shown in Figure 4-8.

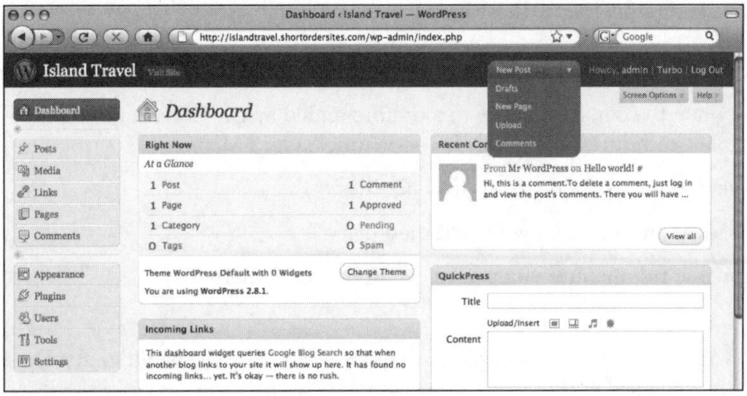

Figure 4-8

This menu contains five items: New Post, Drafts, New Page, New Media, and Comments. You can access them all at any time by mousing over the button, but what's displayed on the button is contextual, based on whatever admin page you're currently viewing.

Try It

In this lesson you try reorganizing your Dashboard and collapsing your side menu.

Lesson Requirements

WordPress installed.

Step-by-Step

To reorganize the Dashboard, follow these steps:

1. Click the header of the QuickPress box and drag it downward.

2. When you get below Other WordPress News, stop and let go.

3. Go back up and double-click the header of the WordPress Development Blog box (which should be at the top of your right-hand column). The WordPress Development Blog should now be collapsed.

4. Do the same for Other WordPress News. You should now be able to see QuickPress without having to scroll.

5. Go to Screen Options and click it.

6. Uncheck Recent Comments and you should see it disappear.

7. Close Screen Options by clicking the button again.

8. Return the Dashboard to the way you want it.

To collapse the side menu, follow these steps:

1. Move your cursor over the light gray line below Dashboard on the side menu.

2. Click when the cursor changes to a double-ended arrow (Internet Explorer — Windows) or a left arrow and upright line (Firefox — Windows and Mac).

3. You should now see only icons and no titles.

4. Mouseover an icon to view the submenu.

5. Restore the full menu if you prefer, using the same method.

 To see some of the examples from this lesson, watch the video for Lesson 4 on the enclosed DVD.

Basic Admin Settings

WordPress has dozens of administrative settings at your disposal, but you'll probably use most of the default settings for as long as you run your site. So the good news is you don't need to mess with more than a few settings as you begin to build your site.

This lesson is to familiarize you with the Settings menu and to show you how to change those truly important few settings. I deal with other admin settings as they're needed in other lessons.

Settings to Get You Started

The Settings heading on the admin menu is where you control various site-wide parameters for WordPress, and its submenus are divided by functions:

- ❏ General
- ❏ Writing
- ❏ Reading
- ❏ Discussion
- ❏ Media
- ❏ Privacy
- ❏ Permalinks
- ❏ Miscellaneous

This is the menu when you first install WordPress. If you add plugins (those extra pieces of software that enable WordPress to do even more) this Settings menu may show more choices depending on the plugins.

The first of the crucial settings to be changed are under Settings ➪ General, where you'll get the screen shown in Figure 5-1.

Figure 5-1

Tagline

The tagline is the text just below the title of your site displayed in the header. This is meant to be a more descriptive phrase about your site and in the case of the Island Travel sample site, Figure 5-2 shows the new tagline as it appears on the site after saving the changes.

Figure 5-2

> By default, the tagline says "just another WordPress blog" and you'll sometimes
> see this on people's sites — they neglected to check their General settings!

WordPress Address (URL)

This is the web address of the directory where you actually installed WordPress. Usually this is already filled in, but you should check, even if it is. If you installed WordPress in the root directory on your server, the URL is simply www.yourdomain.com. If you put WordPress in a separate folder, it would be www.yourdomain/foldername.

Blog Address (URL)

This really means your website address (WordPress assumes you're just creating a blog), so it would be www.yourdomain.com, and again, it's usually already filled in, so you're just making sure it's right.

Don't be concerned if this is the same as the WordPress address; they're used for different purposes, and often are one and the same. The real value of having the two addresses becomes clear when WordPress is installed in a folder or subdirectory.

E-mail Address

Double-check that this is the address you entered when you installed WordPress. Or you can change it, but whatever e-mail you use, remember this is the one where notifications are sent having to do with administrative tasks, such as new users being created.

Timezone

For correctly setting the date and time your content is published or scheduled to be published, you'll want to change the Timezone. WordPress makes this easy by providing a drop-down menu of major cities around the world. Just find a city in your time zone, click Save Changes, and the correct date and time should show up in the Timezone setting area.

Save these new settings before leaving the page; just click Save Changes at the bottom of the page.

And that's it for administrative settings at this point. We'll come back to adjust other settings as needed, but except for completing your personal profile, there's nothing stopping you from publishing content to your site.

Setting Your Personal Profile

When you install WordPress, the system knows you as "admin" but you're more than just an admin, you're a human being with a name, contact information, and color scheme preferences. That's where your profile comes in.

Under the User menu you'll find a link to Your Profile, as shown in Figure 5-3.

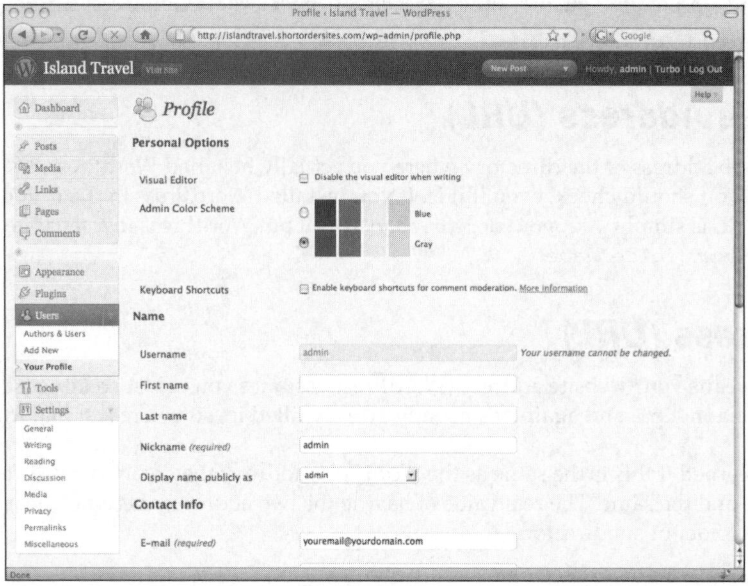

Figure 5-3

This is where you can give yourself a proper name, and most importantly, decide how you want that name to appear on posts and other places on the website. You can enter a First Name, Last Name, and a Nickname. By default, the Nickname is the same as the username, but you can change that (you can't change the username).

Once you've entered whatever names you want they're available under the drop-down menu Display Name Publicly As. If your posts display an author name, this is where you choose what name will be displayed.

There is also a setting that allows users to disable the Visual Editor when writing content (the editor is covered in Lesson 7) and most people will want to leave this box unchecked. The Visual Editor allows you to write in WYSIWYG mode.

Two color schemes are available by default for the admin section: gray and blue. The gray one is selected by default, but users can choose for themselves. Plugins are available for WordPress that allow you to have even more choices. Me, I'm a fan of the default gray.

Finally, it's very important to make sure the correct e-mail address is listed in your profile. You'll see that the e-mail address you entered during installation has been used as your profile e-mail, just as it was for the e-mail under General Settings. The two can be different, but the main thing is that your profile e-mail be, and continue to be, a functioning e-mail address or else you won't be able to recover your password if you ever lose it.

Try It

In this lesson you practice changing the most essential data under General Settings.

Lesson Requirements

WordPress installed.

Step-by-Step

The following is the process for entering important general settings.

1. Drop down the Settings area of the admin menu.
2. Click General.
3. Find the Tagline box and change it to your new tagline.
4. Find the WordPress Address (URL) box and make sure it's correct.
5. Find the Blog Address (URL) box and make sure it's correct.
6. Find the E-mail Address box and make sure it's correct.
7. Find the drop-down menu for Timezone and choose a city in your time zone, or if you know your time zone choose that.
8. If the changes look good, you can click Save Changes at the bottom of the page.

 To see some of the examples from this lesson and to see the setting of a personal profile, watch the video for Lesson 5 on the enclosed DVD.

Part III: Working with Written Content

Adding a New Post — Overview

In this lesson you learn the basics of creating a new post, tagging it and categorizing it, then publishing it to your website. Virtually everything I talk about here applies to writing pages. When I use the term *post*, then, I'm also talking about pages. I'll point out important differences as they come up and then, in Lesson 10, I cover the elements unique to pages.

Anatomy of a New Post

A new post can be started from two locations on the admin screen: the Add New link on the left-hand menu under Posts (or Add New under Pages) and from the drop-down menu at the top of the screen, both shown in Figure 6-1.

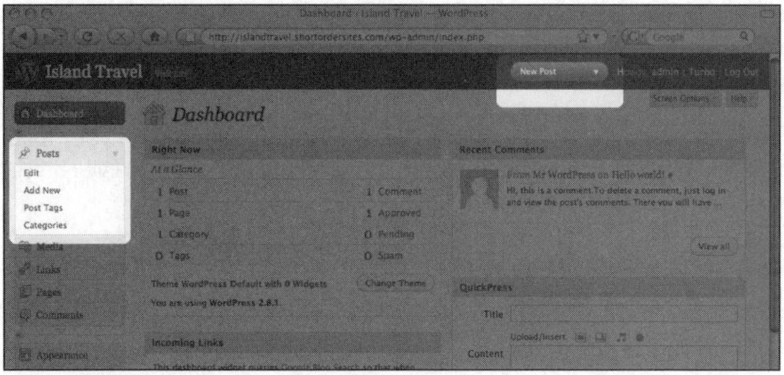

Figure 6-1

Bloggers and others in a hurry should note that posts (but not pages) can also be added from the QuickPress section of the Dashboard as well as from a Press This bookmarklet, if you have it installed in your browser.

Both of these links take you to the Add New Post screen, the top half of which is shown in Figure 6-2.

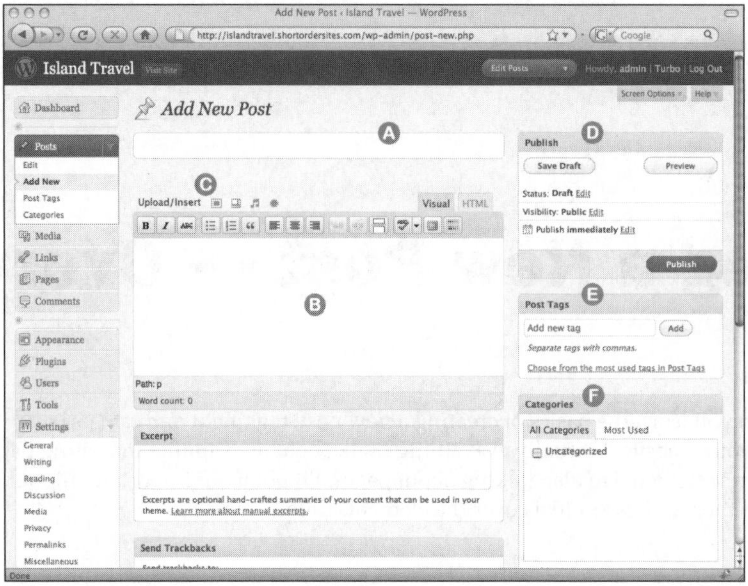

Figure 6-2

The elements on this half of the screen — which I've labeled for ease of reference — are the ones you'll work with the most. The other half of the Add New Post screen has more options that I cover in Lesson 9.

This is how the screen looks by default. You can move elements around by dragging a title bar or you can choose to remove certain elements by using the Screen Options at the top right. In all the installations of WordPress I've done, though, I've rarely moved or removed any of the elements in this top area of the screen because I'm always using them.

Item A is the *title* box (it's not labeled title in case you think that's missing on your installation). The area below the title box is blank when you first open the screen, but after you've entered a title, you'll see the Permalink area, as shown in Figure 6-3.

Figure 6-3

Item B is the primary work area for entering posts: the *Text Editor* or Post Box as it's sometimes described. I'm going to use the term Text Editor partly because it's used mostly for editing and laying out text, but also because it's used for both posts and pages.

By default, the Text Editor displays in Visual mode, which means that text is displayed in a WYSIWYG format, like a word processor — there's even a row of function buttons like on a word processor. You can see the two tabs on the right of the Text Editor header bar and they allow you to switch between Visual and HTML mode. It's handy to be able to see the HTML coding, but for the most part you'll likely work in Visual mode.

Just above the header bar over on the left is Item C — a small menu called *Upload/Insert*. These icons are for working with images and other media you may want to include in a post. I cover this menu in Lesson 11 when I talk about media content — for the moment we'll stick with written content.

At the top right of the Add New Post screen is Item D — the *Publish* box. Publishing a post means making it go live so the world can see it and from this box you control when and how your content is published.

Immediately below the Publish box is Item E, *Post Tags*, and then Item F, *Categories*. As the names suggest, these are used to group posts in any number of ways, and I come back to them after covering the actual writing of a post.

Writing a Post

In this part of the overview I touch on the very basics of using the Text Editor, then in Lessons 7 and 8 I go into more detail about all the functions.

The Button Bar

The heart of the Text Editor is the button bar, from which you access all the functions. By default, WordPress displays a single row of buttons in Visual mode as shown in detail in Figure 6-4.

Figure 6-4

Some of these will be familiar from using word processing programs. Most are used for formatting text, but the one at the far right that I've highlighted is called the Kitchen Sink button and clicking it reveals a second row of buttons, as shown in Figure 6-5.

Figure 6-5

If you log out from WordPress with the second row of buttons displayed, it will still be there when you log in again and until you toggle back at some point to a single row. There is no setting for defaulting to one or two rows of buttons — it's determined by each user's actions.

Before getting to a few of these functions and actually entering some text, it's important to say something about the realities of Visual mode.

What You See Isn't Quite What You Get

On the surface it seems like Visual mode is supposed to show your content as it's going to look when you publish it, just as word processing programs show you what your page will look like when it's printed. However, there are two key ways in which the WordPress Text Editor is not WYSIWYG and I think it's important to get these out of the way early to avoid confusion and disappointment.

1. The Text Editor is not controlled by your style sheet.

    What you see on your live site is formatted by the style sheet of your WordPress theme, but it has no effect on what you see in the Text Editor. There will always be differences between what you see in the Text Editor and what visitors see on the live site, and sometimes those differences can be quite major. That's why WordPress has the Preview button, so that you can see your post the way your style sheet is going to display it. It's important to check Preview before your publish or update a post.

2. The Text Editor thinks of spacing very differently than you.

    You're used to hitting your Enter or Return key on a word processor and getting extra space between paragraphs — the more you do, the more space you get. Not so with the Text Editor.

    Put as many spaces as you like between paragraphs, but when you click Publish or Update, they all disappear. There's a method in this apparent madness, and I explain more in Lessons 7 and 8. I also show you some ways to add that extra space if you're desperate to do so. For the moment it's enough to know that you can avoid frustration by only hitting the Enter key once per paragraph.

Another way of putting these warnings is to say that the role of Visual mode is not to give you exactly what you're going to get, but to make basic formatting obvious and to simplify functions like creating links. For instance, it's much clearer to see that **this is going to be bold text** on my website than to decipher the actual HTML: `<strong>this is going to be bold text</strong>`. And for tasks like creating links or making lists, it's much easier to click a button than to learn HTML coding. So Visual mode is still very useful despite its limits.

Working with Text

To enter text, of course, you just start typing in the Text Editor box. As you type, the box scrolls down as needed (the default size of the Text Editor is quite small, but you can change that in a number of ways — see Lesson 7). You can keep track of your word count at the lower left of the box, while on the right you'll see the last time you saved the current material and the last time the post was edited.

I'm going to create a new post with the title Seven Day Capital Package and enter text about a vacation package in Kingston, Jamaica. When you want to format text you simply highlight the words, press the appropriate button, and you'll see the change. For example, I'll go in and make the name Kingston bold, as shown in Figure 6-6.

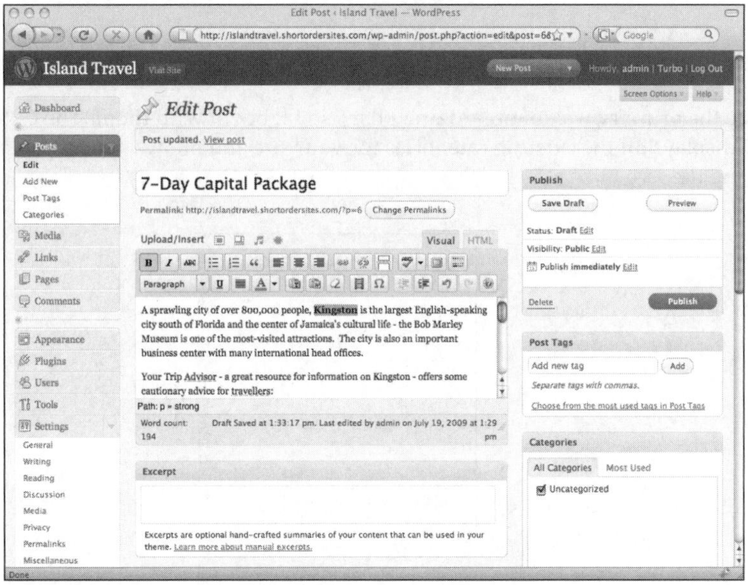

Figure 6-6

When you want to start a new paragraph, you hit Enter on your keyboard. To cut, copy, or paste text you'll need to use the standard keyboard commands — Ctl+x, Ctl+c, Ctl+v — because there are no buttons for these functions.

> For those who like to use keyboard shortcuts, most of the old standbys work in the Visual mode Text Editor, including undoing and saving. You can also access any non-standard function on the button bar using the keyboard — to find out the keyboard commands, just mouse over the button or on the second row of buttons the rightmost button pops up a window with details about the Visual Text Editor, including all keyboard commands.

Before leaving the Text Editor, I make sure I save my work. Because this is a new post but I don't want to publish it yet, I click Save Draft at the top of the Publish box. I would keep using that button until I publish, and at that point, Save Draft disappears and the Publish button changes to Update Post. There is auto-save built into WordPress, but you never know what might interrupt you and cause unsaved changes to be lost, so it's just a good habit save regularly.

Categories and Tags

You can organize posts (but not pages) in two ways: by categorizing and by tagging them. Each fulfills a special role even if they seem quite similar. One way to think of the difference is that categories are like a table of contents whereas tags are like an index — categories are general and tags are specific.

Categories

Categories are the primary way of organizing posts, so I'll begin with them. The Categories box shown in Figure 6-7 displays all the existing categories for your site and allows you to add new categories without leaving the screen.

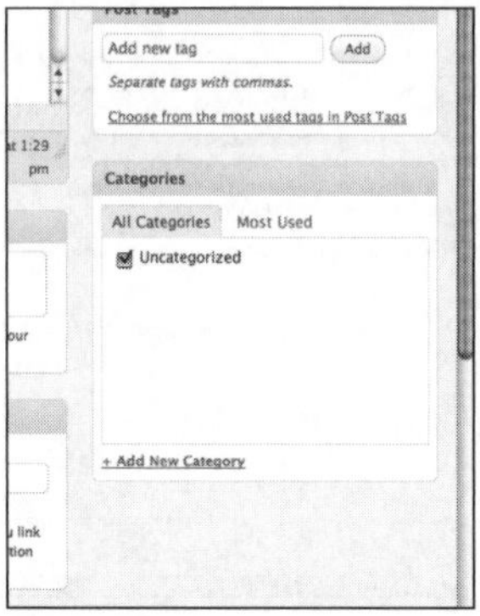

Figure 6-7

Right now there's only one category called Uncategorized. Because posts must be in at least one category, WordPress comes with a category which cannot be deleted. So if you save or publish a post and forget to choose a category, you'll find that WordPress has automatically placed it in the Uncategorized category (see Lesson 20 for ways to handle this category).

The post I'm working on here is about a vacation package, so I'll add a new category called Packages. Click the Add New Category link and you'll see a text box appear like the one in Figure 6-8.

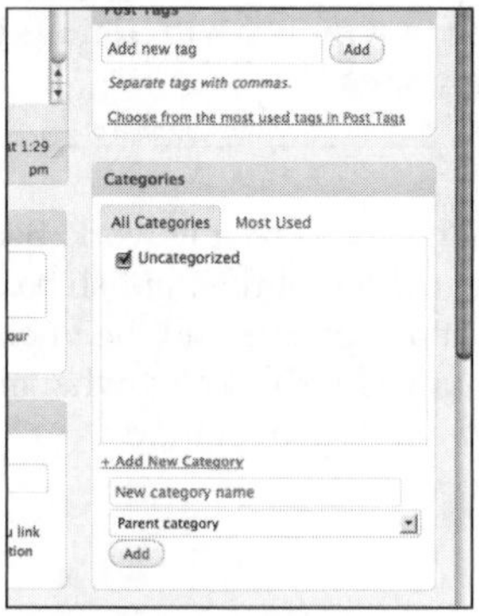

Figure 6-8

You enter the name of your category here. Just below the text box is a drop-down menu called Parent Category. This is used if you want your new category to be a subcategory of something else (you want it to be the child of a parent category). In this particular case, I don't want Packages to be a subcategory of anything else, so I don't touch Parent Category.

When you click Add, you'll see a yellow bar flash at the top of the categories list and your new category appears with a check mark beside it, as shown in Figure 6-9A.

However, I don't want this post in the Packages category, I want it in a child or sub-category of Packages, but because Packages did not exist yet, I had to create it. So I uncheck Packages, go back to the Add New Category link, and enter Jamaica Packages in the new category box. Packages appears in the Parent Category list, so I choose that and click Add. The results are shown in Figure 6-9B (I've added a couple of other child categories under Packages to illustrate a point).

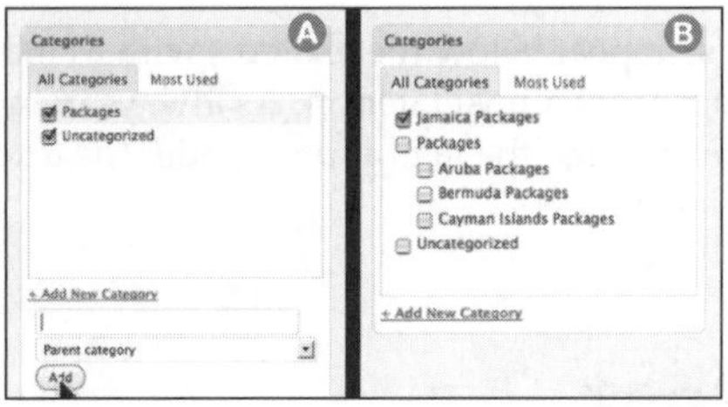

Figure 6-9

Normally categories are shown in alphabetical order, with child categories nested below parents, but notice that Jamaica Packages is listed at the top, out of order. When you have a lot of categories, it can be time consuming to scroll through to find the ones that your post is connected to, so WordPress moves those categories to the top of the list.

Remember too that adding categories, even though they're checked off, does not mean they've been assigned to the post — that only happens when you Save Draft or Publish or Update Post.

> *Something I mentioned in Lesson 2 is worth repeating at this point: posts in child categories automatically are members of their parent categories. So, in the case of my post, I don't need to check Packages — my post is automatically included in that category by being in Jamaica Packages. This is very useful because on the website I could have a listing that shows all Packages, including those for Jamaica, while also showing a list just for Jamaica.*

Tags

Earlier I used the term *specific* to describe tags. In the case of the current post, I categorized it under Jamaica Packages, but in the body of the text it talks about Kingston and all-inclusive resorts. Those are terms for which people might be interested in seeing all similar posts. One option would be to create a Kingston category, but there are so many cities in the Caribbean that the category structure would become bloated. However, if I make Kingston a tag — using the Post Tags box in Figure 6-10A — visitors could still see all posts tagged with "Kingston" just as if it were a category.

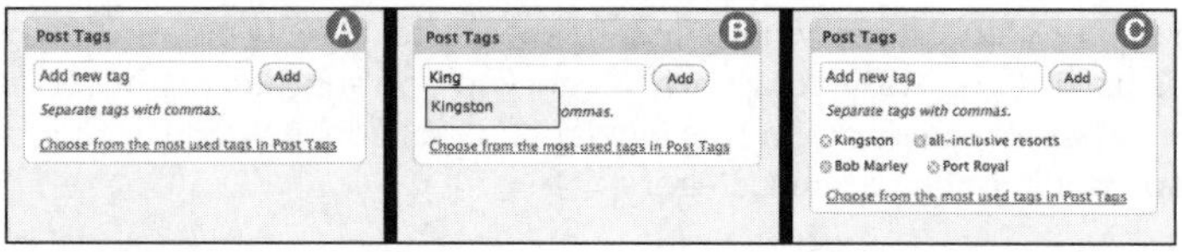

Figure 6-10

All I do is enter the tag in the text box. If you want to enter more tags, WordPress reminds you to separate them with commas.

As you enter a word or phrase, WordPress checks existing tags and displays possible matches in a popup window, from which you can choose, as shown in Figure 6-10B. You can also click Choose from the Most Used Tags in Post Tags to get a list of popular tags on your site.

When you click Add, the tag(s) appear below the text box, with a small x beside them — see Figure 6-10C. This allows you to remove tags from a post later on. As always, remember to Save Draft, or Publish or Update your post because even though the tags appear under the text box, they're not saved in the system until you click "the big blue button."

Publishing a Post

Once you have your post entered, tagged, and categorized, you need to decide what to do with it, and that's where the Publish box comes in. The name is a bit misleading because publishing is only one of the options you have, but because it's the most important of all the options here, it makes sense to use that title.

Figure 6-11 shows the Publish box in detail.

Figure 6-11

What jumps out at you first is the large blue Publish button. Clicking that makes your post live on your site. What's handy about this button is that it will change depending on the context, so it will remind you of what action you're about to take. For instance, once you've published a post, the button will say Update Post, or if you change the date of publication to one in the future, the button will say Schedule.

Starting at the top of the Publish box, the first thing you notice is Save Draft, which I used for the Kingston post. If you're not ready for the world to see your post just yet, you'll want to use this button.

Status

The Status menu allows you to move your post from one state to another depending on the post's current state. In other words, it's a contextual menu. But to see that menu you need to click the Edit link beside the current status, and you get what's shown in Figure 6-12.

Figure 6-12

Once you've chosen the new status, click OK and the menu disappears. If you decide not to change anything, just click Cancel.

A post has four different states:

- Draft
- Pending Review
- Scheduled
- Published

Not all of these are shown at once — as I mentioned, this is a contextual menu — so you only have the possible choices open to you at any particular time.

- **Draft:** This means that the post is still in its early stages and not ready for any eyes, public or otherwise. (Prior to version 2.8 WordPress sometimes uses the term "unpublished" in place of draft.)

- **Pending Review:** This is a state used when you have multiple authors and there's an editor who will review the post before it's published. When the post is ready for review you simply switch it from Draft to Pending Review. Items that are Pending Review are listed separately so, for example, someone who's editing posts knows that those ones are ready to be checked over.

- **Scheduled:** This means the post will be published at a certain date and time in the future. You cannot change the status of a scheduled post by using this drop down menu. You must change the publication date and then update the post.

- **Published:** This means the post is available on the website. Depending on the visibility settings it may not be visible to all visitors, but it's available to whoever has permission to see it.

Visibility

When publishing a post, you need to decide who exactly can see it when it's live, and that's the role of the Visibility menu. Again you'll need to click the Edit link to see the menu shown in Figure 6-13.

Figure 6-13

❑   **Public:** This is the default setting and it means that anyone on the Internet will be able to see the post. You also have the option of making a public post sticky, which simply means that it does not get bumped down by newer posts as it normally would. This stickiness only applies to the front page blog posts, if you've chosen that as the content of your homepage.

❑   **Password Protected:** As the name implies, this means visitors will need to enter a password if they want to see the content of that particular post. You'll need to select Password to see the entry box for the password. Enter it and click OK.

Password-protecting a post is a very handy feature because you might want to provide some exclusive content but don't want to go to the trouble of creating a password-protected directory on the server for a single item or an item you only need protected for a short time. A good example would be a document you want to offer only to subscribers of a newsletter. You simply upload the document to a post, password-protect the post, and then send out the URL and password in the newsletter. After a specified time, you just unpublish or delete the post.

❑   **Private:** This is different from password-protecting because all you need to see the post on the live site is to be logged in to WordPress. However, you must be logged in, either as an Editor or Administrator. Authors, Contributors, and Subscribers cannot see Private posts, though Authors can always see their own posts, even when they're private (see Lesson 26 for the various roles in WordPress).

When you're finished choosing among these, be sure to click the OK button and the new state will display beside Visibility. Remember that although it looks like you're done, *you must click Update Post (or Publish or Save Draft) for the change to actually be made.*

Publish

This setting determines when the post will be published, and the default is immediately. If you want to schedule the post to publish automatically in the future, click the Edit link and you'll see the date display as shown in Figure 6-14.

Figure 6-14

You can even set things up to publish at a specific time of day. For instance, I often set press releases to publish the morning of the day I'm sending out e-mail notices about the release.

> Because you can set any date you like, it's possible to date a post in the past, but why would you want to do that? Suppose you had a press release that had been missed and you want it to appear in your archives in the proper order by date. Simply back date the post and hit publish.

Once you've set the date and time, just click OK and the new time appears next to Publish. And again, *remember to click Schedule or Update Post* (depending on what the big blue button says) or else your change won't be saved.

Try It

In this lesson you create a new post, then schedule it for publishing at a later date.

Lesson Requirements

WordPress installed.

Step-by-Step

Steps for creating and scheduling a post:

1. Click Add New under the Post section of the admin menu.

2. Enter a title for the post.

3. Check that the Text Editor is in Visual mode.

4. Enter some text — try making it bold, italicizing it, or changing its alignment.

5. In the Categories box, click Uncategorized.

6.   In the Publish box, under Visibility, click Edit.

7.   Click Private and then OK.

8.   Still in the Publish box, click Edit beside Publish Immediately.

9.   Choose a date and time in the future.

10.   Click OK. The blue button in the Publish box should now say Schedule.

11.   Click Schedule. When the screen refreshes, you should see a message at the top saying Post Published.

 To see some of the examples from this lesson, such as adding tags and categories or password-protecting a post, watch the video for Lesson 6 on the enclosed DVD.

7

Working with the Text Editor

In Lesson 6 you learned the basics of using the WordPress Text Editor — now it's time to examine its capabilities in detail. You learn the functions of each of the buttons on the button bar, including plenty of little tricks to help make it easier to use this powerful tool. Mostly you'll be working Visual mode, but this lesson also covers a bit of HTML mode.

Anatomy of the Text Editor

As you've seen, the Visual Text Editor has two rows of buttons. By default, only the first row is displayed and you have to access the second row by clicking the Kitchen Sink button (the very last button on the default row). I've created a visual directory of each row, so let's begin with the default one.

> *You may have more buttons on your Text Editor if you have plugins installed on WordPress. If you install the TinyMCE Advanced plugin, you'll also have more rows of buttons and the ability to move buttons around. Some plugins give you a different text box altogether. For the purposes of this lesson, however, I'm only covering the default Text Editor.*

Figure 7-1 shows the functions of the primary button bar

Strike-Through
Puts a line through the selected text.

Align Left
Makes the selected paragraph flush left. Also works with images.

Un-link
Removes link from selected text or image. Button only highlights when a link is selected.

Kitchen Sink
Toggles visibility of the second row of buttons on the Text Editor.

Bold
Bolds the selected text, or if it's already bold, makes it regular.

Numbered List
Creates a list for which each line is automatically numbered.

Align Right
Makes the selected paragraph flush right. Also works with images.

Spell Check
Toggles the spell checking feature and the down arrow changes language.

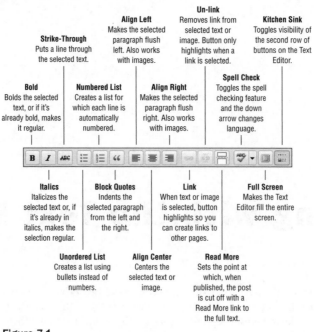

Italics
Italicizes the selected text or, if it's already in italics, makes the selection regular.

Block Quotes
Indents the selected paragraph from the left and the right.

Link
When text or image is selected, button highlights so you can create links to other pages.

Full Screen
Makes the Text Editor fill the entire screen.

Unordered List
Creates a list using bullets instead of numbers.

Align Center
Centers the selected text or image.

Read More
Sets the point at which, when published, the post is cut off with a Read More link to the full text.

Figure 7-1

Figure 7-2 shows the secondary button bar.

Remove Formatting
Clears whatever formatting you have for the selected text.

Indent
Increases the left margin of the selected text. Each click indents the text further right.

Justify
Aligns text flush left and right.

Special Characters
Inserts the proper coding for characters like the copyright symbol.

Redo
Lets you restore the last 10 actions you took in the text editor.

Formatting Menu
Used primarily for various levels of headings.

Paste as Plain Text
Strips absolutely all formatting from text copied from sources like Word.

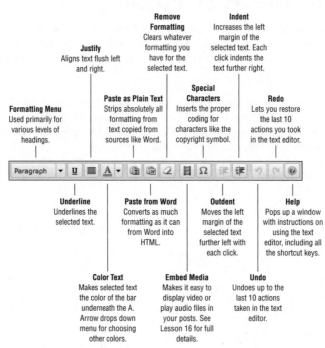

Underline
Underlines the selected text.

Paste from Word
Converts as much formatting as it can from Word into HTML.

Outdent
Moves the left margin of the selected text further left with each click.

Help
Pops up a window with instructions on using the text editor, including all the shortcut keys.

Color Text
Makes selected text the color of the bar underneath the A. Arrow drops down menu for choosing other colors.

Embed Media
Makes it easy to display video or play audio files in your posts. See Lesson 16 for full details.

Undo
Undoes up to the last 10 actions taken in the text editor.

Figure 7-2

Finally, Figure 7-3 shows the single row of buttons for HTML mode.

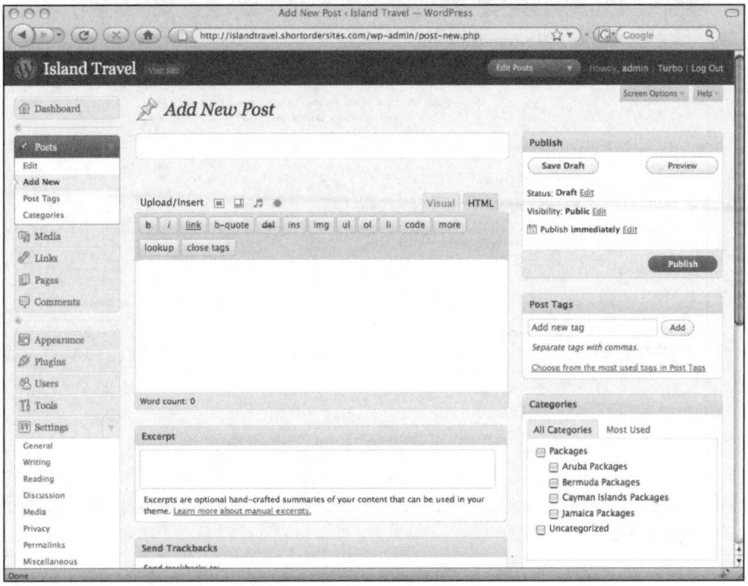

Figure 7-3

Sizing the Text Editor

One way to change the size of the Visual Text Editor so you have more room to work is to locate the three lines on the lower right-hand corner of the editor box, shown in Figure 7-4, click them with your mouse, and drag the box downward (this does not work in HTML mode).

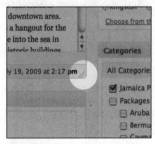

Figure 7-4

WordPress will remember the new height for as long as you're logged in. If you would rather have the Text Editor larger by default each time you log in, you can change that under Settings ➪ Writing as shown in Figure 7-5 (the "Size of the post box" setting).

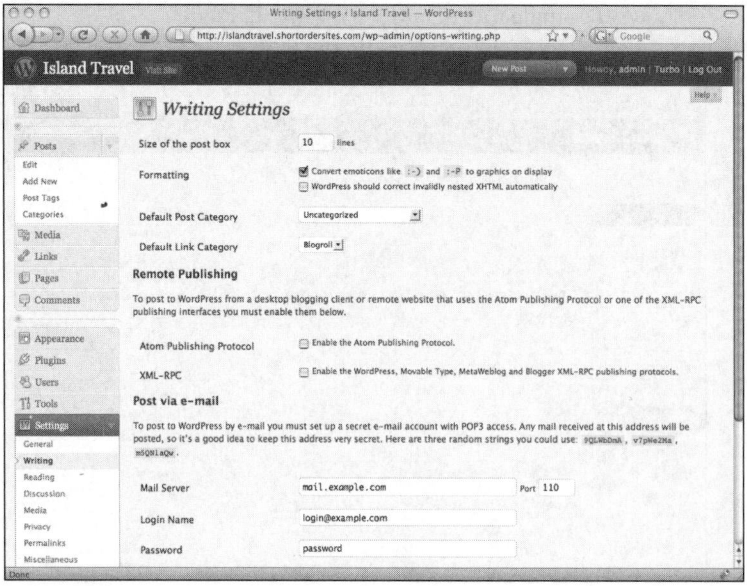

Figure 7-5

Keep in mind that this default sizing will apply to all users on the system, but they'll still have the ability to resize the box each time they log in.

However, height isn't always the only issue you may have with the size of the Text Editor. You could find your screen looking like Figure 7-6 (possible causes: as you add plugins to WordPress, they may place more buttons on your Text Editor or perhaps you've increased the text size of your browser and the button bar gets larger as a result, pushing the Text Editor to the right).

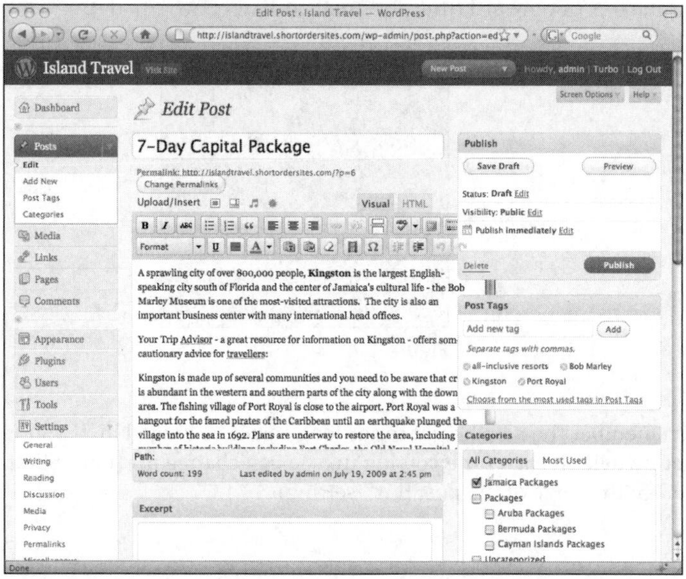

Figure 7-6

Whatever the cause, you need to find more width and for that you have a few options:

1. Increase the width of your browser window — the center column with the Text Editor is fluid and will expand with the window.

2. If you're already at your screen's limit, another option is to collapse the admin menu on the left side of the screen, as shown in Lesson 4.

3. You can set the Text Editor to full screen mode. By clicking the Full Screen button the editor expands to take over the whole of your screen. The button bar remains visible at the top, along with the buttons for the Upload/Insert menu. To get back to the normal screen, just click the Full Screen button again.

4. Finally, a method introduced in WordPress 2.8 is to make the Add New Post page have only one column instead of two. To change the columns, open up Screen Options at the top right and select "Number of Columns: 1". All the boxes on the Add New Post screen will still be there; they're simply moved into a single column with the Title and Text Editor at the top.

> If you do change to a single column and then change back to two columns, WordPress does not automatically restore your screen. Instead it makes space for the second column and you'll need to drag back the boxes you want to appear on the right-hand side.

Styling Text

Whenever you're thinking about styling some text, keep in mind these two points:

❑   Does the styling help visitors understand what you're saying in the post or is it simply adding clutter to what they see, no matter how "pretty" it looks?

   Take the example of making text bold, which was covered in the preceding lesson. If you use too much bold text on a page, the purpose begins to get lost. Everything becomes important so nothing stands out properly. Like that.

❑   Is this styling needed for this post alone or is it something that might better be handled by your theme's style sheet because you want to develop a standard style across multiple posts?

   I often see people create special styles for a section heading on a post. Those headings are already controlled by your theme. Creating a style for a particular heading overrides what's in the style sheet, and that's okay, but maybe what you really want to do is change the style sheet so that all headings of that type look the same.

There isn't time to go through all types of text styling here, and I cover the styling of large bodies of text in the next lesson, so I'll cover just a few common issues.

Underlining

I'm not a fan of using the Underline function at all, at least not on the Web. I think it's just too confusing to your visitors because underlined text spells "link" in their minds. They try clicking the underlined text and you either disappoint or confuse them.

I know some uses of underline are actually required, such as in scholarly documents, but in cases like that, the visitor has some context and is familiar with the underlining. But if you need to emphasize text it's usually best to stick to bold and italics, or perhaps color.

Coloring Text

Having mentioned coloring text, remember a few things before you start doing it:

❑ Don't use the same or similar color as the color of your text links or there's going to be confusion for the visitor.

❑ If you have colored headings in your theme, using the same color for pieces of text can also be confusing, though a shade of that color maybe isn't so bad.

❑ Always think about the background color behind the text. You don't want anything that's going to blend in too much with the background, especially when people are printing the page in black and white.

How, then, do you color text? It's the button with the letter A on the second row of the Text Editor button bar. If you highlight some text and just click that button, it will turn the color of the small bar displayed on the button. If you want to change that color, click the down arrow and you get some preset choices. Click More Colors and you get a popup window where you can choose from any color.

The Formatting Menu

The drop-down menu on the left-hand side of the second row of buttons can be a bit confusing at first. It seems to be, as the name suggests, a way of formatting text in different ways, but the trick is, these formats apply only to paragraphs. So, for example, if you highlight some text to be emphasized, and choose Heading 2, instead of those few words changing, the entire paragraph changes. Styling of paragraphs is covered in more detail the next lesson, so for the moment I'll leave it at this: don't try to use formatting to highlight individual words or phrases.

Working with Text Links

Creating links within the body of your text is important for leading visitors to more information — it's one of the greatest strengths of web-based material. But it's easy to mess up the formatting of links, so thankfully the WordPress Text Editor makes linking very simple. It's not quite as straightforward as bolding, but you're led through every step with an easy-to-use form.

Much of what is said here applies to creating links using images. Details about linking images are covered in Lesson 13.

The first thing to do is highlight the text that's going to be linked. Sometimes deciding which text to link is fairly obvious: "I was reading <u>an article in People magazine</u> today and…" But the best rule of thumb is to link as much of the text as relates to where you want to take your visitor.

Once your text is highlighted and you click the link button, you get a popup window like the one in Figure 7-7.

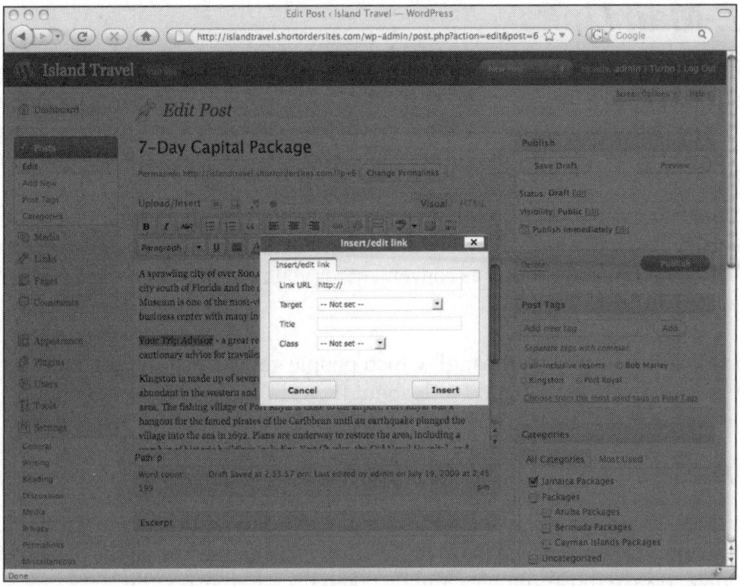

Figure 7-7

As the name Insert/Edit Link suggests, this window is not only for adding new links, but also editing existing ones.

Link URL is obviously where you're going to put the address of the web page you're linking to. WordPress automatically puts in the `http://` so you're not wondering whether it's required. It's also highlighted so that if you're like me and paste URLs copied from your browser address bar, you'll automatically erase the default text and not end up with `http://http://`.

Next, from the Target drop-down menu, you can decide whether you want your visitor to be taken to a new browser window (or tab) or to remain in the current window, with the new content replacing the existing content. If you don't make any choice, the link will automatically stay in the current window and replace its contents.

Either way of handling this has pros and cons. I personally like it when a link opens in a new window or tab — I'm not a big fan of using the back button (which may explain why I have dozens and dozens of tabs and windows open at any one time). Others will say it's confusing for new windows or tabs to be open, particularly when visitors end up with a whole raft of them. Do what you think best.

You can also give your link a *Title*, which is what people will see when they mouse over the link. This can also be helpful in search engine optimization, which I talk about in Lesson 30.

You don't need to worry about the last option in this window — the Class of the link. This can be handy for advanced style sheet work, but mostly you can just leave it at Not Set.

Once you have everything entered, click Insert and you'll see your text underlined and colored. Remember that this link format is just to help you distinguish the link in the Text Editor. How your links look on the web site depends on your style sheet. And of course, before leaving the screen, click Update Post or your nice new link will not be saved.

Creating E-Mail Links

Under the Link URL heading you also have the option of creating a link that starts up the visitors' e-mail program and allows them to send you a message. Instead of a website address, you put this in the Link URL box: `mailto:youremail@you.com`. That will cause the link to open up the user's e-mail program and place the e-mail address in the To: box of the new message.

If you're concerned about spammers grabbing the e-mail address in the link, you have a couple of options: don't create a link, but just put in an e-mail address formatted something like this: `youremailATyouDOTcom`. It doesn't fool all spam robots, and isn't as convenient for your visitors, but it can help control spam harvesting and is simple to do.

A better option is to create a form through which people get in touch with you. A number of plugins for WordPress help you create forms, and I talk about those in Lesson 36.

Editing Links

To edit an existing link, just click it and you'll see the two link buttons highlighted. Click the solid link button to get the popup window you saw earlier. You can change any of the options in the window and then click Update to save those changes and be taken back to the Text Editor.

If you want to change the highlighted link text, you simply erase words or insert words, and the link remains in place. If you want to change all of the wording, highlight the entire link and begin typing the new text. Be careful not to highlight anything beyond the link or else you'll break it and you'll need to create a whole new link.

If you want the link moved to new text elsewhere in the post, you could highlight the link, copy it, and paste it where you want. Then you would change the wording and finally remove the earlier link. It's probably just as easy, however, to copy the URL from the old link, remove it from that text, and create a new link using the copied URL.

Removing Links

I've been careful to use the phrase "remove a link" rather than "delete a link" because removing a link means you're keeping the words that were linked. Deleting a link could mean that you want to get rid of the words as well as the link.

To delete a link you simply highlight words and delete them, but to remove a link you need to click the link itself and then choose the broken link button. You'll see the underlining and the coloring removed from the words — then you know the link is no longer functioning.

When removing links, remember that you need to Update your post for the change to take effect. Because you didn't alter any wording it's easy to forget.

Importing Text

Nobody likes typing when you're just re-entering things into a post, so copying and pasting is a popular sport. Quite often, though, you're copying from a source that can cause you problems by carrying hidden coding with it.

I often have clients say to me that they can't change a certain part of their text, no matter what they try to do in the Text Editor. A look behind the scenes in HTML mode quickly reveals the problem: hidden coding that's controlling the look of the text. In Figure 7-8, compare the text on the left — what the person saw in her word processor and wanted to copy — with the actual coding that got pasted into the WordPress Text Editor.

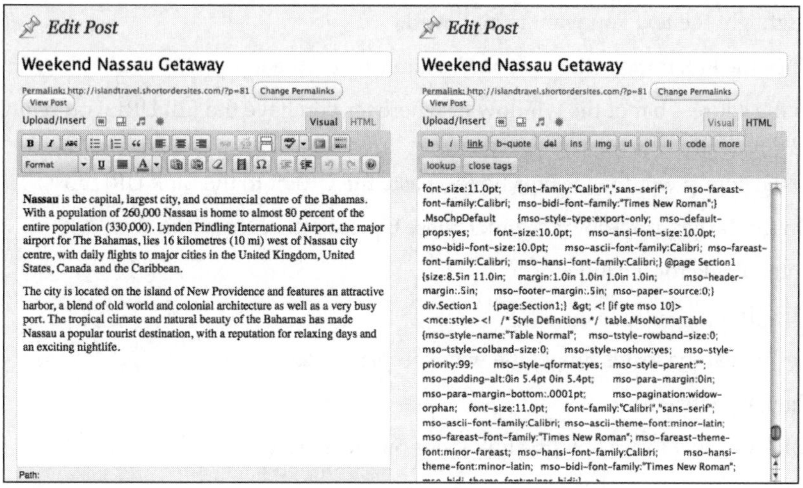

Figure 7-8

Because of the way style sheets work, this coding takes precedence over anything in your style sheet. Then there's the problem of excess coding — you get a few of these on a page and it can make your HTML bloated and slower to load.

One way around the problem is to put any text into a simple text editor program first (such as Notepad on Windows or TextEdit on Mac) and then copy and paste from there. The excess coding will be stripped off in the process, and that includes all formatting, even bold and italics.

If you want to try and preserve some basic formatting, so you don't have to reconstruct it in the Text Editor, you can try using one of the Paste buttons. There's one for text copied from Word and one for pasting text from other sources. The Word button is most commonly used and reports vary on what formatting will be preserved from your document, so it's really a matter of trying it out. Basic things like bold text usually make it through the process, but complex layouts like tables and so on typically do not.

Try It

In this lesson you practice creating a new link.

Lesson Requirements

A post with text.

Step-by-Step

1. Make sure you're in the Visual mode of the Text Editor.
2. Highlight the text you want to be linked.
3. Click the link button (the unbroken chain icon on the top row).
4. In the address bar of the window or wherever you have the full URL you're linking to, copy the web address.
5. In the popup window of WordPress, paste the URL into the Link URL box.
6. On the Target drop-down menu, choose Open Link in New Window.
7. Enter a Title for the link.
8. Click Insert.
9. Verify that the text is linked the way you planned.
10. Click Update Post.
11. Click Preview to see how the link looks on the live site.

 To see some of the examples from this lesson, including how to import text from a Word document, watch the video for Lesson 7 on the enclosed DVD.

8

Laying Out Text

Now that you know how to style bits of text, it's time to look at styling larger blocks using the Text Editor and laying out entire posts. In this lesson you learn how the Text Editor behaves and tips for how to arrange your written content effectively. In the end, it always comes down to what's easiest for your visitors to read.

Styling Paragraphs

I'm using the term *paragraph* to refer to any block of text that you've separated in the Text Editor by using the Enter key. That's because in HTML terms, the Text Editor sees any text separated in that way — even a single sentence — as a paragraph.

Aligning

To change the alignment of a paragraph, you simply need to click anywhere in the paragraph (there's no need to highlight the whole paragraph, though you can) and then click the appropriate alignment button — left, center, and right appear on the top row of the button bar.

There's a fourth alignment button that's only visible on the second row of the button bar, and that's for justified alignment. This is when text lines up flush on the left and the right, as shown in Figure 8-1.

Though the symmetry of this look pleases one part of my brain, there's another part that says "isn't that gap between words the same gap that indicates the end of a sentence?" Still worse is when justification is used on very narrow paragraphs, resulting in gigantic gaps between words. As a rule, I never use justification, but if you do, make sure your aesthetics aren't getting in the way of readability for your visitors.

Figure 8-1

A common misconception is that if you have a paragraph aligned right, center, or justified, to return it to the standard left align, you have to click the Align Left button. However, the default alignment in HTML is to the left, so all you need to do is click the same alignment button (that turns off the alignment) and the text will go back to the left.

Blockquotes

A *blockquote* is an HTML tag for designating a block of quoted text. This is usually displayed indented from both the left and the right. That's certainly how blockquotes display in the WordPress Text Editor, and they're typically used for quoting more than a sentence or two from books or other websites and so on. However, most WordPress themes like to style blockquotes in more creative ways, as you can see in Figure 8-2.

Creating a blockquote is easy. You simply place your cursor in the paragraph you want or highlight multiple paragraphs, and then click Blockquote. On the Jamaica page of Island Travel, I have a quote from a travel guide website. Rather than simply putting quotes around the two paragraphs, I want to really set them apart from the other text, so I use a blockquote — you can see the difference on the live site in Figure 8-3.

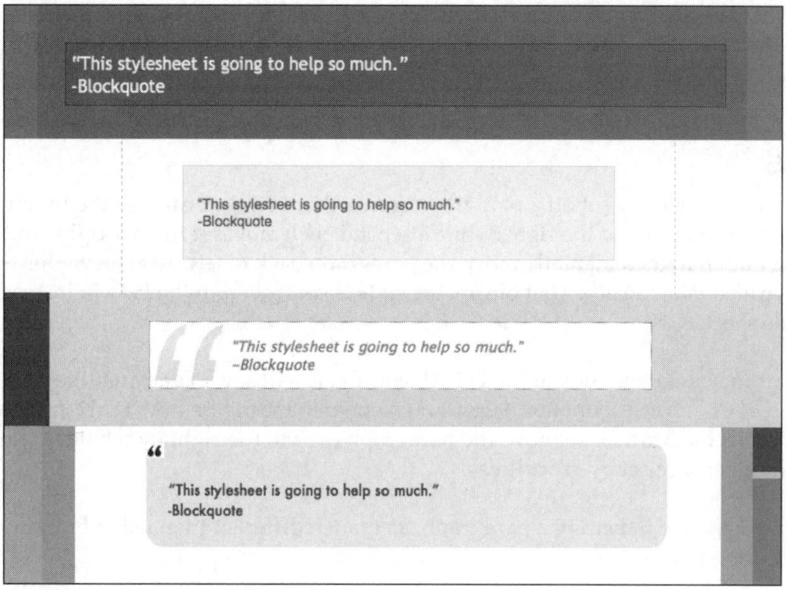

"This stylesheet is going to help so much."
-Blockquote

"This stylesheet is going to help so much."
-Blockquote

"This stylesheet is going to help so much."
~Blockquote

"This stylesheet is going to help so much."
-Blockquote

Figure 8-2

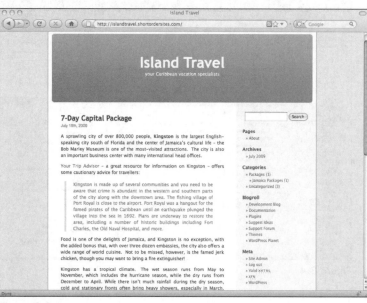

Figure 8-3

Notice too that I created a link to the site where I got the quote. I want to give them credit and it also allows visitors to easily get more information. The other site will also appreciate the link and not just the fact that you quoted them.

Indenting

When you want to visually set off a paragraph from other text, you can use the Indent button. One click moves the paragraph to the right, while a second click moves it further right, and so on. You use the Outdent button to incrementally move the paragraph back to left. To achieve this effect, WordPress uses what's called *inline styling*. That means the style is controlled in the HTML instead of in your theme's style sheet.

If you indent some text and look at the HTML coding, it will say something like `<p style= "padding-left: 30px;">` or 60px, 90px, and so on depending on how far right you're indenting. This coding tells the browser to move the paragraph over to the right by whatever number of pixels, and those numbers are set by WordPress.

At first it may look like indenting a paragraph isn't much different than using blockquotes, as illustrated in Figure 8-4.

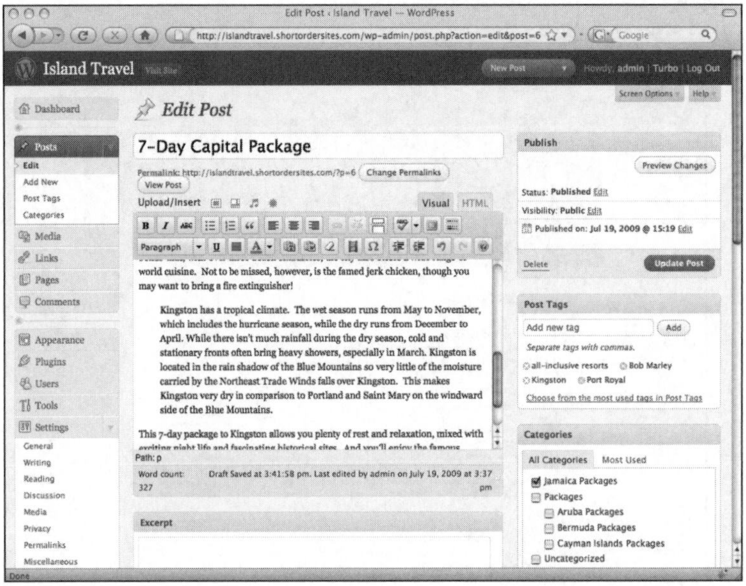

Figure 8-4

The only real difference seems to be that blockquotes are indented from both the left and the right, but as you saw earlier, that right-hand indent may not exist in the styling created by WordPress themes. So what really is different about indenting?

Indenting is meant to set off your own text, while blockquotes are for long quotations of other people's text. This is not a WordPress convention, but a function of the HTML tags that control the two. HTML tags are used not just to control style, but also to convey meaning (to search engine robots for example). The blockquote tag conveys that the text is a quotation from some other source, while the paragraph tags used to create indents do not. From this perspective, using blockquotes for your own text would be confusing, not just to search engines, but visually as well — your text would look the same as quotes you've used from others.

Creating Lists

Lists are very useful because they help break up information into more manageable pieces. On the Web in particular, people have become used to seeing information not only in smaller pieces, but in visually helpful structures, and lists are one of the most important of those.

In HTML, lists are either ordered or unordered, which basically means they're either displayed automatically numbered or with bullets. If you delete an item in an ordered list, the remaining items are automatically renumbered, whereas an unordered list only has the same bullet beside each item and nothing changes if an item is deleted. Figure 8-5 shows an example of each type of list, with its corresponding button highlighted.

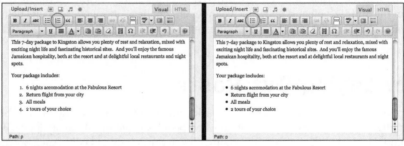

Figure 8-5

If you're not keen on the heavy black bullet effect of the unordered list, rest easy. Your WordPress theme very likely will render that more elegantly, and if it doesn't I will talk about that kind of styling in Lesson 29. You can always check how your list will actually look on your site by clicking Preview.

Beginning a New List

To begin either type of list, start a new paragraph (hit Enter or Return) and then click the appropriate button on the button bar. You'll see the cursor indent with a round black bullet for unordered lists or a number 1 for ordered lists.

If you click a list button while you're at the end of a paragraph (or anywhere inside a paragraph), that paragraph becomes the first item in the list. To return the paragraph to normal, just click the same list button (it'll be highlighted).

After you've entered the first item on your list, simply hit Enter and you'll begin a new list item. Keep doing that until you've entered all the items on your list. To end the list, simply hit Enter after the final list item, as though you're starting a new item, and then hit Enter again. The new item bullet or number disappears and your cursor returns to the far left of the Text Editor, ready to begin a new paragraph.

Working with Existing Text and Lists

If you want to turn existing text into a list, you need to make sure that each item in the list is a paragraph, which really means that each item has to be separated by hitting Enter after it. For example, if I have a paragraph describing the features of a resort, I can't simply highlight the paragraph and click a list button. The entire paragraph would become a single list item. What I need to do is go through the paragraph and hit Enter after each sentence, then highlight all these "paragraphs" and click a list button.

Converting an existing list to the other type of list is even simpler. Just highlight all the list items and click the other list button. Your ordered list instantly becomes an unordered list, or vice versa. Unlike paragraphs, for which you can place the cursor anywhere in the paragraph and apply certain styling to the whole (such as alignment or making it a blockquote), you must highlight the entire list to convert it. If you just place your cursor somewhere in the list, you'll only convert the list item you're on.

If you want to de-list some or all items in a list, highlight the ones to be converted and click the appropriate list button. Each list item becomes an individual paragraph. If you've only de-listed some items, the rest remain in list format and, if it's an ordered list, they automatically renumber. If the de-listed item(s) is in the middle, you end up with two independent lists, one above and one below, and if the original was an ordered list, the two remaining lists will renumber themselves separately.

Tips for Laying Out Posts

My first tip for laying out the text in a post is to ask yourself whether you might not be better off with one or more smaller posts. I say this because often when people are asking about layout it's because they have a lot of material to deal with and they're not sure how to break it up visually. And sometimes the answer to that is to break it up into separate posts or pages.

In the case of posts, for example, I talked about testimonials when I was planning the Island Travel site in Lesson 2. Instead of having all the testimonials on a single page in WordPress, I talked about how useful it would be to put each individual testimonial into a post. Part of that usefulness is that I don't have to figure out how to lay out a giant page of testimonials — the work is done for me when I call up the Testimonials category, and all of the testimonials are displayed as individual posts with headings and other visual separators.

In the case of pages, when there's a lot of content on a single page, ask yourself whether your visitors wouldn't be better served by breaking it up into separate pages, each with its own focus. The goal here is not to save yourself the trouble of laying out a lot of text on a page — that's just a side benefit of thinking about whether your visitors are having to sift through a lot of material that could be in relevant chunks.

Advanced Post Options

We've been looking at the most commonly used functions of the Add New Post or Edit Post screens; time now to look at the remaining functions.

Advanced Options Overview

In Figure 9-1 you have a visual overview of the lower portion of the Add New Post screen.

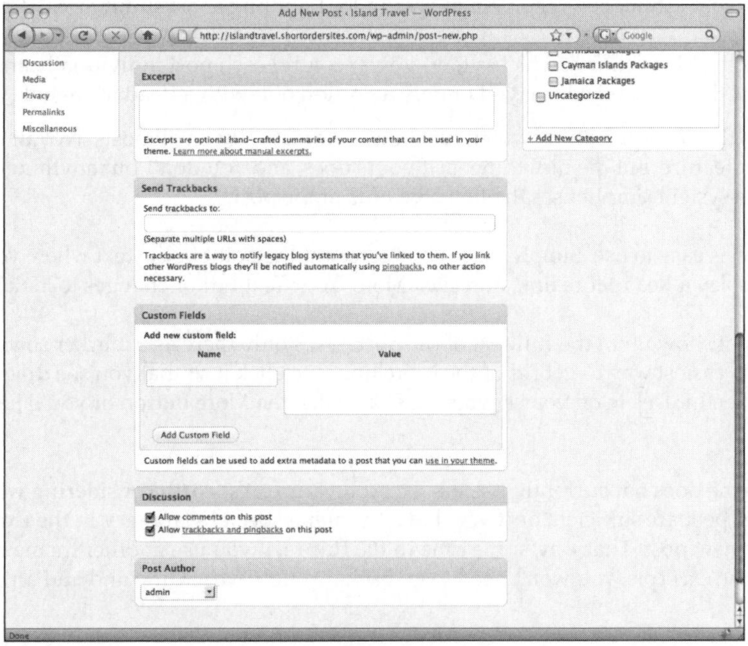

Figure 9-1

Because you have to scroll down on most screens to see these additional boxes, I usually don't bother collapsing or hiding them, but you can arrange things however you want. If anything, I might hide the Send Trackbacks box because it's the one I use the least. I discuss the role of Trackbacks in Lesson 25 so I'll pass over it here.

Custom Fields is a feature that allows users to create fields in the WordPress database for storing additional information. You would only be creating new fields if you learned how to incorporate them into your Theme files, but that's beyond the scope of this book.

However, you may well use the Custom Fields box depending on what plugins you install. Some of them will use Custom Fields, either to display information about a post or to ask you to enter information. Sometimes a theme author will use Custom Fields and provide you with instructions on using the fields he's set.

Typically, though, you won't need to deal with the Custom Fields box at all.

The *Post Author* box should show whatever name you've selected in your personal profile as your display name. If you haven't made any choice, the default is to show your WordPress username. If you have multiple users who are able to write or edit posts, their names will appear on this drop down list. In the case of the Island Travel site, for example, you might create a post for a press release and then change the author to a different staff member so they have permission to go in and edit the release. There may also be instances when you're ghost-writing an item for another user, so you change the author drop down to give them the credit for the post.

Excerpts and the More Button

WordPress has what I think is a very elegant system for handling short summaries of posts:

❑ There's the More button, which allows you to control each post individually and decide whether the full text is displayed or only a portion of it with a Read More link.

❑ There's the Excerpt feature, which functions automatically on all posts. Not all themes use the Excerpt feature, but the nice thing is, if yours does, and you don't put anything in the Excerpt box, the system simply uses the first 55 words of the post.

The More button is easy to use. Simply place your cursor at the point in the text where you want to cut off the post and display a Read More link, and click More. Your Text Editor changes to look like Figure 9-2.

That line does not show up in the full text of the post — it's only there as a marker so you know where you've set it. The easiest way to get rid of the More line is to click it so that you see drag points around its edges, and then hit Delete on your keyboard. Don't click the More button or you'll just get another More line.

Even if your theme does not currently use the Excerpt feature, it's worth considering whether the opening lines of your post are sufficient or if you'd like to enter a special summary in the Excerpt box while you're adding a new post. That way, some time in the future, if you use another theme or modify the current one to use excerpts, you won't need to go back through everything and add an excerpt where you want one.

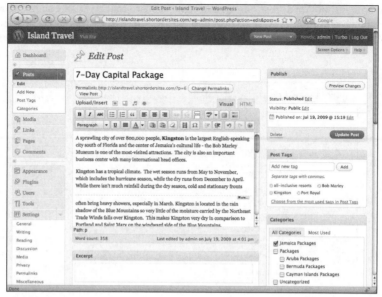

Figure 9-2

Discussion and Comments

The Discussion box is the place where you can override two of the site-wide parameters set under Settings ➪ Discussion: comments and trackbacks/pingbacks. By default WordPress allows both for all posts or pages, so unless you've changed anything in Settings, both boxes will be checked, as you saw in Figure 9-1.

It might be tempting to use your Screen Options and get rid of this box altogether — the general discussion settings are set up so why bother having this box at all? I find it's helpful, however, to be reminded that these options are available whenever adding or editing a post.

> You've probably seen blogs where it says that comments are now closed. On WordPress you can set comments to automatically close after a fixed period of time — see under Settings ➪ Discussion — or if you want individual control just go to the post and uncheck the Allow Comments box. Existing comments will continue to display but no new ones can be entered.

Handling Revisions

Has this ever happened to you? You completely rewrite something on a web page, save it, and then discover a week later that the new information is wrong and you don't have a copy of the original. That's where WordPress's revision feature comes in handy.

You may remember that WordPress has an auto-save feature that regularly saves what you're working on, but once you've published, saved, or updated a post, WordPress also starts keeping a copy of earlier versions of the post. A list of these revisions displays at the bottom of your post as you can see in Figure 9-3.

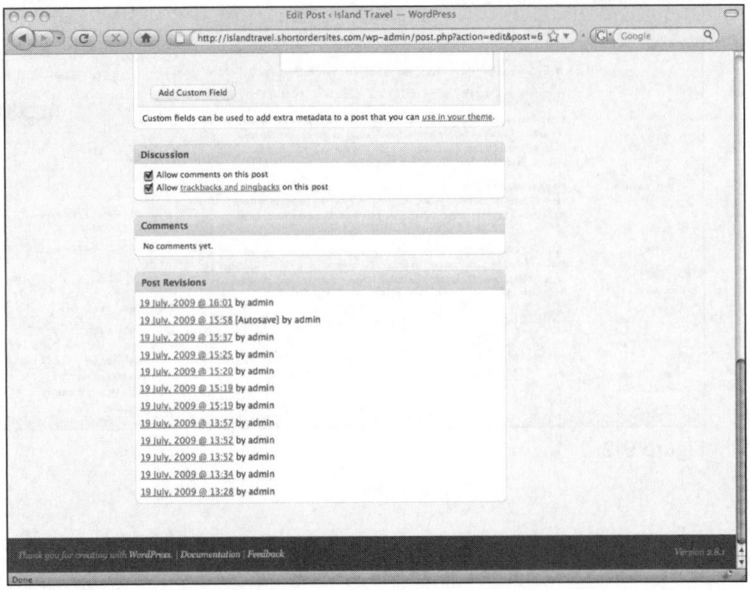

Figure 9-3

This box did not show in the overview image because there are no revisions when you're creating a new post. Once you save it and make your first changes, the revisions begin to accumulate and show up on this list.

The process of changing a page back to an earlier state is called *restoring* and the way to do that is to click the revision you want. If you're not sure which revision it is, don't worry, clicking here does not restore anything yet. What you get is the HTML for the earlier version of the post, as shown in Figure 9-4.

If this isn't the right version, you can look at others until you find the right one. I've trimmed the height of the screen so you can also see the bottom menu, where all the revisions are listed again. You'll see that the revision you chose has one of the radio buttons highlighted, and at the top of the list is the current version of the post and it too has a highlighted radio button. Those highlighted buttons mean you can compare those two versions by clicking Compare Revisions. If you want to compare two different revisions, click their respective radio buttons, one in the left column and one in the right.

When you do a comparison between two revisions, you get the HTML of each one side by side with different colored backgrounds for paragraphs with differences, and the text that's different in each is highlighted in a darker color, as demonstrated in Figure 9-5.

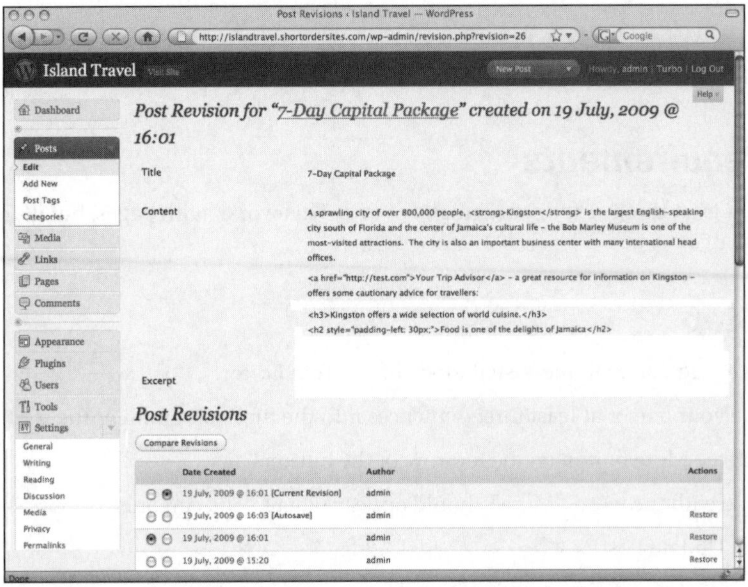

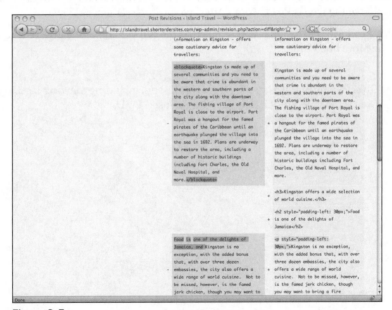

Figure 9-4

Figure 9-5

If you want to use a revision, simply click the Restore link to the right of the revision date. If you decide you want the current post to stay as it is, just click the date of the current post (always at the top and labeled "current") and you'll return to the Edit Post screen.

Try It

In this lesson you create a Read More breakpoint in the text of a post.

Lesson Requirements

A post with at least three or four paragraphs of text. This works with pages, but it's easier to see the effect quickly in a post.

Step-by-Step

1. Make sure you're in the Visual mode of the Text Editor.

2. Place your cursor at least three sentences into the first paragraph of the post.

3. Click the More button on the top row of the button bar.

4. A line with the word "More" should appear where your cursor is.

5. Click Update Post.

6. Navigate to a category that contains the post you just edited.

7. Unless you have a lot of posts in that category, the one you edited should be near the top. You should see the words Read More... after two or three sentences (55 words).

8. Click Read More to test that you're taken to the full version of the post (without the Read More or the More line visible).

 To see some of the examples from this lesson, including viewing revisions, watch the video for Lesson 9 on the enclosed DVD.

10

Adding a New Page

Virtually everything covered so far about writing content applies to both posts and pages in WordPress. I've also covered the key functions unique to posts, such as categories and tags. Now, in this lesson, it's time to cover the functions unique to WordPress pages, such as using page templates or creating sub-pages.

Pages vs. Posts

In older versions of WordPress there was often only one word on the entire screen to visually tell you whether you were about to add a post or a page. In the most recent versions there are enough differences to easily avoid that confusion, as you can see from the tops of both screens shown in Figure 10-1.

Figure 10-1

The more common problem these days is a conceptual one: how exactly do posts and pages differ? A detailed discussion of this was covered in Lesson 1, but it's worth running over a couple of points again here.

If you're simply running a blog, the distinction is fairly clear: most of the content of your site is in the form of posts, with the newest ones displaying on the homepage, whereas pages are used occasionally for content that rarely changes. However, if you're using WordPress to run a website (assuming for a moment that it has no blog section), pages take on a more important role and posts are more isolated bits of information rather than all belonging to "a blog."

Organizational structure — categories and tags vs. pages and sub-pages — is the primary difference between posts and pages, but a couple of other differences exist when working in the Add/Edit screens. Let's have a look at those next.

The Add Page Options

The first thing you notice is that there are fewer options on an Add New Page screen, as this overview in Figure 10-2 demonstrates.

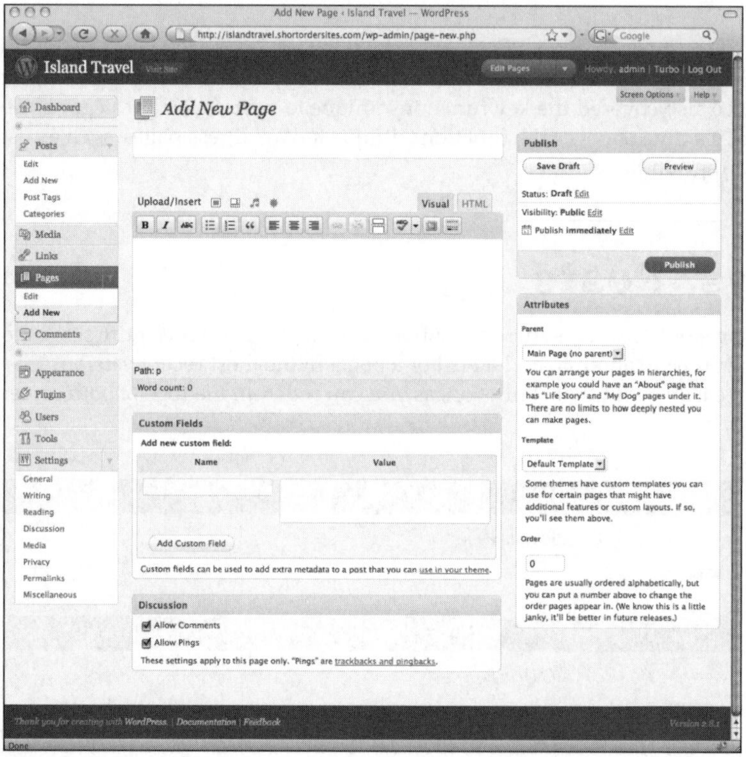

Figure 10-2

Gone from this screen are Tags and Categories, Excerpts, and Trackbacks. There are several new options over on the right-hand side in the Attributes box.

I'll leave the first of these — Parent — for the next section. The option below it is the Template menu. This displays all the page templates available for the theme you're currently using. For the default theme, the drop-down looks like Figure 10-3.

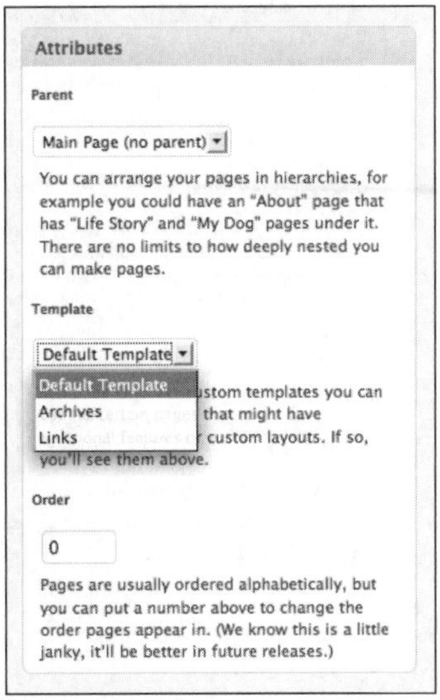

Figure 10-3

Page templates have layouts that can differ from the default page layout as much as the theme developer likes, though typically what these templates do is display specific information. In the case of the default theme, for example, the Links template shows all of the link categories as a series of lists. You wouldn't even need to enter any text for that page, other than the title.

Below the Template menu is the Order input box. In the automatic page menu that WordPress generates, pages are ordered alphabetically according to their titles. You can override that by entering numbers in the Order boxes for each page. It can be a bit cumbersome if you have a lot of pages and need to change the order at some point, but it works. Plugins are available for WordPress that offer simpler ways of handling this, the most popular of which is My Page Order.

Creating Sub-Pages

The other option in the Attributes box of the Add New Page screen is the Parent menu. This drop down — shown in Figure 10-4 — allows you to choose a parent for the page you're creating; that is, you can make it a sub-page of some existing page.

As you can see from this, some of the pages are shown with an indent. That means they're sub-pages of the first flush-left page above it. In a very complex web setup you could have sub-pages of sub-pages, as deeply nested as you need.

You can change the relationship of a page to other pages at any time by using this same drop-down menu while editing the page.

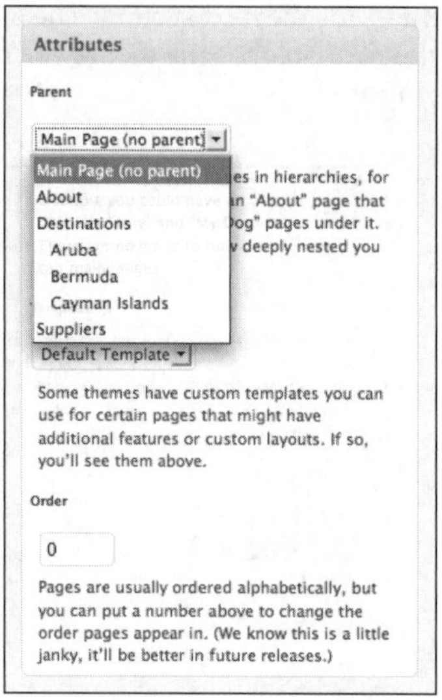

Attributes

Parent

Main Page (no parent) ▾

Main Page (no parent)
About
Destinations
Aruba
Bermuda
Cayman Islands
Suppliers

es in hierarchies, for
an "About" page that
og" pages under it.
y deeply nested you

Default Template ▾

Some themes have custom templates you can
use for certain pages that might have
additional features or custom layouts. If so,
you'll see them above.

Order

0

Pages are usually ordered alphabetically, but
you can put a number above to change the
order pages appear in. (We know this is a little
janky, it'll be better in future releases.)

Figure 10-4

Try It

In this lesson you practice making a new page a child of an existing page.

Lesson Requirements

At least one page already in the system.

Step-by-Step

1. Click Add New on the Page area of the Admin menu.

2. Enter a title and then some text.

3. In the Attributes box, drop down the Parent menu.

4. Choose a page to be the parent of your new page.

5. Click Publish.

6. Refresh the home page on your live site and see how the page menu looks — you should see your new sub-page.

 To see some of the examples from this lesson, including making a Links page using the Links template, watch the video for Lesson 10 on the enclosed DVD.

Part IV: Working with Media Content

11

The Basics of Handling Media Files

Up to now you've learned about entering, editing, styling, and laying out text content. In this lesson you begin the same process for media files, which primarily means images, but also includes video, audio, and documents. It's important to understand how WordPress organizes these files so I'll start with that, and then you will learn the basics of uploading and inserting an image into a post.

The Media Library vs. Galleries

As you explore the admin section of WordPress you'll notice a number of places for adding images and other media files. There's the Add New button in the Media area of the side menu or the short-cut menu at the top, both shown in Figure 11-1.

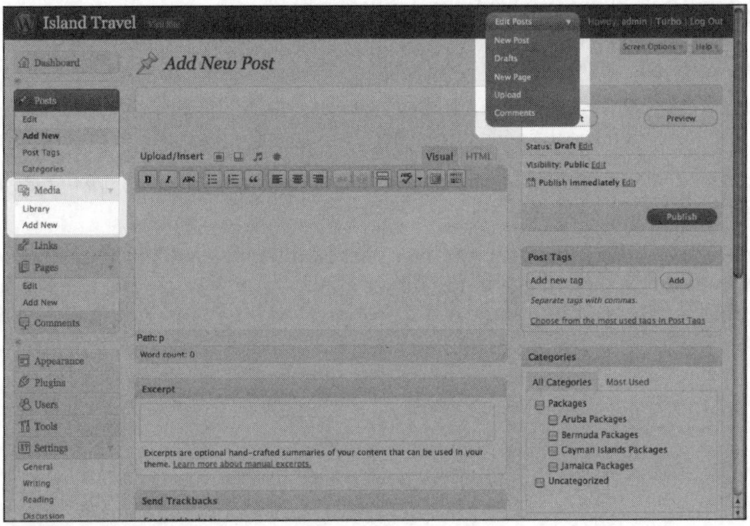

Figure 11-1

As you saw in earlier lessons, there is also the Upload/Insert menu of the Text Editor for posts (as always I'm using "posts" to mean posts or pages).

But before you go crazy with uploading from any of these spots, let's take a moment and talk about how WordPress thinks about media files and organizes them. You'll see that, when it comes to uploading, what matters is location, location, location.

WordPress organizes media files in two ways: the media library and galleries.

The media library is a list of every file you've ever uploaded to your site and from it you can access those files from anywhere on the site.

A gallery, on the other hand, lists only the media files associated with that gallery's post.

What do I mean by associated? That's where things get a little complicated. A media file becomes associated with a post by 1) being uploaded into WordPress through the Upload/Insert menu for that post or 2) having its first insertion from the media library into that post (it can be inserted into other posts later, but will only be associated with that first post).

Think of it this way: whenever you upload a file into WordPress, you're uploading it into the media library. But if the upload is done through the Upload/Insert menu of a particular post, the file is also associated with that and only that post. This means that all media files necessarily are in the media library, but not all files are necessarily in a gallery.

Why have galleries at all? Why not just a media library? Galleries are useful because they group related files together for easier retrieval and also allow you to easily display sets of images — image galleries — with just a click of a button, a topic I cover in detail in Lesson 15.

You'll sometimes see the term *attachments* used to refer to files that are in a gallery. It's just another way of describing the relationship of certain media files to a post, and this relationship is used by plugins and customizations to do all sorts of cool things.

Understanding these relationships will not only help you think of ways to use media files in WordPress, but it will help avoid two common confusions:

> *I inserted a photo into a post but it doesn't show up in the gallery.*
>
> That's because you "borrowed" an image from the media library that had already been inserted into at least one other post, so it's permanently associated with some other post.
>
> *I uploaded an image to a post for a particular use and now it's also showing up in the gallery of images I created for that post.*
>
> Any image you upload to a post becomes part of any image gallery in the body of the post. If you don't want this new image in the image gallery, you would need to upload it to the media library instead, insert it into some other post first, and then insert it into the post you're dealing with.

The Upload/Insert Menu

You saw the Upload/Insert menu when you explored the WordPress Text Editor, but look at it in detail now using Figure 11-2.

Figure 11-2

The title of this menu is important because it's a reminder that it fulfills two functions, both of which are completely separate: uploading media files and inserting them into the post. You can upload media files and not insert them into the post, and you can insert media files that were previously uploaded.

The four icons represent four types of media files. From left to right (with examples of file types) they are:

❑   Images (photos, graphics — jpg, gif, png)

❑   Video (swf, mp4, wmv, avi, mov, and so on)

❑   Audio (mp3, ram, and so on)

❑   Other Media (doc, ppt, xls, zip, and so on)

If you forget which is which, you just need to mouseover one and you'll see the name of it.

Click any of these icons and you get a popup screen where you perform the upload or insert functions. I go into all the details of those screens in Lessons 12 and 13. For the moment, I want to show you the basic steps for getting an image into a post.

Inserting an Image into a Post

The most common way you'll add images is when you're working on a post, so to demonstrate I'll upload a photo as part of a post about a vacation package on the Island Travel site. I begin by locating the Image icon of the Upload/Insert menu that you saw in Figure 11-2.

Clicking that icon produces the popup window in Figure 11-3.

Figure 11-3

The photos are on my computer, so I can use the default From Computer tab.

I click the Choose button and up pops a browse window showing my computer. I locate the image I want, highlight it, and click the Select button (or whatever your browser displays), as shown in Figure 11-4.

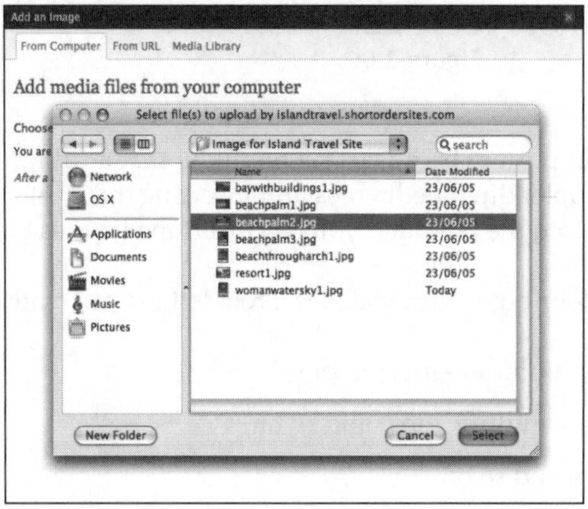

Figure 11-4

At that point the browse window disappears and WordPress displays a progress bar for the uploading of the images. Depending on the size of the image it could take a little while. When it's finished, you see a thumbnail of the image with a whole lot of options, as shown in Figure 11-5 (you'll probably need to scroll to see all this, depending on the size of your screen).

Don't worry about all those options right now. What I'm looking for is the Insert Into Post button down at the bottom left. I click that, the popup window disappears, and I see the image in the body of my post, as in Figure 11-6.

Remember to click the post's Update button and you can click Preview to see what your image will look like on the live site.

Figure 11-5

Figure 11-6

Try It

I've just run through the basics of uploading an image to a post and then inserting it, so for practice, try uploading to the media library first and then inserting into a post.

Lesson Requirements

A post with text.

Step-by-Step

1. Find the Add New link under the Media section of the admin menu and click it.

2. Click Select Files.

3. In the popup window, choose the file to upload and click Select. You should see a progress bar for the upload. When the upload is complete, you'll see a series of options.

4. Fill in any of the fields you choose.

5. Click Save All Changes.

6. Navigate to the post where you want to insert the image.

7. Click the Image icon of the Upload/Insert menu.

8. Click Media Library.

9. Locate the image you just uploaded and click Show.

10. Click Insert Into Post. You should see your image in the body of the post.

 To see some of the examples from this lesson, watch the video for Lesson 11 on the enclosed DVD.

12

The Upload/Insert Window Tabs

When you click one of the icons on the Upload/Insert menu and the window pops up, you see tabs in that window, and in this lesson you learn what they each mean. Briefly, here's what they do in order from left to right:

❑ **From Computer:** This is for uploading files from your computer.

❑ **From URL:** This is for creating links to files elsewhere on the Web.

❑ **Gallery:** This displays a list of every media file (not just images) that has been uploaded to this post. They may not all have been inserted into the text, but they were all uploaded in WordPress through this post. This Gallery tab is also used to insert a thumbnail list of all images into the post.

❑ **Media Library:** This is for inserting any files already listed in your media library.

The following sections cover each of these tabs in some detail.

The From Computer Tab

Because the From Computer tab is the one you'll use the most, and it's the default tab when the window opens, let's start with it, as shown in Figure 12-1.

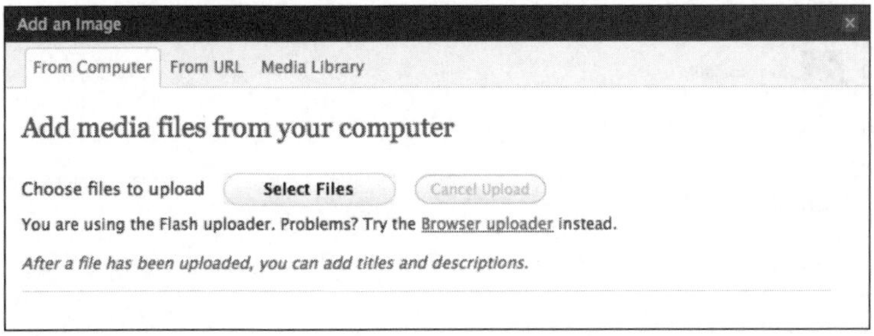

Figure 12-1

You're told to "Choose files to upload" and the good news is that they really do mean files, so you can process many files at one time instead of having to choose them one by one. The not so good news is that this uploading system, which uses Flash, doesn't always work on every browser. In fact, WordPress even tells you that and offers an alternative Browser Uploader link. So if you don't see a Choose button, just click the browser link and you'll get a regular upload function — only you'll have to do it one file at a time.

As you saw earlier, the upload window displays a bar showing the progress of the upload, shown in Figure 12-2.

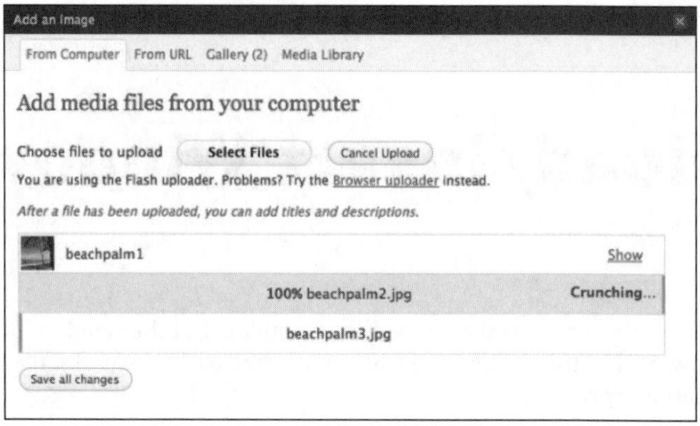

Figure 12-2

If you're uploading multiple files, there will be a separate progress bar for each one, all running at the same time.

What you see after uploading is finished depends on whether you're uploading multiple files or just one. If it's several files, you'll see a thumbnail for each file with a Show link, as illustrated in Figure 12-3.

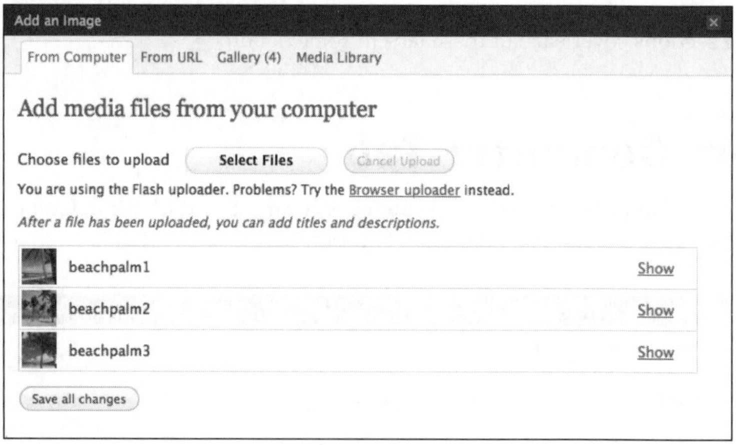

Figure 12-3

If you're uploading just one file, you'll get a larger thumbnail and a whole series of options (the ones you would see if you clicked the Show link for multiple files). These options will vary depending on the type of media file you're uploading. I cover the options for images in Lesson 13, and the others I cover at points when I'm talking about that particular file type.

The one option shared by all screens is the ability to either Insert the file into your post or Save it for future use.

The From URL Tab

This is the place to insert media files that are located on a site other than your own. You may want to use this option in cases where you run multiple websites and have an image or document common to all, so you simply use the URL on all the sites. Another example is when a company whose product you're selling provides you with a URL to an image of the product — this is where you'd insert that URL.

> You can't just start grabbing images from anywhere — you need to have permission to use the image, not just for copyright reasons, but because you're using their server's bandwidth to load the image.

As you can see in Figure 12-4, unlike the From Computer tab, you're presented with all the options right up front.

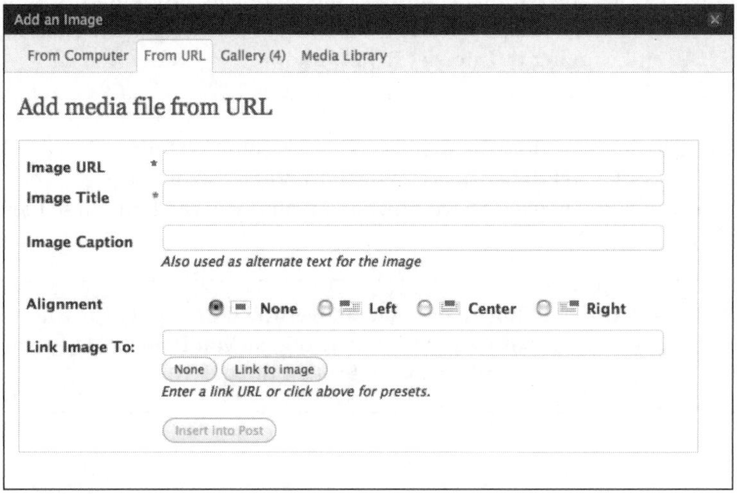

Figure 12-4

Notice that the title says "Add media file from URL" and the options say "Image." The reason for that is you'll have different options in the From URL tab depending on which icon you chose from the Upload/Insert menu. In this case I had chosen the image icon.

I cover the details of each type of option in the lesson for that particular media type, but there is one option that's the same on all From URL tabs, and that's the URL box.

You'll need the full URL for the media file in a form like this: `http://www.somedomain.com/folder/filename.extension`. (The extension is the .jpg, .avi, .pdf, and so on.)

Type or paste that URL into the URL box. As soon as you move your cursor off that box, you'll see a tiny spinning graphic to the left of the URL box. If WordPress successfully locates the file, you'll see a green check mark — if not you'll see a red X after a certain amount of trying. An example of each is shown in Figure 12-5.

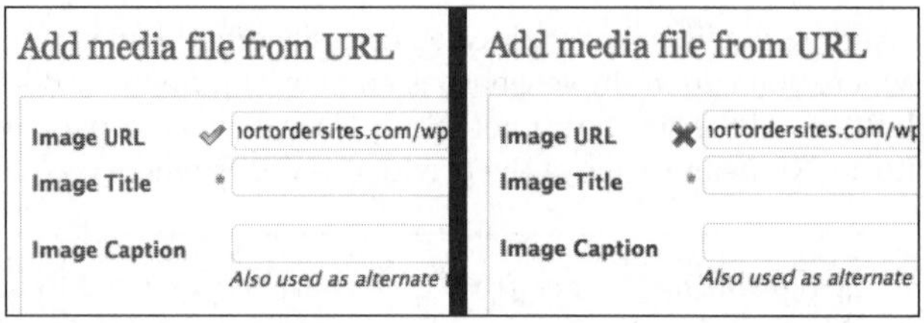

Figure 12-5

If you get the red X, you'll need to make sure you typed in the URL correctly (that's why I prefer to copy and paste) or that you've actually copied the right URL.

> You can usually get the URL by right-clicking an image, pdf, video, or other media file and selecting Copy Image Location (Firefox), or Properties and then highlighting the URL and copying it (Internet Explorer).

The other option that all From URL tabs share is the Insert Into Post button. It will remain grayed out until WordPress has confirmed the existence of the file and given you the green check mark. At that point you can do the insert. There's no Save function because you can't put these files into the gallery or the media library.

> Keep in mind that if you don't have control over the URL where the file is located, it could disappear in the future without warning, so you'll need to keep an eye on such files so your visitors aren't left with broken images/links.

The Gallery Tab

You will not always see a Gallery tab when you click a button on the Upload/Insert menu. Only if there is at least one item already in the gallery will you see the tab. The number in the bracket on the tab title is the total number of media files in the post's gallery — that's all media files, not just images.

Figure 12-6 shows an example of the screen you get when you click the Gallery tab.

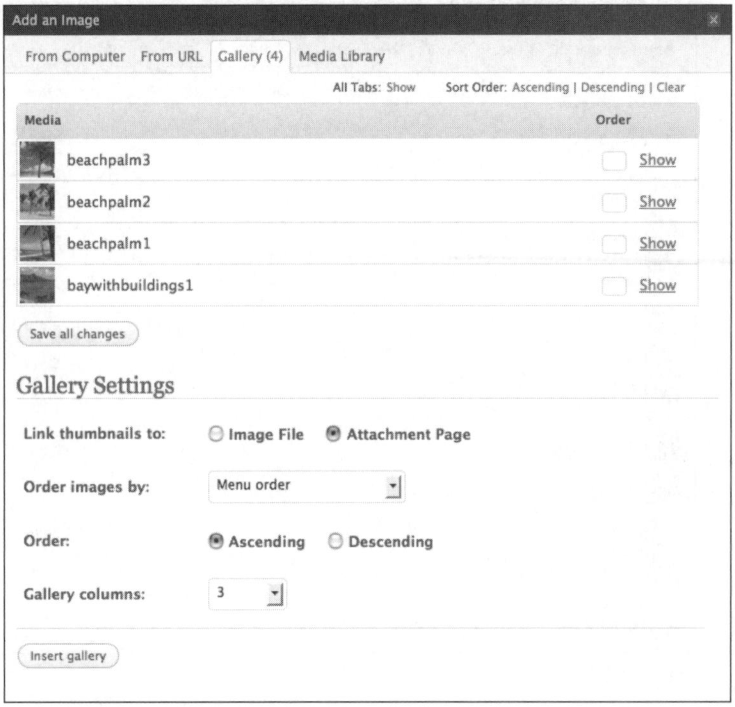

Figure 12-6

The Gallery Settings area at the bottom is where you create image galleries for your posts, and I deal with that in Lesson 15. Right now, I'm focused on the top area, which, as I said, displays all media, not just images.

On the left-hand side you'll see image thumbnails or icons representing other types of media files. On the right of each file is a Show link. Clicking that reveals all the options for the particular type of file, including the option to insert the file into the post. While the options are displayed, this link will say Hide — click it to hide the options.

There's also the option at the top of the screen called All Tabs: Show, and by clicking that you'll open the options for all files at one time. Just click Hide to close them all up again.

Next to All Tabs is a small menu called Sort Order and this is part of how you control the order of images when you've inserted an image gallery into a post — something I cover in Lesson 15 — so you don't need to worry about it at this point.

The Media Library Tab

What you get in this tab is a quickie version of what you would see under Media ➪ Library in the main admin menu. It allows you to see every media file that's been uploaded to your site and use it in the post you're working on. An example is shown in Figure 12-7.

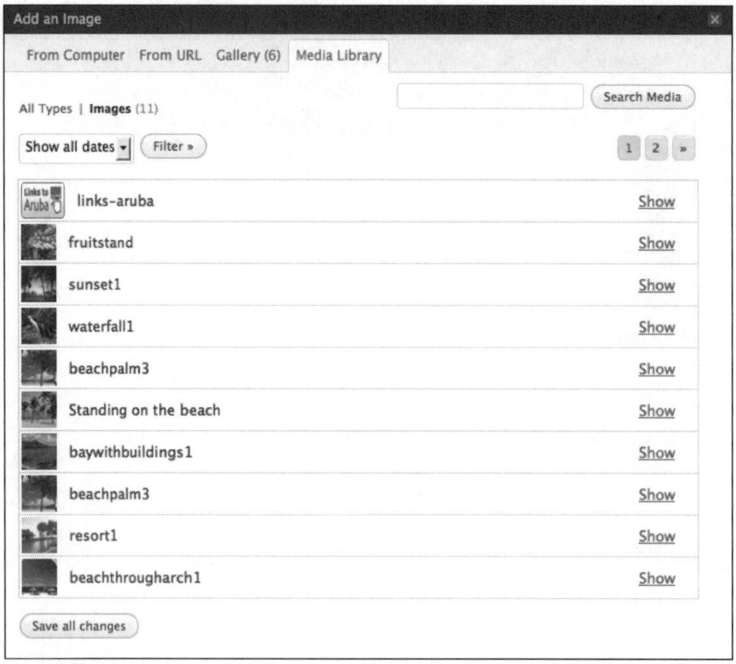

Figure 12-7

As you can see it's very similar to the Gallery tab with the thumbnails on the left and the Show link on the right. If there are more than 10 items in the library, you'll see pagination at the top right, allowing you to navigate through numerous screens of file listings.

> Most of the time you'll be working with images and if you click the Media Library tab, you might wonder where all your PDFs or other media files have gone. That's because by default WordPress shows you only the file type you're working on. You need to click All Types at the top right of the Media Library tab to see every file in the library.

From this tab you can not only insert a media file into your post, but you can change the options on those files whether or not you're inserting them. Whether you change the options on one or more files, be sure to click Save Changes at the bottom left. It may or may not be visible depending on the height of your screen, so you may need to scroll down to see it.

I've been talking here about the Media Library tab, but in Lesson 19 I cover the media library itself, which you access from the Admin menu.

Try It

In this lesson you practice inserting an image into a post using the From URL tab.

Lesson Requirements

An existing post and have in mind an image on your website that you'd like to insert into your post (or if you have permission for an image on another site).

Step-by-Step

1. Open a post for editing.

2. Click the image icon of the Upload/Insert menu.

3. Click From URL.

4. In a separate tab of your browser, find the page with the image you want to insert.

5. Right-click the image and choose View Image or Show Picture — if neither is available, choose Properties and highlight the URL in the popup window.

6. If View Image or Show Picture works, you'll see the image by itself in your browser — copy the URL in the address bar.

7. Paste the address for the image into the Image URL field.

8. Click the Image Title or any other field.

9. A small spinning circle displays beside Image URL, indicating it's checking that your image is where you say it is.

10. If the image is found, you'll see a green check mark.

11. If the image is not found, you'll see a red X.

12. Assuming you get a check mark, choose an Alignment.

13. If you want the image to link somewhere, enter that URL in the Link Image To field.

14. Click Insert Into Post.

15. Click Preview to see the image in your post.

 To see some of the examples from this lesson, watch the video for Lesson 12 on the enclosed DVD.

Image Options in Detail

When I showed you the procedure for uploading and inserting an image into a post, you briefly saw the options screen for the image, and I talked about some of the choices you could make. This lesson examines those options in detail.

Titles, Captions, and Descriptions

WordPress makes it easy to add various types of text to your image — shown in Figure 13-1 — each of which serves a particular function.

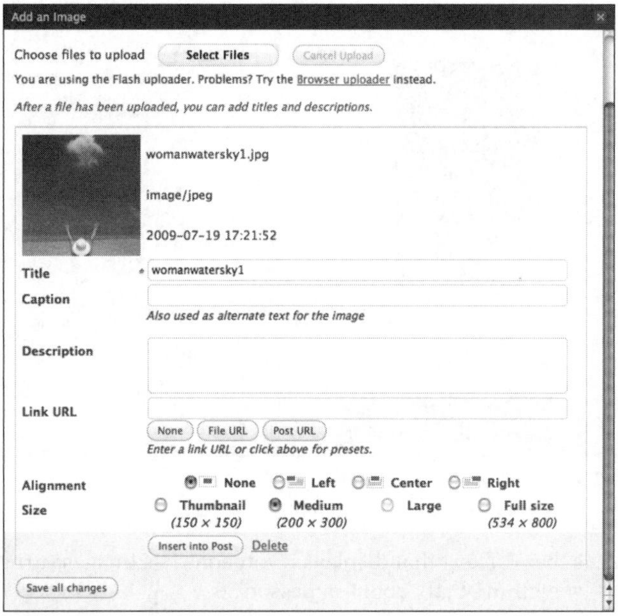

Figure 13-1

WordPress automatically extracts some of the data embedded in digital images (aperture, shutter speed, and so on) and stores it in its database. If your image has an embedded title and caption, they'll be displayed in the screen shown in Figure 13-1. The other data are used by plugins or you could make use of them through customized theme files.

Title

WordPress automatically gives the image a title, using the name of the file minus its extension (.jpg, .gif, and so on). You don't have to change the image title, but it makes a lot of sense because it's the wording that will show up when people mouseover the image and it's also used for the name of the image in various contexts, such as when you create image galleries. Besides, six months later when you're looking through the media library, you'll appreciate "Sailboat off Cape Cod" much more than "img000534."

If the default title does not look exactly like the name of the file you uploaded, that's because WordPress cleans up names by stripping them of spaces, changing upper- to lowercase, and adding numbers if there's a file of that name already in the system.

Caption

As the name suggests, any text entered here automatically displays as a caption when you insert an image into a post or beneath the thumbnail when you insert a gallery. Figure 13-2 shows the actual placement of the caption in a published post and a common way of styling it (this will vary depending on your theme's style sheet).

Figure 13-2

The caption also serves as the ALT text that displays if someone has images turned off and it's also useful for search engines — something I talk about in Lesson 30.

In the case of thumbnails for an image gallery, the only way to prevent a caption from appearing is to delete the content from this field. For single inserted images, you can remove the caption from that instance of the image by going into the HTML editor view and deleting the caption text. That way the caption is still available for the image's thumbnail in an image gallery or another use of the image in another post.

Description

This setting allows you to provide a lot more detail about the file. Where or if the description gets used will depend on your theme. In the case of default WordPress theme used on the Island Travel site, the description is displayed on the page that's created by using the Post URL button described in the Linking Images section below. Even if your theme doesn't currently make use of descriptions, you might want them later if you customize WordPress, so if you have time, enter a description when you upload/insert the image.

Linking Images

The address placed in the Link URL field, shown in Figure 13-3 is used to automatically create a link for your image. For instance, you might want to link an image of a product to a page on your site with more details or to a manufacturer's website.

Figure 13-3

WordPress also offers a couple of automated buttons for creating links. *File URL* links to a blank browser window displaying the full-size version of the image, and *Post URL* displays the image in the size you set, on a web page that typically looks the way one of your posts would look. Some themes come with a template file that displays images in a special way or you can have one made.

Why is there a None button for the Link URL? WordPress remembers how you configured the last image, and if you chose a link option, it does the same again for the new image. If you don't want any link, just click None.

Choosing an Alignment

I've already spoken briefly about choosing alignment options, but Figure 13-4 provides a quick reminder of what they look like.

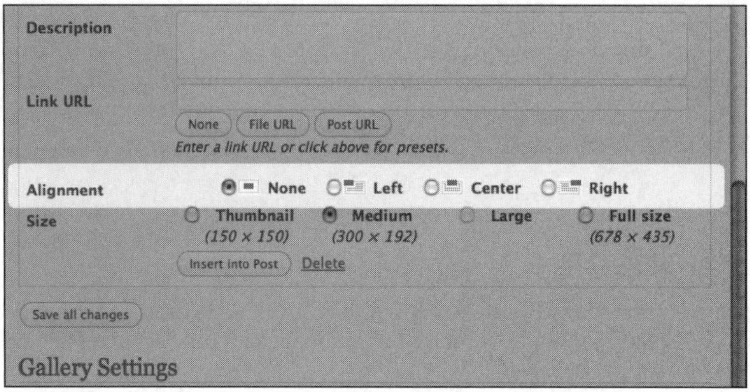

Figure 13-4

This setting tells WordPress how to place your image relative to the text and other images on the page. The Left and Right options place the image to one side of the text and the text flows around the image. The Center option places the image in the center of the screen with text above and below it. Selecting None also breaks up text above and below the image, but the image sits over on the left (the default position in HTML).

As with Link URL, WordPress remembers the last way you aligned an image and repeats that setting. So always check this option and don't take for granted that it will default to None.

Choosing an alignment option does not do the actual aligning — it assigns a class to the image. Your theme's style sheet must have those classes set up or else the alignment won't occur in the published version of the post. Most themes do have these CSS styles, but it's something to be aware of, especially when modifying or creating a theme.

Choosing a Size

You're given a choice of one or more sizes for the image you're going to insert, with the pixel size shown in brackets. Not all sizes will be available for all images, as shown in Figure 13-5. The choices depend on how large the original was. Keep in mind that the available sizes represent physically resized copies of your original.

When you upload an image, WordPress automatically creates other versions of it, depending on how large the original is and depending on what values are in Settings ⇨ Media (I look at those settings in Lesson 19). By default, WordPress creates Thumbnails of 150 pixels, Medium images of 300 pixels, and Large images of 1024 pixels.

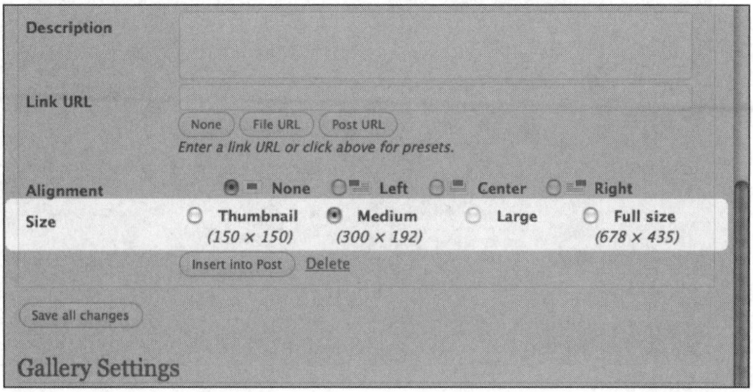

Figure 13-5

Based on those settings, if your image is 800 pixels wide, you'll have a choice of Thumbnail, Medium, and Full-Size. If you upload an image of 125 pixels, you would only have the choice of Full-Size. If a sizing option is not available it won't have any dimensions listed below it and you won't be able to choose it, as in the case of Figure 13-5 where there is no choice for Large.

How Large Do Images Need to Be?

Before leaving this discussion of sizing, it's important to say something about the size of images you upload to your site. As the average digital camera offers increasingly larger pixel sizes, I see clients uploading image files from which you could print a poster! Though it's possible your image might be rejected by WordPress for exceeding the server upload settings, there's still no need, in the vast majority of cases, to upload a 2MB or even a 500K image file.

Unless you intend visitors to be able to download print-quality photos (for example, on a media page where magazines and newspapers would download material for print), you should be keeping the files you upload as small as possible. That does not mean you can't display huge photos on the Web; you just need to understand how even a small file will produce gigantic web images — an image of just 100K could fill your entire screen.

This is not the place to discuss the details of file compression for the Web. The simplest answer is to think in terms of pixels. In your image editing program, check the longest side of the image — if it's more than 1600 pixels, reduce it to at most 1600 before uploading. Even 800 pixels is probably more than enough for most situations.

Currently the average screen is 1024 pixels wide, so 800 would fill the majority of the screen. It's true that WordPress creates small versions for you to use in your posts, but you don't want people waiting for long downloads when they click to view the full-size image, and you also don't want to be using up valuable storage space on your server.

Insert vs. Save

These two buttons, shown in Figure 13-6, can sometimes cause confusion.

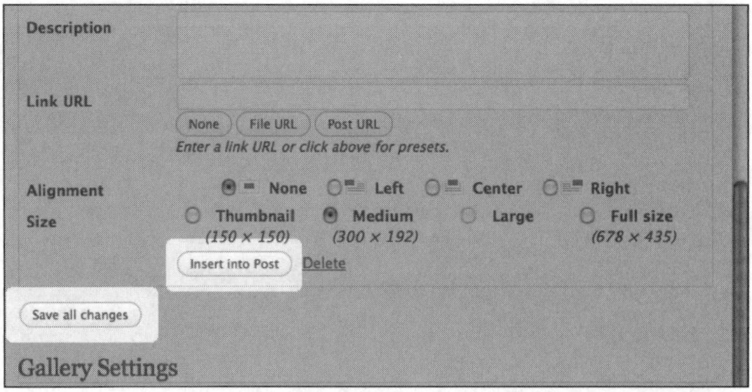

Figure 13-6

Insert Into Post

Clicking this button places the image into the text at whatever point the cursor currently sits. Don't worry if the image doesn't end up in the right place; as you'll see in Lesson 14, it's easy to move. In addition to inserting the image, this button simultaneously saves all the text you entered and the options you chose.

Sometimes people look at the Save All Changes button at the very bottom of the popup window and see the word Save, but clicking that does not put the image into the text of the post. You must click Insert Post.

Save All Changes

The word *Changes* might be a bit confusing if this is the first time you're uploading this image; you're not changing existing information. More to the point, though, if Save All Changes doesn't insert the image into the post, why use it? Why else would I be uploading an image if not to insert it?

Suppose you've already inserted an image gallery in the post — like the one for the Jamaican travel package. You want the thumbnail of this new picture to appear with the others, but nowhere else in the post. If you use Insert Into Post, the image will show up in the body of the text as well as in the image gallery. Using the Save All Changes feature, it will only show up in the image gallery.

If it turns out you want to get rid of the image — erase it from WordPress completely — there is a Delete function. A new line will appear warning you that you're about to delete the image, with a Continue link and a Cancel link. As a further warning, the Continue button turns red as you're about to click it. Don't say you weren't warned.

Try It

In this lesson you practice uploading and inserting an image with a number of options.

Lesson Requirements

A post with text and an image to use for uploading.

Step-by-Step

1.   Find the post you'll upload to and click Edit.

2.   Make sure you're in the Visual mode of the Text Editor.

3.   Click the image icon of the Upload/Insert menu.

4.   Using the From Computer option, upload your image.

5.   Change the Title from the filename to something else.

6.   Enter a short Caption for the image.

7.   Enter a Description for the image.

8.   If there is a URL in Link URL, click None to clear the field.

9.   Choose Alignment Right.

10. Choose the Medium size if it's not already selected.

11. Click Insert Into Post.

12. View the image in the Text Editor — the caption should be displayed.

 To see some of the examples from this lesson, including a quick demonstration of how different-sized images display on the Web, see Lesson 13 on the enclosed DVD.

14

Editing and Laying Out Images

Having inserted an image into a post you may need to make some changes once you see the image in relationship to the text and other images. You'll want a layout that's pleasing to the eye and easy for your visitors to read. WordPress provides a number of options for editing images within the body of the post. How you choose to layout the page is up to you, but in this lesson I go over some ideas to help get you started.

Align and Resize — An Overview

Two of the most common tasks you'll do when editing images are aligning and resizing, so let's take a quick look at them. I've started a page for biographies of the Island Travel staff, including their photos. As you can see in Figure 14-1, the image doesn't look all that great in relationship to the text.

Diana Smith

Email Diana
Diana's background includes a BA from Overton College majoring in Hotel, Restaurant & Institutional Management with a focus on Travel & Tourism. After graduating, she worked in corporate travel and meeting planning for Donnair Travel in Houston. She came to Island Travel in 1998 and coordinated group

Figure 14-1

An easy way to improve this layout would be to move the image over to the right-hand side of the page and let the text flow around it. In other words, you need to change the alignment of the image relative to the text. Here's how.

Just click the image and you'll see several things — a set of two buttons at the top left and a number of squares around the edges of the image, called drag points, as shown in Figure 14-2.

Figure 14-2

Unfortunately, Safari users will not see any drag points. As of this date, the browser has not implemented the creation of the resize box. See http://tinymce.moxiecode.com/punbb/viewtopic.php?id=15126.

Click the left-hand button — the one that looks like a little picture — and up pops the editing options window as shown in Figure 14-3.

There's a lot going on in this window — I go over it in detail later — but for now, find the Alignment options. Choose Right, and then click Update at the bottom left. As you can see in Figure 14-4, the photo is now over at the right side of the editor and the text flows around it.

With the photo aligned the way you want, it's obviously a bit big for that spot, so let's resize it. If your image isn't showing the drag points, just click it again. Place your cursor over any of the corner squares, and when the cursor looks like Figure 14-5 you can click and drag.

Drag the image inward until you get the size you want and let the cursor go. *Remember to update your post.* The finished version, shown in Figure 14-6, looks much better.

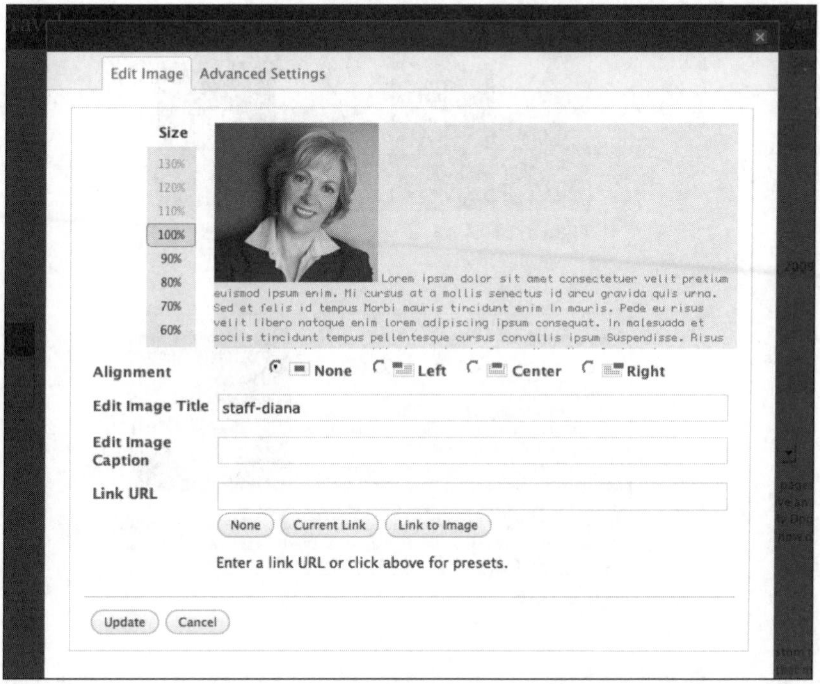

Size

130%
120%
110%
100%
90%
80%
70%
60%

Lorem ipsum dolor sit amet consectetuer velit pretium euismod ipsum enim. Mi cursus at a mollis senectus id arcu gravida quis urna. Sed et felis id tempus Morbi mauris tincidunt enim in mauris. Pede eu risus velit libero natoque enim lorem adipiscing ipsum consequat. In malesuada et sociis tincidunt tempus pellentesque cursus convallis ipsum Suspendisse. Risus

Alignment   ⦿ None   ⦾ Left   ⦾ Center   ⦾ Right

Edit Image Title   staff-diana

Edit Image Caption

Link URL

(None) (Current Link) (Link to Image)

Enter a link URL or click above for presets.

(Update) (Cancel)

Figure 14-3

Diana Smith

Email Diana
Diana's background includes a BA from Overton College majoring in Hotel, Restaurant & Institutional Management with a focus on Travel & Tourism. After graduating, she worked in corporate travel and meeting planning for Donnair Travel in Houston. She came to Island Travel in 1998 and coordinated group programs until 2002. After taking a break to travel round the world with her husband, Diana was excited to return to Island Travel in 2004. Her extensive travel background

Figure 14-4

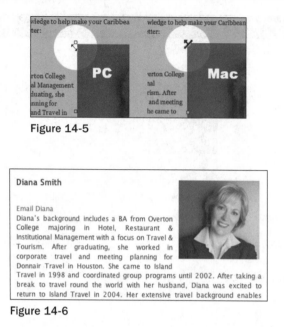

Figure 14-5

Figure 14-6

That's a quick overview of the basic tools needed for editing and laying out an image in a post. Let's go back now and look at all the possibilities in some detail.

The Popup Image Editor

To access the popup image editor you need to click an image so that you get a set of drag points around the edges and two icons at the top right. Before clicking the left-hand icon and popping up the editor, let me say something about the other icon — the red circle with a slash shown in Figure 14-7.

Figure 14-7

You probably guessed that it's for deleting the image, but only from the body of the post. Clicking this icon does not delete the image from the post's gallery. If you want to physically remove the image from WordPress, you'll need to go into the gallery or the media library and delete it from there.

Getting back to the left-hand icon — the one that looks like a picture — as you saw before, clicking it pops up the image editor. At first glance the window shown in Figure 14-8 looks quite different from the window used to upload and insert an image, but it performs virtually all the same functions.

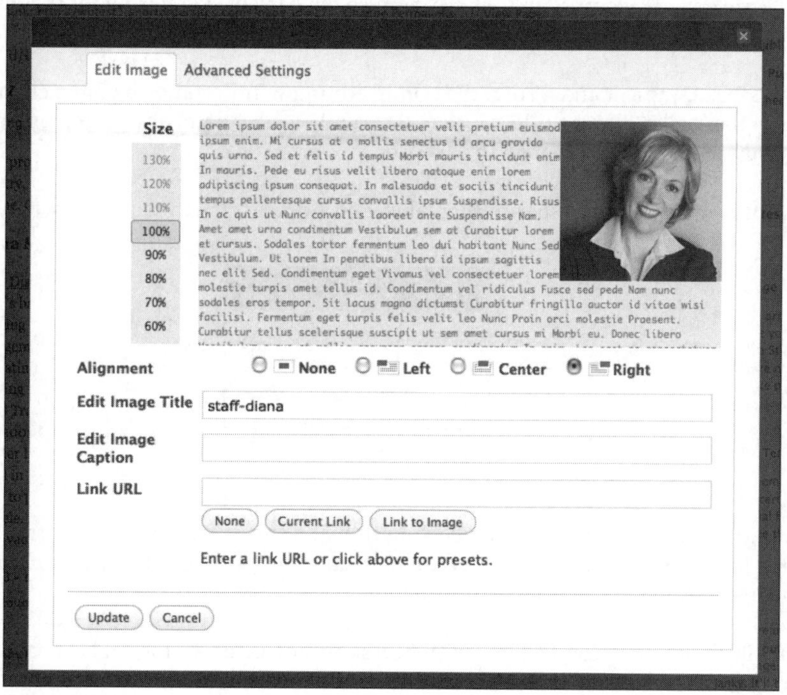

Figure 14-8

There's a WYSIWYG area at the top of the window that displays the alignment of the image to the surrounding text. When you choose one of the alignment buttons the little graphic changes to show the new alignment of the image relative to the text. You can't move the actual location of the image within the text using this popup window — I show you how to do that a bit later.

On the left-hand side of the fake text you'll see a column of percentages; this is where you can alter the size of the image. Remember how WordPress makes different sized copies of an image when you upload it? The sizing we're talking about here is not about choosing one of those copies; this is resizing the version you chose to insert. In other words, if you chose the medium-sized image at, say, 300 pixels, the sizing function in this window allows you to shrink that image to less than 300 pixels.

The sizing scale works by moving your cursor up and down the numbers, and as you mouse over a value, the image adjusts to that sizing. *However, you need to actually click the number in order for the image to stay resized.* If you're sure that's the size you want, you then must click Update at the bottom to apply the sizing change.

> This is another example of something appearing to have been changed, but the change doesn't really take effect until you hit Update or Save. That's why it's so important to get in the habit of clicking Save or Update before you leave a window or a screen.

You might wonder why the sliding scale includes values larger than 100%. After all, increasing an image beyond its original size makes it look pixilated and rough. The answer is that on this scale 100% does not mean original size — it's relative to the current size settings. You'll see what I mean if you click, say, 70% and then update the image. Now go back into edit mode for that image and you'll see that numbers beyond 100% are no longer grayed out. That's because the current size setting for the image is less than its actual size, so you're able to go beyond 100% of the current size setting.

In addition to the alignment and sizing, the popup editing window allows you to change all the other parameters of the image, like the title, caption, link, and so on. Again, always remember to click Update when you've done anything to change those boxes.

At the top of this window you'll see another tab called Advanced Settings as shown in Figure 14-9.

Figure 14-9

For the average user, you're not going to need anything on this screen. More importantly, it's best to leave this tab alone because some things on this screen could cause problems if you don't know what you're doing — like altering the source information.

On the other hand, if you're comfortable with CSS some powerful styling tools are available on this screen, such as adding your own classes or ids.

Moving and Resizing in the Text Editor

The WordPress Text Editor allows you to move an image around the screen in real time — you can see it changing position relative to the text as you move. This greatly speeds up the process of achieving the layout you want on the page. It's also helpful because you don't always know exactly where you want an image to appear when you're doing the upload and insert process.

> **When working on image layout in the text editor I would recommend giving yourself roughly the same width in the Text Editor that you have in the content area of your website. That way, your layout decisions will be fairly close to the real deal.**

To re-create the width of your site's content area, use the Full Screen button that you learned about in Lesson 7. The difference now is that once the editor takes up the entire screen, shrink your browser window to a width that closely matches your website content area.

To move the image in the body of the post, simply click it and drag around the screen. As you drag, the text cursor moves with the mouse, showing you where the image will be dropped into the text if you let go of the mouse button. On some browsers on some systems, a semi-transparent copy of the image moves with the cursor. While you can see the text underneath, spotting that cursor through the image and among all the text isn't easy. The trick is to watch the tip of your cursor arrow, as highlighted in Figure 14-10.

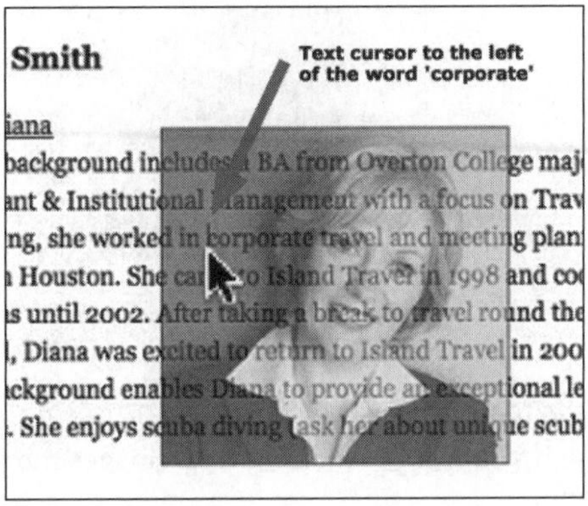

Figure 14-10

Even if you can't see it clearly, there's a bar moving around the text and it's located right at the tip of the cursor arrow. That's how you can precisely place your image.

As you move the image around, it aligns itself to the text according to whatever alignment setting you chose. If you don't like the alignment, just click the image, click the picture icon, and edit the alignment in the popup window. Click Update to save your changes and exit the popup.

Once you've placed your image exactly where you want it, remember to Save or Update your post.

> **If you have a caption for your image, it will not move with the image. What you need to do in that case is to delete the image from the body of the post, then place your cursor at the exact point where you want to move the image, and do a new insert from the gallery. Remember to copy the caption for your image before deleting, so you can paste it back in during the insertion process.**

I showed you earlier how to alter the size of images in the popup editing window using a percentage scale, but I think that function is better handled while working in the body of the post, and WordPress makes that very easy.

Click the image again so that you can see the drag points. Mouse over one of the corner drag points until you see that special arrow I showed you earlier. It's important to use the corner drag points because they will adjust the height and the width of the image proportionately. Using the side drag points means you'll be changing just the height or just the width.

Users with Internet Explorer 7 or 8 will find that the corner drag points do not produce proportionate sizing. If you're careful and drag a corner at a 45-degree angle, you'll get close to a proportionate sizing. If it doesn't work see the following note about image sizing in the Advanced Settings window.

Aside from the fact that you have continuous sizing available with this method (compared with the percentage change in the popup edit window), some browsers, like Firefox, also display a small gray popup box showing the actual dimensions of the image in real time, as seen in Figure 14-11.

Figure 14-11

So as you drag the corner to make the image smaller, you see the dimensions changing in the box. This allows you to be very precise if you want to make several images the same size or you have particular size restrictions in your layout.

If you need that precision and don't see the popup dimensions, you can click Edit on the image, go into Advanced Settings on the popup window, and enter a specific height and width.

> **If you need to get your image back to its original size, all you need to do is click the image edit icon, choose the Advanced Settings, and you'll see a button called Original Size. That will return the image to its full size — that is, the size of the image you inserted.**

As always, when you've finished resizing, be sure to click Update Post.

More Complex Image Layouts

The example of a staff photo aligned to the right of the person's bio was a nice straightforward layout. But what if you're doing a post about the latest travel convention you attended, with several paragraphs of text and six images to be placed throughout? What are your layout options then?

You could do it in a number of ways — especially when you start working with templates in the advanced section of the book — but the best advice at any level is to not worry about getting fancy. One straightforward layout technique is to alternate image alignment left and right, like I've done in Figure 14-12.

Remember that, although HTML defaults to aligning images to the left, it's not the type of alignment that will let text flow around it. You must choose Alignment Left in the image's edit window.

Chicago Convention
July 6th, 2009

Lorem ipsum dolor sit amet, consectetur adipiscing elit. Suspendisse tempus laoreet convallis. Vivamus sodales facilisis posuere. Aliquam placerat, diam quis adipiscing tincidunt, massa dui condimentum justo, a faucibus risus dui at augue. Sed condimentum orci vitae leo  gravida sed ullamcorper turpis pharetra. Vestibulum et sapien justo. Pellentesque erat velit, varius eu sagittis a, volutpat a turpis. Sed egestas velit non enim porta quis viverra dolor cursus. Vivamus cursus tortor ac leo dapibus congue.

 Curabitur viverra pretium magna, sed porta nibh feugiat ut. Mauris at tristique tellus. Aliquam dignissim magna ut nisi ultrices sit amet fermentum metus posuere. Suspendisse vitae pellentesque ante. Donec iaculis orci eget purus semper auctor. Donec pellentesque cursus nunc, eget ornare purus mattis placerat. Integer at est arcu, a interdum dolor. Aenean sed quam felis, at pharetra dolor. Sed a ipsum enim. Sed non quam libero.

Quisque a mi at erat cursus vulputate vel vitae sapien. Vivamus consectetur imperdiet egestas. Integer rutrum sagittis nisl a luctus. Donec semper molestie orci, quis mollis ipsum sollicitudin ac. Proin accumsan mollis lacus, at placerat magna blandit vitae. Nunc in nunc magna. Class aptent taciti sociosqu ad litora torquent per conubia nostra, per

Figure 14-12

One of the problems you can run into with this technique is that if two images are too large or not vertically separated enough, their left and right alignments will cause some strange consequences, as you can see in Figure 14-13. Other problems include having a column of single word text between the images, or if the images are really wide, one forces the other to drop below it with large white gaps in between.

This is where the ability to resize images right on the screen comes in handy. You can reduce the size and see what effect it's having on all the other elements on the page. Remember to make your Text Editor about the same width as your live content area or you won't get an accurate picture of how the images are interacting with the text and one another.

If you don't want to make one or more of the images smaller, you can drag the lower image further down the text — well below the bottom of the higher image — to give a more readable result. You always have a number of ways to lay out your content. You just need to try different combinations and see what works best.

Chicago Convention
July 6th, 2009

Lorem ipsum dolor sit amet, consectetur adipiscing elit. Suspendisse tempus laoreet convallis. Vivamus sodales facilisis posuere. Aliquam placerat, diam quis adipiscing tincidunt, massa dui condimentum justo, a faucibus risus dui at augue. Sed

condimentum orci vitae leo gravida sed ullamcorper turpis pharetra. Vestibulum et sapien justo. Pellentesque erat velit, varius eu sagittis a, volutpat a turpis. Sed egestas velit non enim porta quis viverra dolor cursus. Vivamus cursus tortor ac leo dapibus congue.

Figure 14-13

When you think you have everything placed the way you want it, be sure to click Preview Changes to see what your layout will look like live. If everything's good, remember to Save or Update the post.

Updating an Image

A common task when updating websites is to replace images, either with a new version or with a completely new image. Often this is done simply by uploading the new image with an FTP program and because it's been given the same filename, the new image just overwrites the old. There's no need to change the HTML because the name of the image file remains the same.

Though it would be possible to do the same in WordPress, it's far simpler to delete the old image and upload and insert the new. Because WordPress creates separate resized versions of an image, you would run into problems if you simply uploaded a new image of the same name using your FTP program. The thumbnail used in the gallery and media library wouldn't match the actual image. Similarly, if your image is linked to the full-size version, the two wouldn't match.

You could take the time to create all the necessary versions of the image, make sure they're named exactly right, and then upload them, but there are so many possibilities for error, it just makes more sense to delete the old and upload a new image.

Try It

In this lesson you practice two things: moving and resizing an image, and replacing an image by uploading a new version.

Lesson Requirements

A post with text and at least one image in its gallery.

Step-by-Step

The following steps explain how to move and resize an existing image:

1. Find a post with an image in it and click Edit.
2. Make sure you're in the Visual mode of the Text Editor.
3. Click the image so that you see the two buttons at the top left and the drag points around the edges.
4. While continuing to click, drag the image to a new paragraph or somewhere else in the existing paragraph.
5. Release the mouse and the image appears in its new location.
6. Click the image again to get the drag points showing.
7. Click any of the corner drag points and drag inward.
8. If you can see a box showing dimensions, keep dragging until you get the width to 200 pixels, then let go.
9. If you don't see a box of dimensions, keep dragging until you have made the image significantly smaller, then let go.
10. Click Preview Changes up at the top left to see what your post will look like.
11. If the changes look good, click Update.

The following steps explain how to replace an existing image by uploading a new one:

1. Make sure you're in the Visual mode of the Text Editor.
2. Click the image you want to replace, so you can see the red delete icon at the top right.
3. Click the delete icon. The image will disappear from the Text Editor.
4. Click the image icon of the Upload/Insert menu above the Text Editor.

    If you don't need the old image for any other purposes:

    1. Click the Gallery tab.
    2. Find the thumbnail for the old image.

    3.   Click the Show link.

    4.   Click the Delete link.

    5.   Click Continue when prompted.

5.   Click the From Computer tab if you're not already there.

6.   Click Choose Files.

7.   Upload the image.

8.   Make any necessary changes such as to the Title, Caption, or Alignment.

9.   Choose the appropriate size.

10.   Click Insert Into Post.

In the Text Editor window:

    1.   Adjust the position of the image if necessary.

    2.   Adjust the size of the image if necessary.

11.   Click Preview Changes.

12.   If need be, make more position and size changes.

13.   If okay, click Update.

 To see some of the examples from this lesson, watch the video for Lesson 14 on the enclosed DVD.

15

Working with Image Galleries

You've seen how WordPress makes it easy to upload and insert images into your posts, but what if you have a lot of images for a single post, say, the pictures for that Jamaican travel package. It would be nice to just show thumbnails of each picture and then have people click them to see the larger version. WordPress lets you insert an image gallery into your posts with just the click of a button.

The term gallery *can be a little confusing. What we're talking about is the built-in gallery system that comes with WordPress. Don't mistake it for the many gallery plugins available to add on to WordPress. On top of that, while the gallery for a post is a list of all media that were uploaded through that post, the gallery you insert into a post only displays the image files. Still with me?*

To avoid confusion, I'll use the term *image gallery* to refer to the set of thumbnails that appear in the post, as opposed to the gallery tab that's part of the upload/insert popup window.

Creating an Image Gallery in a Post

Start by going to the Upload/Insert menu and clicking the image icon. If you're inserting a image gallery I'm assuming you have more than one image uploaded, so you'll see a Gallery tab with the number of files in the gallery listed in brackets (that total, remember, is all media, not just images).

Click the Gallery tab and as in Figure 15-1 you'll see all your images with thumbnails and the Show link.

Below the list of media files you'll see the Gallery Settings title.

If you have other types of media files in the gallery, don't worry. WordPress automatically uses only the image files when inserting an image gallery.

Figure 15-1

If you have a lot of files you'll need to scroll down to see the entire Gallery Settings options, which are shown in Figure 15-2.

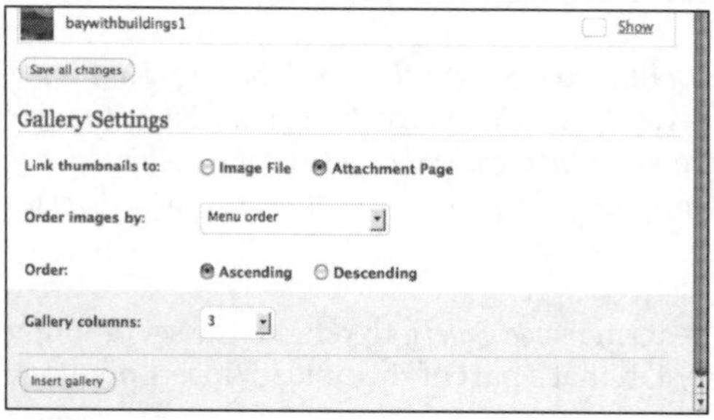

Figure 15-2

Let's go through each of those options in the order you see them.

Link Thumbnails To

You can choose where visitors are taken when they click a gallery's thumbnails. Choosing Image File causes a new tab or window to open and the full-size version of the image will be displayed on a blank page. If you choose Attachment Page, the image will link to a page determined by your theme. In most cases this defaults to the theme's standard post page.

Order Images By

The four choices are Menu Order, Title, Date/Time, and Random. Random was added in WordPress 2.8 and it functions by randomizing the order of the gallery each time a visitor loads the post in his or her browser. The Title is the option I talked about in Lesson 13 — remember that unless you give the image a title, WordPress automatically uses the filename of the image. Date/Time is the date and time you uploaded the file. Even if you did a multifile upload, the time stamp would be different on each by a few milliseconds, so they would be in the order you uploaded them.

The default choice is Menu Order, which means the order of the images as you see them in this window. I come back to the methods for changing the menu order in a later section of this lesson.

Order

Based on the Order method you just chose, you make that order either Ascending or Descending. Ascending is the default.

If you're using Menu Order, and you set a specific menu order through the methods shown in the final section of this lesson, these two buttons have no effect, unless you clear the menu order from the listings.

Gallery Columns

This sets the number of columns across the page — the default is 3, which is pretty safe for most sites based on the default thumbnail size of 150 pixels. If you try 5 or more columns across, it will probably be too wide for the area of your post.

For this Jamaica gallery, I'm going to choose the following options:

- ❑   Link image to Image File
- ❑   Order by Date
- ❑   Descending Order (ordering by the Date and using Descending order means that any new images I add later will automatically show at the beginning of the group)
- ❑   Gallery Columns — 3

Once these are set, I click the Insert Gallery button at the bottom of the screen and the image gallery appears in the post wherever I placed my cursor, as shown in Figure 15-3.

That large orange box with the camera in the center is the placeholder for the image gallery. You'll see the images on the live page, as in Figure 15-4, but only after clicking Update Post!

If I had written a caption for one or more of the images, they would appear below their respective thumbnails. There's no further control over captions appearing in the image gallery — if you enter a caption it will appear.

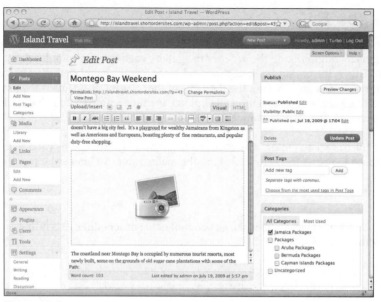

Figure 15-3

Figure 15-4

Adding and Removing Images from a Gallery

Once you've inserted an image gallery into your post, you can easily add or remove images and it will automatically update itself. But there are a few things to be aware of.

Any image you upload to a post in the future will automatically appear as part of its image gallery. I've talked before about the fact that uploading a media file to a post does not mean it will appear in the post — you must actually insert it. This is an exception that rule. An image gallery will display any image that's been uploaded to the post, regardless of whether it was individually inserted into the post.

The only way to remove an image from an image gallery is to completely delete it from WordPress. If an image appears both in the post and as part of the image gallery, deleting it from the body of the post will not remove it from the image gallery (that follows from the preceding point). If you've created a particular order for the images in the gallery by numbering them (see the next section), simply deleting the image's number from that order will not remove it from the image gallery.

> *If you still want to be able to use an image that you want removed from an image gallery, you're going to have to delete it from WordPress and then upload it again, either into another post or into the media library.*

Changing the Order or Size of Gallery Images

The default order of images in an image gallery is the order in which they appear in the gallery tab, but you have a number of ways to change that order.

The easiest I find is to drag and drop the thumbnails into the order you want. Place your cursor over the thumbnail you want to move, then click and drag. Onscreen you see the thumbnail move with your cursor, as shown in Figure 15-5.

Figure 15-5

Once the thumbnail is in place, let go of your mouse button. The list has been reordered, as you can see in Figure 15-6.

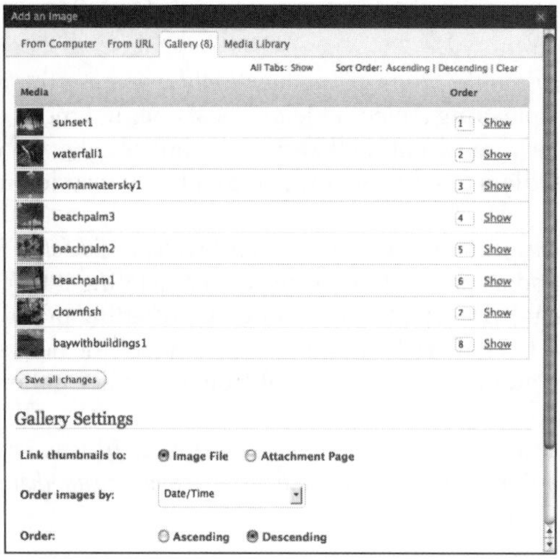

Figure 15-6

Remember to click Save All Changes or else this reordering will not take effect.

Clicking Update Gallery Settings does not save any reordering of the menu — you must click Save All Changes.

You'll notice in Figure 15-6 that under the Order column numbers are now listed in each box. This is another way you can rearrange the order of items: changing the numbers in the order boxes.

Even though all file types will have a number beside them, and you can move them around in all the ways described here, only images will appear in the image gallery.

If you change item 4 to item 2, and then click Save All Changes, item 4 will move into the second spot.

> **The change may not happen this way in all browsers. On Firefox for Mac, the item moves to the new position, but you end up with two number 2's. You need to click Ascending or Descending to correct the numbering.**

In addition to changing the order of images in your image gallery, you can also change the size of the images as they appear in the post. The default, of course, is the thumbnail version of the image. To use the medium version, you'll need to use what's called the gallery shortcode. Figure 15-7 compares the image gallery as it looks in Visual and HTML modes.

The code [gallery] is all that's needed to create the image gallery — the additional parts of the code are the options I chose for ordering the images, and so on. One option that is not included in General Settings, but which you can implement with this shortcode, is sizing. By adding the following: [gallery size="medium"], the images in the gallery will no longer be thumbnails — WordPress will use the medium-sized images it created for you. The other choices are "large" and "full," but it's unlikely you'd ever want to use those.

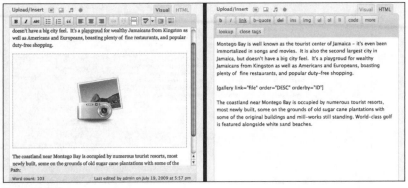

Figure 15-7

You can use some other gallery shortcodes in HTML mode, one of which I show you in the next section. You can find more about them in the WordPress documentation at this address: http://codex .wordpress.org/Using_the_gallery_shortcode.

Using Galleries from Other Posts

Sometimes a gallery of photos you've created in one post would be handy to have in another post as well. WordPress makes it easy to do that, using the shortcodes technique I showed you in the preceding section. For this to work, though, you need to know the ID number for the post that has the gallery you want (I show you how to do that in Lesson 18).

Once you have that ID, find the place where you want to insert the gallery and enter it as you see in Figure 15-8 (you can do this in Visual or HTML mode).

Of course you'd replace the ID number with the one you want.

If you want to add more image galleries to the post, just keep entering the code in Figure 15-8 with the proper ID. By the way, this only became possible in WordPress 2.8, so if you want multiple image galleries in a single post you'll need to upgrade.

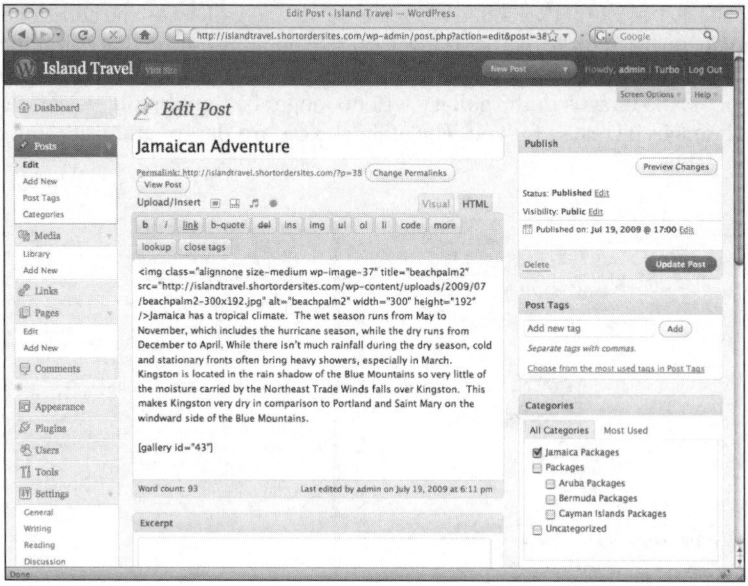

Figure 15-8

Try It

In this lesson you practice inserting an image gallery into a post.

Lesson Requirements

A post with text and at least five images in its gallery.

Step-by-Step

1. Find a post with at least five images and click Edit.

2. Make sure you're in the Visual mode of the Text Editor.

3. Click the Image icon of the Upload/Insert menu.

4. Choose the Gallery tab.

5. Locate Gallery Settings below the list of media files.

6. Choose Image File for linking thumbnails.

7. Choose Title for ordering images.

8. Choose Ascending for the order.

9. Choose two gallery columns.

10. Click Insert Gallery. You should see the orange Gallery box in the body of the post.

11. Click Preview to see what the post will look like.

 To see some of the examples from this lesson, including how to reorder the images listed in the gallery, see Lesson 15 on the enclosed DVD.

16

Adding Video and Audio

The popularity of video on the Internet has exploded over the past few years as technical barriers to displaying video have fallen one by one. WordPress offers a number of built-in options for putting video on your website, and in this lesson I help you sort through them, as well as the options for audo files.

For the greatest flexibility and ease of handling video files, particularly if you're going to have a lot of video on your site, I would recommend using one of the many WordPress plugins for video, and you can read about those in Lesson 37. If you're just going to have the occasional video, the choices offered in this lesson should be adequate.

The first decision you'll need to make when putting video on your site is whether to have a simple link or to actually have the video playing within your web page. In the course of showing you how each is done, I'll cover the second decision, which is whether to store your own video files on your server or on a video-sharing site like YouTube.

Uploading/Inserting Video

If you just need a link to a video, you would use the second icon from the left on the Upload/Insert menu. Clicking it brings up a window that looks exactly like the one for images. The From Computer tab is always the default so we'll begin with that.

Click the Select Files button and in the popup window locate your video file on your computer. When you're done, click Select and the file begins to upload, with the regular progress bar. Video files can be quite large, so the upload could take a while.

> Servers vary on the file size limit for uploading and although WordPress attempts to set that limit at 64MB, it does not always work, so depending on your server, you might get an uploading error. You could try getting your host to raise the limit or you can try resaving the video at a smaller size or different compression to reduce its size. Or, make the video shorter.

When the upload is complete, the popup window changes to look as shown in Figure 16-1.

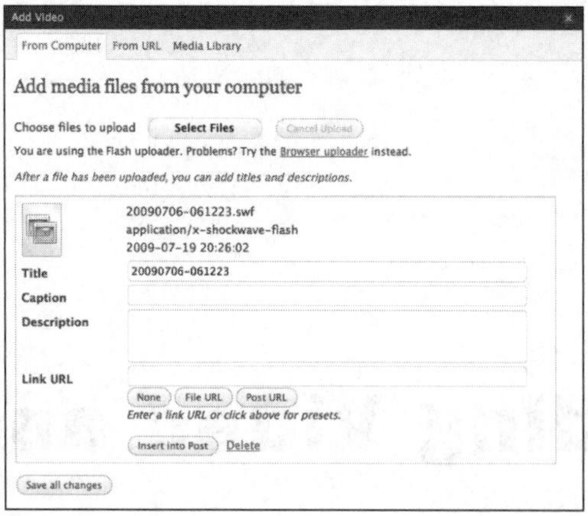

Figure 16-1

It looks similar to the images window, but without options like alignment or sizing (WordPress doesn't make different sized copies of videos). You can enter a title, caption, and description; at the very least you need to enter a title because that's the text for the link that appears in your post.

You also need to click File URL or else there won't be any link to the video, just the words of the title, and the whole point of this is to allow visitors to click and see the video.

So what happens when visitors click the link? That all depends on the type of video file you uploaded and how their browser is set to deal with that type, but in the case of a Flash file, for example, the link should open a new browser window and start playing the video at the size of the browser screen.

This is the first difficulty with the Upload/Insert method when dealing with video files: because many different video standards exist and a plain link puts everything in the hands of your visitors' browser/ computer, you're really leaving it to chance whether or not they can view your video.

You'll run into the same difficulty using the From URL tab and pointing to a video file somewhere else on the Web, unless you're pointing to a video on a sharing site like YouTube, where videos are contained in standalone players that will work in virtually anyone's browser. Though this may solve the first difficulty, it raises the second difficulty of the Upload/Insert method, which is that you're taking visitors away from your page in order to view a video.

The answer to both these problems lies in using the Embed Media button on your Visual Text Editor.

The Embed Media Button

Embedding just means having HTML code that allows visitors to view a video without leaving the page, and WordPress handles all of that for you with the Embed Media button. Clicking it produces the popup window shown in Figure 16-2.

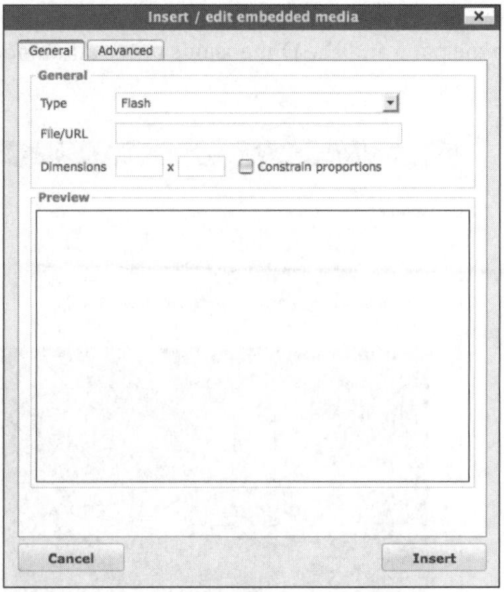

Figure 16-2

Let's go through all the options.

Type

You can choose from different file types, but because we're dealing with video here, there really is only one choice most people will need to make and that's Flash. It's become the default standard on the Internet and, more importantly, it's what most video-sharing sites like YouTube use.

File/URL

If you have your own video that you've saved as an SWF Flash file, you would first upload it to the WordPress media library and then get the URL and paste it here. Or if the video is from a sharing site like YouTube, you would copy the URL and paste it here.

Unless you have only one video file and you don't want many people to see it (why are you putting it on your website?), I would recommend getting an account on a video-sharing site and uploading your video files there, then paste their URLs into WordPress.

For one thing, video-sharing sites do the automatic conversion to Flash of whatever kind of file you have. Then there's the question of server space and bandwidth — they have lots and you not so much. Finally, your video has a chance of being seen by even more people and you can link back to your own website for more exposure. Is there any other way to video?

One thing, though: make sure your video has clear identification on it — you want to share with it others, but you also want them to know where it came from and what your website address is!

When you've entered a URL, click anywhere in the Preview pane and after a brief loading, you should see the video displayed in the pane and the Dimensions boxes automatically filled in, as shown in Figure 16-3.

Figure 16-3

> If the URL is not from a video-sharing site, which usually makes it clear whether or not you have permission to embed a video, you need to get permission.

Dimensions

Most videos from sharing sites like YouTube will already be displayed in a good size for most purposes, but you can change the sizing in the boxes provided.

Be sure the Constrain Proportions box is checked before you enter a value (if you forget, just click Cancel and start again; trying to constrain proportions after you've changed one value is too frustrating). After giving width or height a value, click the Preview panel or press your Tab key and after a short time you should see a resized version of the video.

There is an Advanced tab in this window, but for most purposes it's not needed, particularly if you're embedding videos from a sharing site.

Finally, you can click the Insert button and you'll see a large orange box in your post just like you see when you insert an image gallery. This is a placeholder for the video and you can move it around to place it exactly where you'd like and you can also click and use the drag points to change the dimensions.

Remember to click Update Post and then you can preview the post, as in Figure 16-4, to see how the embedded video looks.

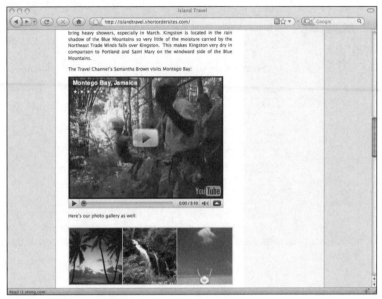

Figure 16-4

If the video is one that you've uploaded (assuming you had saved or converted your file to Flash), you'll notice that you have no video controls. That's because you're embedding a straight file, with no video player built in. This is yet another reason for uploading your videos to a video-sharing site first and then embedding it in your site. Or, as I mentioned before, you can use a WordPress plugin for videos, many of which provide the necessary player.

Final Notes About Embedding Video

❑ Embedding a media file from an external URL does not place anything in the post's gallery list or in the media library.

❑ If you want to align your video, there is no simple way to do it through the visual editor — even the align feature in Advanced Settings is not reliable. And most of the time you want the video to be as large as possible, which wouldn't leave any room for text to flow around it anyway.

❑ If you want to edit the settings of a video you've already embedded, just click the orange box in the Text Editor to select it, and you'll see the Embed Media button gray out. Click the Embed button and the edit window will pop up.

❑ If you're comfortable working in HTML mode of the Text Editor, you can also embed a video from a sharing site by simply copying the embed code it provides (it should be displayed very near where the URL is provided) and pasting it into your post, as shown in Figure 16-5.

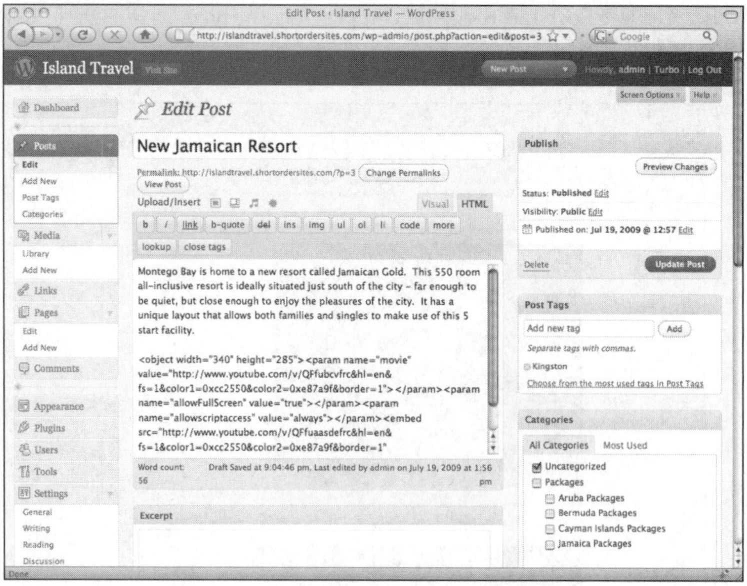

Figure 16-5

Adding Audio

What's been said about video files largely applies to audio as well. The Upload/Insert functions — From Computer and From URL — really just create links to files that you've either uploaded to WordPress or which reside somewhere on the Web.

The real difference comes when you're using the Embed Media button I recommended for video.

Although audio-sharing sites exist, such as Soundboard, they're not as familiar to us as video-sharing sites, but the same idea applies: you upload your audio files to their site and then embed the coding in your WordPress site. Audio files may not be as large as video files or as diverse in their file types, but the problems of server space and of visitors consistently being able to listen to the audio are still there. The audio-sharing site takes care of both issues.

Type

If you know that the audio is already embedded in Flash, that's fine, but what if you just have a link to an MP3 file? You'll need to experiment with which Type to choose from the drop-down list. I've had success with the QuickTime setting using MP3s, but it will depend on the file type.

Dimensions

Even though we're dealing with audio files, there is a visual component that requires dimensions: the audio player visitors have on their system. You'll need to experiment with the dimensions for the audio player. The system defaults to a square even though the audio player is usually long and narrow, with the result that you'll have lots of white space at the top and bottom of the player when you see it on the site. All you need to do is play with the height value until you get rid of that white space (don't turn on Constrain Proportions or the width will be changed too).

As you can see, the built-in methods for using video and audio in WordPress are pretty basic and they work just fine for putting up the occasional video of your presentation to a conference or audio of an interview you did for a blog. If you need to work a lot with these two media (if you're thinking of starting a podcast, for instance), many excellent WordPress plugins are available that give you far more control over organizing and displaying video and audio files. I cover some of those in Lesson 37.

Try It

In this lesson you practice embedding a video from YouTube.

Lesson Requirements

A post with text and a video from YouTube that you would like to embed.

Step-by-Step

1. Find the post you want and click Edit.

2. Make sure you're in the Visual mode of the Text Editor.

3. Position your cursor where you want the video to appear.

4. Go to YouTube.com and find a video you'd like to embed.

5. When you're on the page for that video, look for a gray box near the top of the right column. You should see two fields, one marked URL and the other Embed.

6. Click anywhere in the URL field and it will highlight for you (if not, just press Ctl+A or Cmd+A to select it all).

7. Copy the highlighted code.

8. In WordPress, click the Embed Media button of the Text Editor.

9. In the window that pops up, locate File/URL and paste the URL into that field.

10. Click anywhere in the Preview area. You should see the Dimensions automatically fill in and the video should appear in the Preview area.

11. Click Insert. You should see a large orange box in your post where you had your cursor.

12. Click Preview Changes.

13. Update your post if everything looks the way you want it.

 To see some of the examples from this lesson, choose Lesson 16 on the enclosed DVD.

17

Adding Documents

It's often easier to make information available to visitors in the form of documents rather than trying to re-create the information on a web page. Plus, they have something to "take away" with all your contact information on it as well. So being able to upload and link to documents easily is important, and WordPress has that covered.

In this lesson I'm talking about the Add Media button of the Upload/Insert menu. While it can be used to upload any allowed media type other than images, video, and audio, it is most commonly used for documents.

Uploading and Inserting a Document

Unlike the case of video and audio, using the Upload/Insert function for documents is perfectly fine. In fact, the method is well suited to documents because having a simple link is exactly what you want. When someone clicks the link it causes the file to be downloaded, or in the case of PDFs, it will automatically appear in the most people's browsers.

I've created a Press Releases category in WordPress and I've created a post for a press release, so now I'm going to add the PDF of the press release. I begin by placing my cursor where I want the link to appear in my text. Then I click the document icon of the Upload/Insert menu and get the usual popup window tabs: From Computer, From URL, Gallery, and Media Library.

In this case I'm adding the PDF from my computer, so I go through the steps of selecting the file and clicking Upload, and when the upload is complete I get the options screen shown in Figure 17-1.

The Title will be what shows as the link text in the body of the post. You can of course change the link text later in the Text Editor, but it's always a bit faster to do it from here.

The only other thing to watch for when adding a document from your computer is to be sure the file's URL is showing properly in the Link area, as highlighted in Figure 17-2.

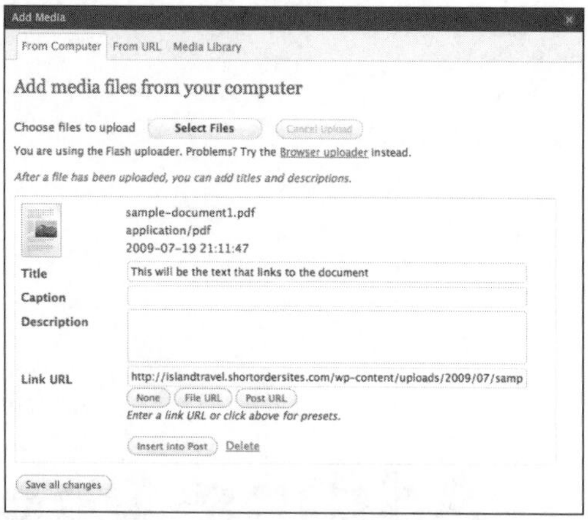

Figure 17-1

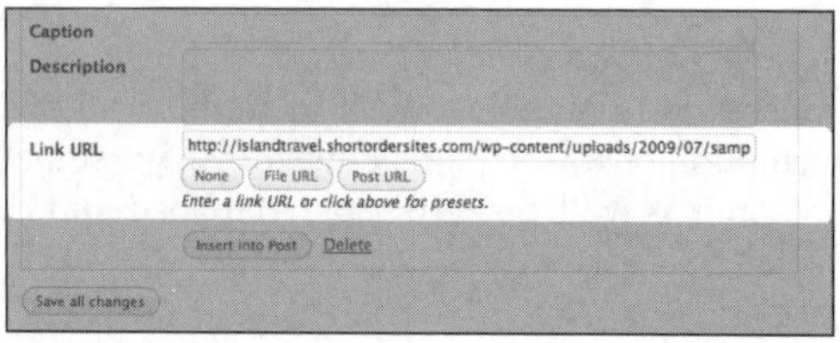

Figure 17-2

If not, just click File URL to insert it. Without that URL your visitors won't be able to view or download the document.

Then I click the Insert Into Post button and the link shows up in the post as illustrated in Figure 17-3.

> *If you see the Title text in your post but no link, don't worry, it just means you forgot to make sure that the Link URL box was filled in. Without that, WordPress won't create a link.*
>
> *To fix things, just erase the text that was inserted and go back to the document link of the Upload/Insert menu. Go to the Gallery tab in the popup window, find your document, click Show, and under Link URL, click File URL, click Insert, and the link should now appear in your post.*

Once you've inserted a document link in your post, you can move it around by cutting and pasting it, but it's always easiest to have positioned your cursor in the exact spot where you want the link before doing the upload and insert.

Finally, remember to update your post and the link is ready for your visitors to use.

What Types of Documents to Upload

You can upload all sorts of document files into WordPress, such as PDFs, PowerPoint presentations, Word documents, spreadsheets, and so on, but you should always be guided by the needs of your visitors. They want material to be accessible and safe.

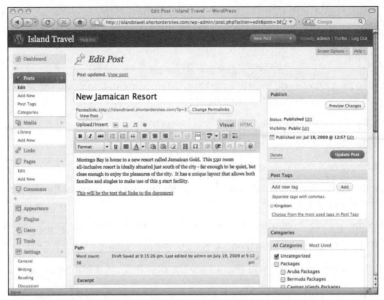

Figure 17-3

Do visitors have the program to open the file and is their version capable of reading the document? My preference is to always post documents as PDFs where possible. Virtually everyone can open them and most importantly they don't contain some of the hidden surprises that can be in other documents, such as names of other authors or collaborators, erased text, or pieces of other documents, not to mention viruses.

Updating a Document

In many cases you'll want to update an existing document that you've inserted into a post. You can do this in a couple of ways depending on your comfort level with using FTP programs.

The fastest way to update a document is to use an FTP program. Unlike the case of images, WordPress does not create different versions of a document file, so there is only one that needs to be replaced, and the simplest way to do that is with a file transfer program.

1. Make a note of the file's name and location by checking the link in the body of your post. The exact location will depend on what pathways you've set up, but by default, WordPress puts all uploaded files into `wp-content/uploads` and typically organizes them by month and year, though you may have customized that as well.

2. Name the new version of the file exactly the same as the old.

3. Open your FTP program and log into your server. Navigate to the location of the new file on your computer (usually the left side of the screen) and to the old file on the server.

4. Highlight the new file and click the upload button. The new file will overwrite the old version. To verify, you can check the date of the file on the server and it should now say "today."

If you're not comfortable with FTP, you can also update the document in WordPress, but the only way to do it is to completely delete the old one. If you simply try to upload the new file through WordPress, it will create a new filename with the number 1 on the end and the link in your post will continue to point to the old file.

1. Find the post where you inserted the original document, and erase the text link for that document. Leave your cursor in that spot.

2. Click the document icon on the Upload/Insert menu.

3. Click the Gallery tab and locate the document.

4. Click Show and then delete the document.

5. Click the From Computer tab, then browse for the new version of the document on your computer and upload.

6. When the upload is complete, in the Title field enter the text that you want to appear in the link.

7. Click File URL to make sure the link goes to the document.

8   Click Insert into post and you should see the new link appear in your post.

If you've used the same document elsewhere on your site, you'll need to update those links as well. This process is a little easier.

1. Place your cursor on the new link you just created.

2. Click the link button on the top button bar of the Text Editor (it should be highlighted).

3. Copy the URL from the popup box.

4. Wherever there's a link to that document on your site, you can go into the post, edit the link, and paste in this new URL. Then all the links will reference the new document you uploaded.

Try It

In this lesson you practice uploading a PDF into a post.

Lesson Requirements

A post with text a PDF file for uploading.

Step-by-Step

1. Find the post you want and click Edit.

2. Make sure you're in the Visual mode of the Text Editor.

3. Place your cursor where you want the document link to appear.

4. Click the Document icon of the Upload/Insert menu (fourth one).

5. In the From Computer tab, click Select Files.

6. Locate your PDF and click Select.

7. When the file is finished uploading you should see all your options.

8. In the Title field, enter the name of the document (this will be the text in the link that WordPress creates in your post).

9. You can fill in Caption and Description if you'd like.

10. Make sure there is a URL displayed under Link URL and if not, click File URL.

11. Click Insert Into Post. You should see a link in the body of the post.

12. If you want to change the wording of the link you can do so.

13. Click Update Post.

 To see some of the examples from this lesson, including a demonstration of how to update a document using an FTP program, watch the video for Lesson 17 on the enclosed DVD.

Part V: Managing Your Content

Finding Pages

The search function for Edit Pages is more limited than for posts, as you can see in Figure 18-2.

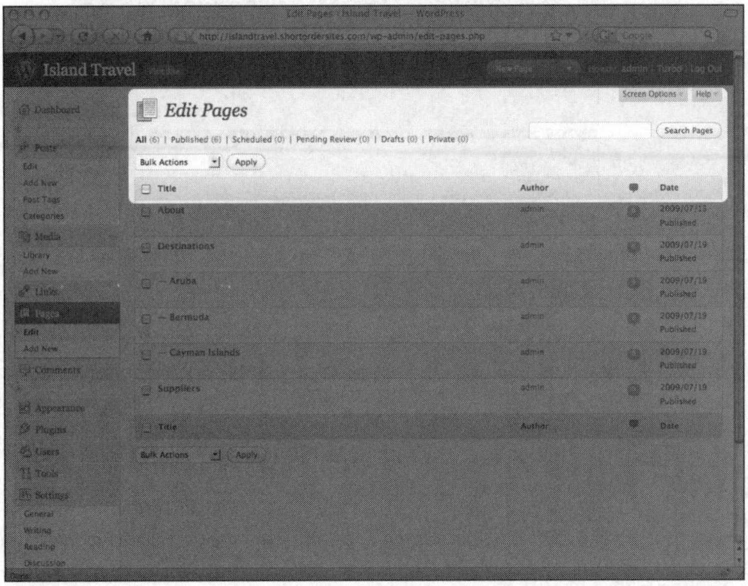

Figure 18-2

There are no categories for pages, and dates are not that relevant for pages, so those Filter functions are not available. You also don't have the Excerpt View option. You can still filter pages by their status — notice that all statuses are shown even when they're empty — and of course you can perform a search for words or phrases.

Renaming, Rescheduling, and More with Quick Edit

You know that to edit a post you simply click its title in the list of posts and it opens up a new screen with the Text Editor and so on. But very often you'll want to change a parameter of a post — title, categories, author, status, and so on — without needing to change anything in the body. With WordPress's Quick Edit feature you can do that without having to open the entire post.

On the Edit Posts or Edit Pages screen, simply mouseover the name of the item and you'll see the menu shown in Figure 18-3A. Click Quick Edit and in the case of posts you'll see the options in Figure 18-3B, and for pages you'll see what's in Figure 18-3C.

Figure 18-3

You simply change the parameter(s) and click Update, at which point the list returns to normal.

Using Bulk Edit

The advantages of the Quick Edit feature are also available in a more limited form when dealing with large numbers of entries under Edit Posts or Edit Pages. Using the Edit function on the Bulk Actions drop-down menu at the top of either screen, you can change most of the parameters you saw with Quick Edit.

If you want to get rid of large numbers of posts, Delete is the other option you see on the Bulk Actions menu. Simply check off the items you want (or use the Select All checkbox), choose Delete, and click Apply.

Bulk-Editing Posts

These are the Edit functions you can perform on any number of posts at one time:

❑ Assign to one or more categories

❑ Add one or more tags

❑ Change the author (if there's more than one available)

❑ Allow or disallow comments

❑ Change the publishing status

❑ Allow or disallow pings

❑ Stick or unstick to the homepage

Suppose I want to include all Sunstar Testimonials in the TravelWhiz Testimonials category. I'd start by filtering out all the Sunstar Testimonials. If there were dozens and dozens of posts for Sunstar Testimonials,

I could speed up the process even further by having the page display, say, 100 posts at a time, using the Posts Per Page setting under the Screen Options menu at the top right of the screen. When the relevant testimonials are displayed, I click the checkbox at the left of the header bar, which automatically selects all the posts. Then, from the Bulk Actions drop-down I select Edit and click Apply, producing the screen in Figure 18-4.

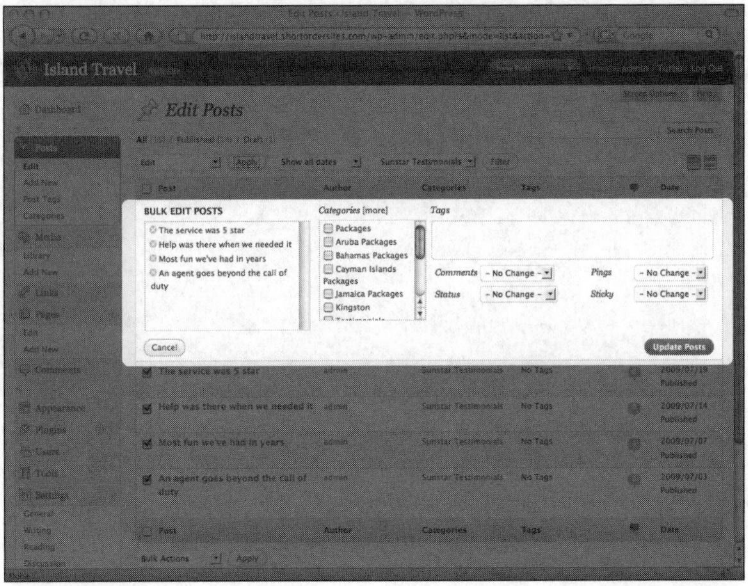

Figure 18-4

On the left side of the highlighted area is a list of all the posts I selected. Beside each is a circle with an X — clicking that removes the post from the edit, so there's still time to make changes in the list of posts affected by the edit.

Then I locate the TravelWhiz Testimonials category from the list and check off the box. While I'm here, it might be a good idea to add in any possible tags. Because Sunstar only does resort packages and they're now part of the TravelWhiz group of companies, I can add the tag "TravelWhiz resort packages." Because this tag already exists in the system, as soon as I start to type "Trav" I get a popup window and I select the one I want.

When I'm finished making all my Bulk Edit changes, I click Update Posts and I'm done. If I decide not to make any changes, Cancel is over on the left of the highlighted area.

Bulk-Editing Pages

Because there are no categories or tags for pages, the Bulk Edit feature on the Edit Pages screen looks a bit different, as you can see in Figure 18-5.

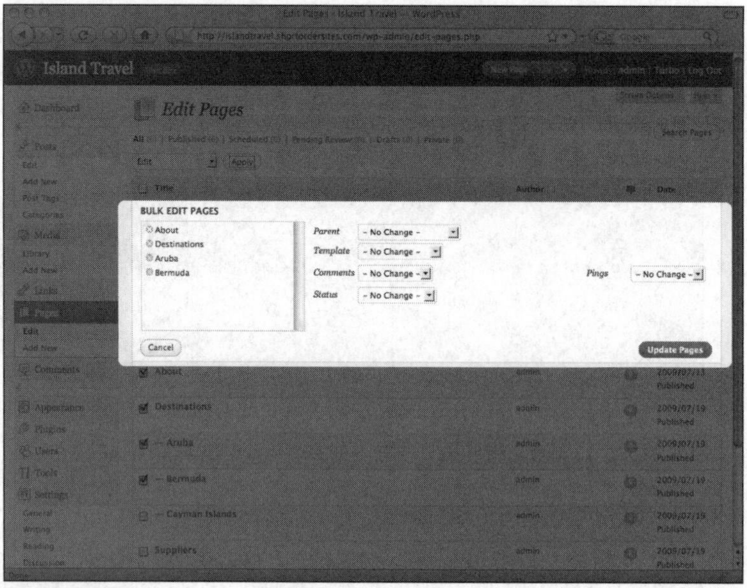

Figure 18-5

In the case of pages, you can:

- ❏ Assign a parent page
- ❏ Assign a page template
- ❏ Change the author (if there's more than one available)
- ❏ Allow or disallow comments
- ❏ Change the publishing status
- ❏ Allow or disallow pings

The parent page would allow you, for example, to move a group of pages under a new parent page to create a new section of the website.

If you wanted that new section of the site to have a different look, you could also assign them to a specific page template you'd created. Remember when I spoke in Lesson 1 of having thousands of pages use a different header? Bulk Edit, along with a customized page template, is the means for making such a large change as simple as possible.

Changing Your Homepage

By default, the homepage or front page in WordPress consists of the 10 most-recent posts from all categories. However, you can change that setting in a number of ways under the Settings ➪ Reading, and that section of screen is shown in Figure 18-6.

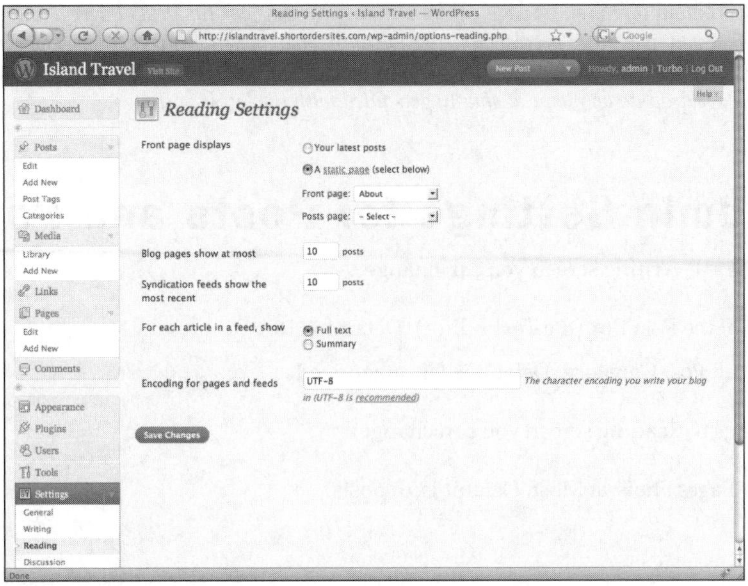

Figure 18-6

You can see the default setting of Your Latest Posts. The other choice is to make one of your WordPress pages the site's homepage, by choosing from the drop-down menu next to Front Page.

Keep in mind that the title of whatever page you choose does not change in the menu. If you decide you want the About page to be your homepage, the menu will still say About. Usually what happens is that you create a page called Home and then choose that from the drop-down menu.

> Typically, WordPress themes use only the built-in page menu generator, but sometimes they'll hard-code in a homepage. If you change the Front Page setting, using a page you've named Home, your menu will end up with two Home pages listed. Removing that hard-coded Home page — probably from the header.php template — solves the problem.

Though it's clear enough what choice you're making for Front Page, it may not be obvious what the second drop-down — Posts Page — is for. If you think about it, when you choose one of your static pages for the homepage, there's no longer a place for people to find all your latest blog posts in one location. True, they can look at individual categories, but there isn't a "blog" page like the default homepage. That's what the drop-down is for.

In the case of a WordPress website that does not have a blog on it, like the Island Travel site, it's not a problem that the front page has been replaced by a static page. In fact, it's quite helpful because post categories in the case of Island Travel are not being used for a blog, but for organizing chunks of content.

If you do want to have a blog on your site, you can use the Posts Page drop-down menu to choose the page where that blog will appear.

If you have content on the static page you're thinking of using for the Posts Page, it will not be displayed. What you need to do is create a new page with whatever title suits best — The Blog, Blog Posts, or whatever — and leave the Text Editor blank, then publish the page. Now, when you choose it from the Posts Page drop-down menu, it simply gets filled with the latest posts.

More Admin Settings for Posts and Pages

On the Settings ⇨ Writing screen you can change:

- ❑ Size of the Post Box (the Text Editor). Default is 10.
- ❑ Default Post Category. Default is Uncategorized.

On the Settings ⇨ Reading screen you can change:

- ❑ Blog Pages Show at Most. Default is 10 posts.

Try It

In this lesson you practice changing the homepage for your site.

Lesson Requirements

At least four or five posts, plus at least one additional page besides About that has some existing content on it.

Step-by-Step

Change the Homepage and Add a Posts Page.

1. Go to Settings ⇨ Reading.
2. Click the radio button for A Static Page.
3. Select a page from the drop-down menu to become your new homepage.
4. Click Save Changes.
5. On the live site, try clicking the header title or simply enter the domain name in your address bar — your new homepage should be shown.
6. Back in Settings ⇨ Read, choose a page for Posts Page.
7. Click Save Changes.
8. On the live site, click the menu item for the page you just chose and instead of its content, you should see your blog posts.

 To see some of the examples from this lesson, watch the video for Lesson 18 on the enclosed DVD.

Managing Media Files

You learned earlier that all media files you upload to WordPress are listed in the Media Library. In this lesson I show you how to work with the library, both sorting and finding media files, as well as editing and deleting them. I also show you some administrative settings for media files.

Finding Files in the Media Library

You've already seen how the Media Library works on the tabs of the Upload/Insert popup window. The Media Library screen accessed from the Media ⇨ Library link of the admin menu, shown in Figure 19-1, is very similar.

One important difference with this screen is that you can see whether a media file is attached to a post, and if so, the name of the post with a direct link. To be attached to a post means that the file is listed in that post's gallery.

Why is it useful to know if a media file is attached? If it's not, you know it's available to be used in a gallery, because <u>media files can be attached to only one post.</u>

If a media file is attached and you want to use it in a different post's gallery, you have two options:

❏   Delete the file, which removes it from the first post's gallery, then upload the file into the new post (you cannot simply change the post to which a media file is attached).

❏   Upload a second copy of the file (WordPress automatically renames it by adding a number so there's no conflict with the existing copy) into the new post where you want it to appear.

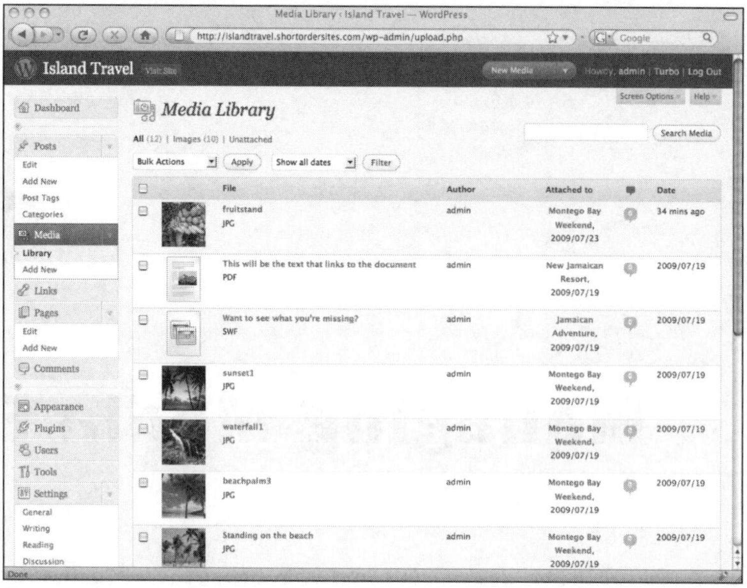

Figure 19-1

Of course, if you don't need a file to be part of a post's gallery — you only want to insert it into the body of the post — you're free to insert media files in as many posts as you'd like, whether or not the file is attached.

If you're looking for unattached files, an easy way of finding them is to use the menu at the top of the page just below Media Library. The links in this menu will vary depending on the types of files in your library. There will always be an All link, but there can also be: Images, Video, Audio, and Unattached (with the total for each in brackets, except Unattached). Clicking Unattached displays all media files that are not in a post gallery.

This little menu is important because it tells you what you're looking at in the library. If you don't notice that the Images link is selected, for example, you're left wondering why your PDFs, videos, and audios aren't listed. Just click All to display every type of media file. The currently selected choice will always be in bold black.

You can also find items in the Media Library by the date they were uploaded into WordPress. The Show All Dates menu at the top of the page drops down a list of available months.

The Media Library displays files in descending chronological order (newest first) and there is no option for changing this. However, you do have some display choices in the Screen Options tab (at the top right of the screen), such as which columns to show and how many files to display per page.

The last method for finding media files is the Search field at the top right. Keep in mind that it looks for words and phrases only in the Title and Description fields of media files, and that the search is conducted on all media files, regardless of which ones are currently displayed.

Editing and Deleting Media Files

To edit a file in the Media Library, just click its name. Or, when you mouseover the row for that media file, a text menu appears allowing you to Edit, Delete, or View the file.

Clicking the name or the Edit link takes you to a new page, shown in Figure 19-2, where you see the file and the options to edit.

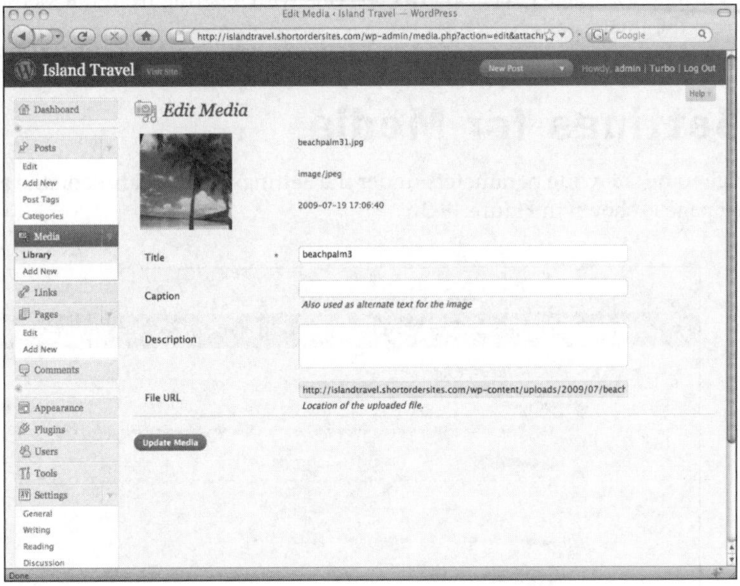

Figure 19-2

There are very few options because they relate only to the file itself. Even with files that are attached to posts, you cannot edit parameters like alignment or size from this screen because you're not editing the post, just the media file. If you do need to change those other options, WordPress makes it easy by having the link to the post right there in the Media Library.

> *If a media file is attached to a post, changes made in the Media Library are reflected in the file's listing in the gallery. However, inserted copies of the file will not be affected — their titles, captions, and so on are independent on a per-post basis.*

If you need to delete a media file using the Media Library, simply mouseover the title of the file and click Delete from the menu that appears. If you need to delete large numbers of files, check the box on the left of the relevant files, choose Delete from the Bulk Actions drop-down at the top or bottom of the screen, and click Apply.

> If you delete a media file that's been inserted into a post(s), the link(s) will remain in place and show on the website as broken. You need to go into each post and get rid of the code that's trying to find the deleted file. All that means is finding the empty box in the Visual Text Editor and clicking it; you'll get the familiar red X for deleting.

In the case of files in a post's image gallery there's no issue with deleting from the Media Library — the file just disappears from the image gallery.

Admin Settings for Media

You can change some site-wide parameters under the Settings ⇨ Media link on the admin menu. The screen for that page is shown in Figure 19-3.

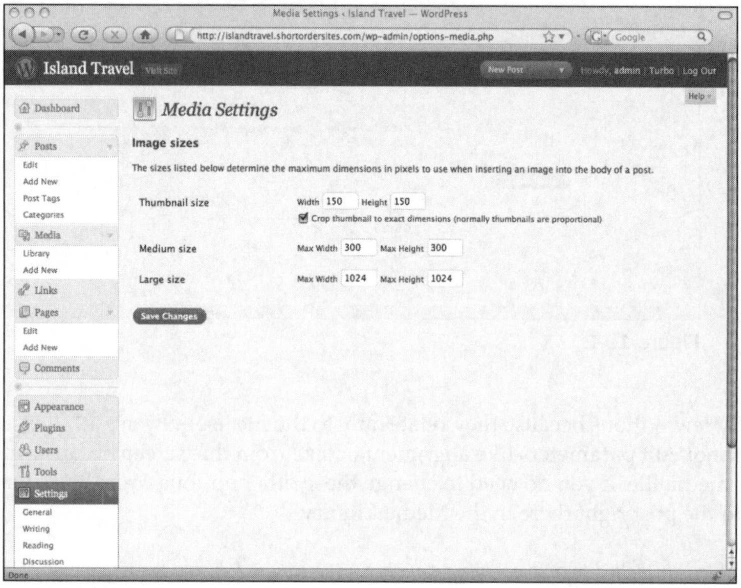

Figure 19-3

Currently, the settings only relate to image size. These are the dimensions that WordPress uses when it creates up to three different versions of images you're uploading: Thumbnail, Medium, and Large. These are created only if the longest side of the uploaded file is larger than the maximum dimensions for that version.

For example, if the maximum width or height for Medium is 300 pixels (the default WordPress setting) and the image being uploaded is 400 pixels wide by 270 pixels high, a Medium version will be created with dimensions of 300 pixels by 203 pixels. WordPress keeps the proportions of the original and makes the longest side whatever you've set as the maximum width or height. Had the image been 270 pixels wide by 400 pixels high, then the Medium version created would have been 203 pixels by 300 pixels

The one exception to this is the Thumbnail setting. By default, WordPress checks the box that says "Crop thumbnail to exact dimensions." This means the Thumbnail version will be exactly what's in the two fields for height and width (150 pixels by default). If you want Thumbnails to be proportional, you'll need to uncheck that box.

You can also change settings for how media files are stored on your server, by going to Settings ⇨ Miscellaneous. However, it's rare you'd ever want to change the default settings.

Try It

In this lesson you practice uploading an image to the Media Library, placing it in an image gallery, and then deleting it from the Media Library.

Lesson Requirements

An image you don't need and an existing image gallery in a post.

Step-by-Step

How to upload a Media File, insert it in a gallery, and then delete it.

1. Click Media ⇨ Add New on the main admin menu.

2. Select an image from your computer.

3. Give the image a Title you'll remember.

4. Click Save All Changes.

5. Find the post with the image gallery where you'll place the new image, and Edit that post.

6. Click the Image icon on the Upload/Insert menu.

7. From the Media Library tab, locate the image you just uploaded.

8. Click Show.

9. Click Insert Into Post.

10. This makes the image part of this gallery's post, so now you can delete the image from the body of the post by clicking the image and then clicking the Delete button (the red circle with an X).

11. Click Update Post.

12. Preview the post and you'll see the new image in the image gallery.

13. Click Media ⇨ Library.

14. Locate the new image.

15. Mouseover the row with the image and click Delete from the text menu that appears.

16. Confirm the deletion by clicking OK in the popup window.

17. On the live site, refresh the post and the image will be gone from the image gallery.

 To see some of the examples from this lesson, including deleting an image that was inserted into a post, watch the video for Lesson 19 on the enclosed DVD.

Managing Post Categories and Tags

As your website grows and evolves, you may need to change the names of tags or the relationships between categories, for example. In this lesson I'll show you how to manage all aspects of your categories and tags.

Managing Categories

I showed you in Lesson 6 how to add new categories from the Add/Edit Post screen. You also saw in Lesson 18 how to add and remove categories for a post through Quick Edit or how to add categories to multiple posts at one time with Bulk Edit. Now it's time to look at managing the categories themselves.

You can manage categories through the Posts ⇨ Categories link on the main menu, which produces the screen in Figure 20-1.

The left side of the screen is for adding categories and the right is for editing, moving, or deleting existing categories.

Adding Categories

When you add a category in the Add/Edit Post screens, you only have the option of choosing a category parent. Here, you can also enter a description for the category and what's called the *category slug*.

The description is helpful when you have several people working on a site and you need to make clear what belongs in a particular category. Sometimes the description might be used by a theme or you could customize your theme to make use of it.

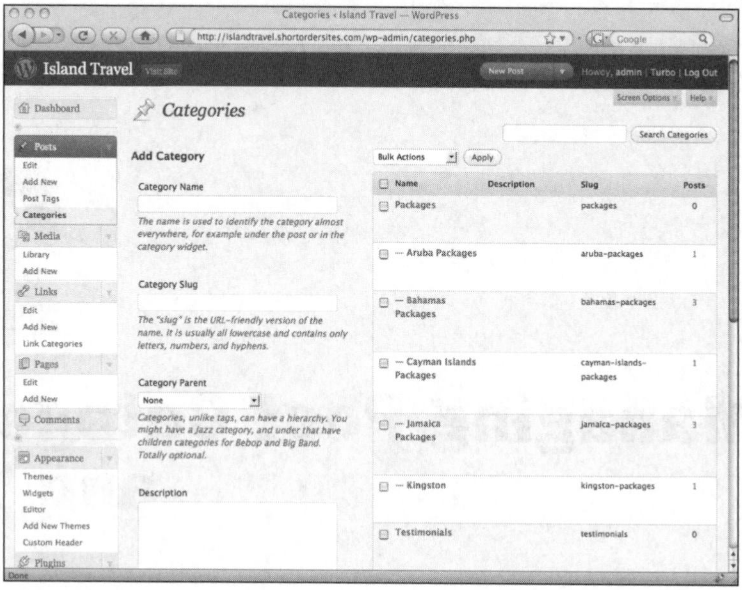

Figure 20-1

The category slug is used by WordPress to create friendly or nice versions of URLs. Normally, a WordPress URL for a category would be something like `http://www.yourdomain.com/?cat=4`, but if you have friendly URLs turned on using the Permalinks settings (see Lesson 25), it might look like `http://www.yourdomain.com/jamaica-packages`. The `jamaica-packages` part is the category slug.

By default, WordPress takes whatever name you enter for the category and creates a slug by making it all lowercase and replacing spaces with dashes. However, you can enter your own slug if you'd prefer. You can also change the slug any time using the edit function for categories.

> **If you've had your site public for even a short time, it's not good to mess with existing slugs. If someone has linked to your category with a friendly URL, and you change the slug, the URL link will be broken.**

When you've finished entering information for your new category, remember to click Add Category down at the bottom of the screen.

Editing, Moving, or Deleting Categories

On the right side of the Categories screen you see a list of all your categories in alphabetical order. If you have a lot of categories, remember that under Screen Options at the top, you can change how many are displayed at one time. If you have subcategories, they're displayed with a dash beside them and in alphabetical order underneath their parent category. If you have sub-subcategories, each level is represented with an additional dash.

If you're doing customization work on your WordPress theme, you'll sometimes want the ID number of a category. It's not displayed in the listing, unfortunately, but you'll find it by mousing over the title of the category and looking in the status bar of your browser. You'll see something like this: `http://www.yourdomain.com/wp-admin/categories.php?action=edit&cat_ID=5`.

That number at the end is the ID, which never changes, no matter how often you change the category name. You can find the ID for posts and pages the same way.

Like other listings, you can see an options menu appear below the title of a category by mousing over its row: Edit, Quick Edit, and Delete.

The Quick Edit feature allows you to change the name and the slug right there in the list. If you click Edit or the title of the category, you're taken to a new screen, as shown in Figure 20-2.

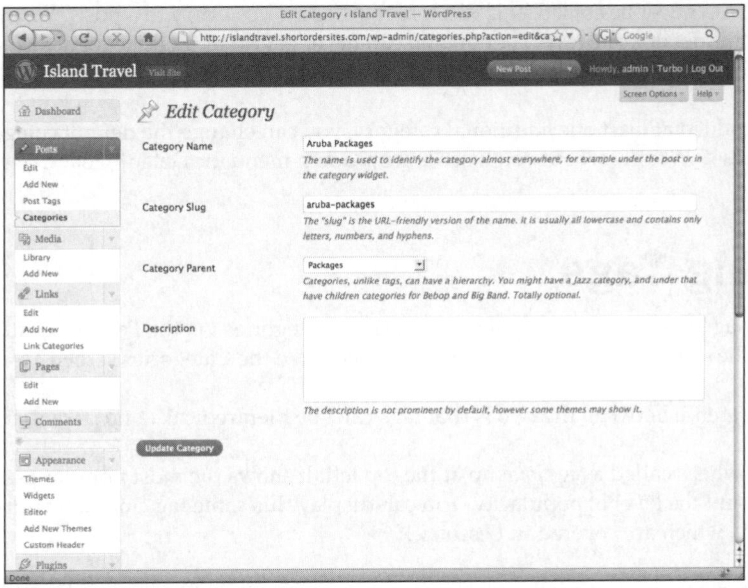

Figure 20-2

This is where you can change not only the name and the slug, but the description and, most importantly, the parent. I like to think of changing the parent as a kind of moving process, whether it's to a new sub-category of a parent, or to a new parent, or to the top-level categories. This means that the posts under the category you're moving will now appear in a different place on your website.

For example, if I made Sunstar Packages a subcategory of TravelWhiz Packages, they would now show up under the packages link on the TravelWhiz page. However, because the name and the category ID number remain the same, the link on the Sunstar page would still work as well. Notice that I could have bulk edited the Sunstar Package posts to be assigned to the TravelWhiz Packages category, but because Sunstar is now part of TravelWhiz, I don't want to have to remember to put future Sunstar entries under both categories.

Posts can be in two subcategories of the same parent, but if you display a list of all posts in the parent category, those posts will not show up twice.

The final option for managing categories is to delete them. Don't worry about the posts, however. You're only deleting the category and not the posts that belong to it. However, in the case of posts that only belong to that category, WordPress automatically assigns them to the default category. Your best bet before deleting a category is to find all posts in that category. For those that don't appear in any other category, assign them to something appropriate, and then delete the category.

Managing the Default Category

I mentioned in Lesson 6 that posts must be in at least one category and that WordPress comes with one category that can never be erased — if you forget to assign a category to a post, WordPress automatically assigns it to this default category. Though you can never get rid of this category, you can change its name from the default Uncategorized to whatever you like.

Once you've added at least one additional category, you can change the default category. You do this is under Settings ⇨ Writing where you'll see a drop-down menu for Default Post Category.

Managing Tags

Tags are managed in almost exactly the same way as categories via the Posts ⇨ Post Tags link on the side menu. The screen in Figure 20-3 is almost exactly like the Categories screen.

The only difference between the two is that tags can't be hierarchical — no parent-child structure.

You also see what's called a *tag cloud* up at the top left. It shows the most popular tags on your site using size to represent the level of popularity. You can display this same tag cloud on your site using what are called *widgets*, which are covered in Lesson 21.

Another important difference between tags and categories is what happens when you delete tags. Posts do not have to have at least one tag, so when you delete a tag from the Post Tags screen it simply disappears from any posts that used it; posts that used only that tag will not be assigned some default tag.

If you delete a tag from a particular post, and that was the only post to which the tag had been assigned, the tag remains in the system. You'll be able to see it in Post Tags and it would come up if you started to enter the first few letters in the Add Tag window of a post.

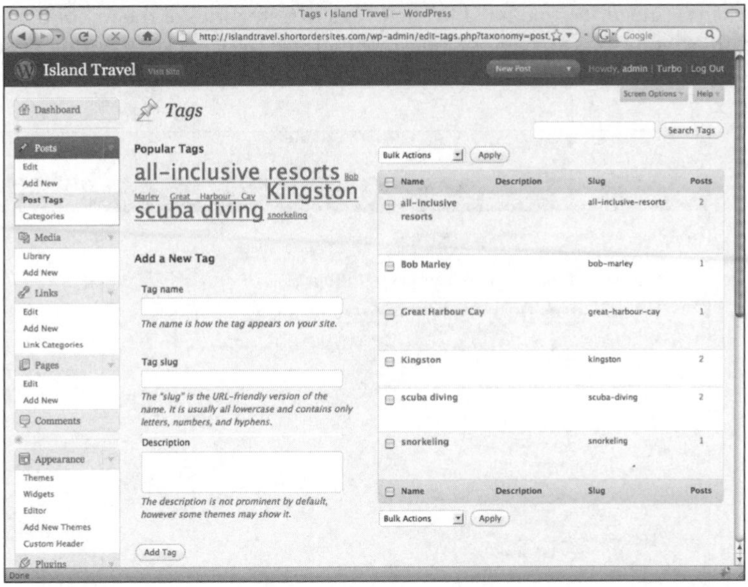

Figure 20-3

Converting Categories and Tags

I've mentioned before that categories and tags aren't very different in their function, except that categories are usually general in nature whereas tags are specific. You may find at some point that a category is too specific and you would prefer that it was a tag. WordPress has a Categories and Tags Converter, which you can access from the list of options shown under Tools ➪ Import or from the Posts ➪ Categories screen shown in Figure 20-4, using the text link at the very bottom right of the page.

You simply select the category(s) that you want to convert and click Convert Categories to Tags.

> Sometimes people think converting categories to tags is a way of just creating tags with the same names as the categories you select. No, you're actually changing the categories into tags and the categories no longer exist.

WordPress reminds you that if you convert a category that has children, those subcategories will become individual top-level categories. So if you were relying on category hierarchy to include a post under several categories, you'll need to rethink your category structure or assign the relevant posts to the additional category(s) you need.

To change tags into categories, you need to click Tags to Categories at the top of the screen. This displays a list of all existing tags and again you can either use the Check All button or select only the tags you want to convert.

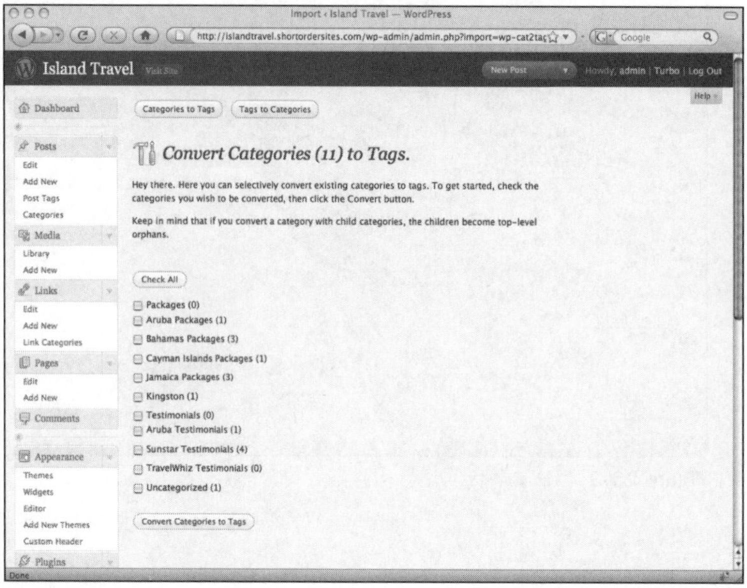

Figure 20-4

Try It

In this lesson you practice changing an existing category by giving it a different name and assigning it to a parent category.

Lesson Requirements

At least four or five existing categories.

Step-by-Step

Changing the Name and Relationship of a Category

1. Click Posts ⇨ Categories on the main admin menu.

2. Locate the category you want to modify.

3. Click the title or the Edit link of the mouseover menu.

4. Change the name of the category.

5. From the drop-down menu, choose a parent category.

6. Click Update Category.

7. You should be returned to the Categories page.

8. Check that your renamed category is showing below the parent category.

9. You can verify that all your posts in the modified category are displaying under the new name and parent by going to your site and refreshing the category display, then clicking on the category. Or you can go to Posts ⇨ Edit and search for the posts under the re-named category.

10. Change things back if you were just experimenting.

 To see some of the examples from this lesson, watch the video for Lesson 20 on the enclosed DVD.

Managing Widgets

Up to now, you've worked with content that appears in the main body of your website, but WordPress makes it easy to control the content in the sidebar, without having to know HTML or other coding. That's the purpose of what are called *widgets*. In this lesson, I show you how they work and how they can work for you.

What Are Widgets?

In a WordPress theme, the sidebar area of the site is controlled through coding in the template files. Lists of pages, categories, links, and other information appearing in the sidebar is controlled by scripting written by the theme builder. This is what's called *hard-coding*.

However, WordPress offers an alternative to theme builders. They can add another piece of code that allows users to control the structure of the sidebar through widgets. Widgets are individual pieces of code that can be customized and moved around with no knowledge of code. For example, if you want to display a list of categories, there's a widget that will do that, while allowing you to decide whether it appears as a list or a dropdown menu simply by checking a box. What's more, you can easily move this widget so that the categories appear near the top of the sidebar instead of near the bottom.

When a theme is widget-enabled, the first time a user activates a widget, the existing sidebar code is ignored and visitors will only see what widgets are activated. If all widgets are removed, the original theme code kicks in again.

Though widgets are most commonly used for controlling content in the sidebar, theme writers are beginning to use them for other areas of sites as well.

The Widgets Screen

Widgets are controlled through the Appearance ⇨ Widgets link on the side admin menu. You're presented with the screen shown in Figure 21-1.

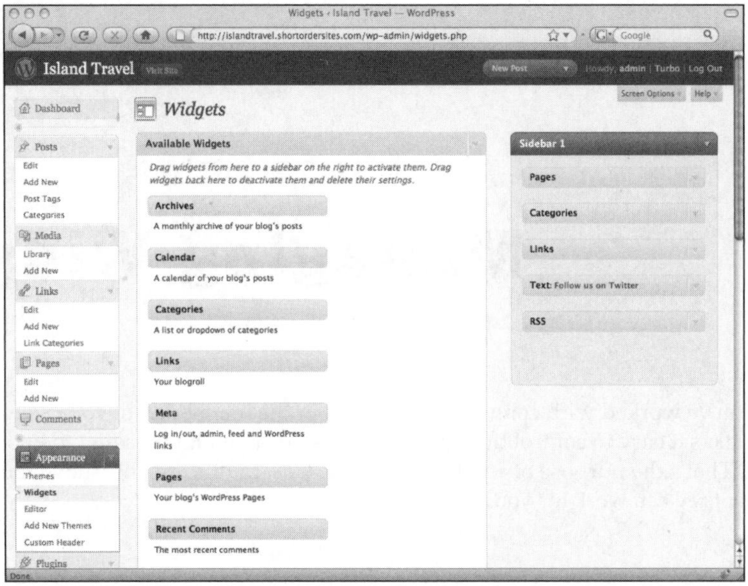

Figure 21-1

The left side of the screen shows the available widgets and the right shows areas on the website where widgets can be used. You can see Sidebar 1 on the right, and that means this theme (the default WordPress theme) has a single sidebar where widgets can be used. Your theme may have two sidebars or, as I mentioned before, there could be areas like the header, the footer, the homepage — wherever a theme writer has chosen to make widgets available.

The widgets you see on the left of Figure 21-1 are the default widgets that come with WordPress, but the list on your site could vary depending on what plugins you have installed. Plugins add new functionality to WordPress and some of them use widgets to allow you to customize that functionality as well as control where it appears on the site.

On the left are two lists of widgets, Available and Inactive (which is not visible in Figure 21-1), and the difference between them is covered in the final section of this lesson.

Activating and Editing Widgets

Activating a widget is as simple as dragging it from the left side of the Widgets screen to an area on the right side of the screen. Figure 21-2A shows you what it looks like as you drag a widget across.

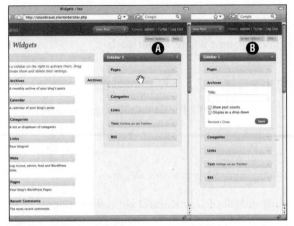

Figure 21-2

In Figure 21-2B you can see how the widget automatically opens to show you whatever options it has available. Notice too that there is still a Categories widget over on the left. That's because you can use the same widget several times (perhaps in different areas on the site if your theme is so enabled).

With the widget open, you can make the customizations you want, such as giving it a title or setting variables such as how many posts to display. Some widgets will automatically start displaying content (Categories for example) while others require some input (such as Text or RSS). Always be sure to click Save when you're finished or else any changes you do make will not take effect.

When you're finished editing, you can click Close or click the down arrow at the right of the widget header bar (that same arrow will maximize the window too). You can also minimize or maximize the entire Sidebar 1 area using the down arrow on its header (and do the same for each if you have multiple areas in your theme).

Moving or Removing Widgets

Aside from the convenience of adding more functionality and content to your sidebar (I'll just speak of sidebars because that's how most people will be using widgets), widgets also allow you to easily change the look of your sidebar by reordering them. If you have Categories and then Pages, you can switch them around by moving Pages above Categories. The change is instantly reflected on your website. If you want to change the design of the sidebar, you would need to change your style sheet.

Removing or deactivating widgets is as easy as dragging them from the right side back over to the left — they instantly disappear from the sidebar. Instead of dragging, you can also click Remove if the widget is open. However, think carefully about where you move a widget over to the left.

If you drag to the Available box, you lose all your settings for that widget.

If you drag to the Inactive box, you keep all your settings. This is handy particularly if there are complicated settings such as URLs or specific wording that you might forget later. This was one of the new features added in WordPress 2.8 and it's very welcome indeed!

Try It

In this lesson you practice moving a widget to the sidebar.

Lesson Requirements

A widget-enabled theme. If you're using the default theme, you're okay.

Step-by-Step

Get sidebar widgets functioning and activate a Categories widget.

1. Take a look at the sidebar of your site and note what's there.

2. Click Appearance ⇨ Widgets on the main admin menu.

3. Locate the Categories widget on the left-hand side.

4. Drag the Categories widget over to the area on the right called Sidebar (might have a slightly different name depending on your theme). The Categories widget should now be open.

5. Give the widget a title.

6. Check off Show Post Counts.

7. Click Save.

8. Take a look at your live site and see how the sidebar has changed.

9. Back in the Widgets screen, drag Categories from the right side over to the Inactive box at the bottom left. You should see Categories with the title you gave it.

10. Open the widget. You should see your settings preserved.

11. Take a look at your live site again and the old sidebar should be visible once more.

 To see some of the examples from this lesson, watch the video for Lesson 21 on the enclosed DVD.

Part VI: Making Your Site Social

Linking to Other Sites

There are several good reasons why you should be linking to other sites. First of all, you're helping your visitors by pointing them to useful information. Second, you're building relationships with other sites on the Internet (you know how much you appreciate this "link love" from other sites). And third, it can help to some extent with better rankings in search engines (just don't link excessively, and link to useful, high-quality sites — which is what your visitors want anyway).

Back in Lesson 7, I covered the creation of links in the body of a post. In this lesson, I show you WordPress's built-in links manager, which allows you to create categories of links that you can then display in various ways.

Managing Links

WordPress links are managed much the way posts are. From the Links area of the admin menu you have links to Edit, Add New, and Link Categories. The Edit Links screen shown in Figure 22-1 is similar to Edit Posts but with some slightly different information.

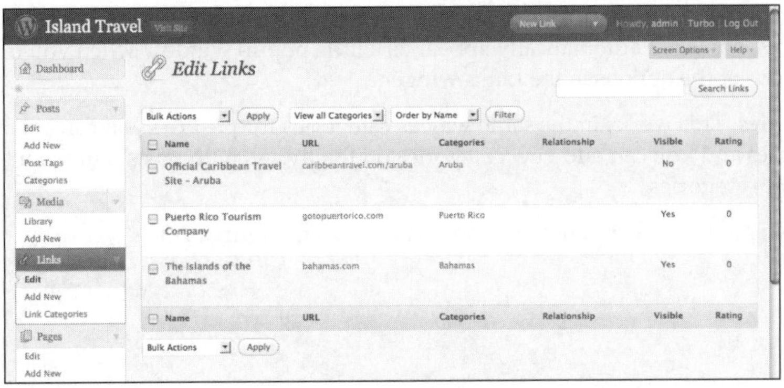

Figure 22-1

The navigation should be familiar from earlier lessons — filtering by category, searching, and so on. To edit a particular link you click the Name or click Edit in the text menu that appears when you mouseover a row. For the key elements of a link listing, look at the top region of the Links ⟶ Add New screen in Figure 22-2.

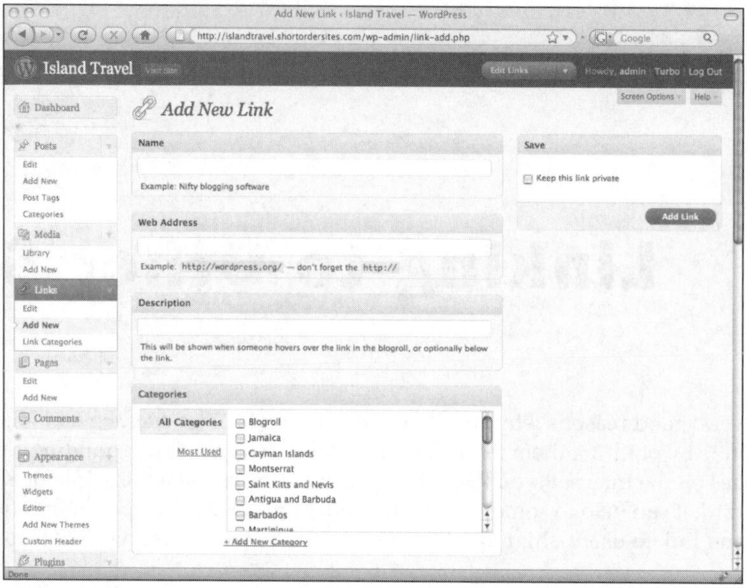

Figure 22-2

Here's an overview of all your options:

Name: This is entirely up to you — it's the title for the link that'll appear on your Links page or in the sidebar.

Web Address: This is the URL of the website. WordPress reminds you to include the `http://` at the beginning. The simplest thing of course is to highlight and copy the address out of your browser's address bar, or in the case of a text link, just right-click and choose Copy Link Location.

Description: This is a short summary of or comment on the site. Not all themes make use of this for their Links page template, but it's available to use if you're customizing a theme. The description does, however, automatically appear as a little popup window when you mouseover the link and is one of the options in the Links widget.

Categories: This works in the same way as categories for posts — you can choose one or several categories and you can add new categories on the fly. As with posts, links can be assigned to multiple categories.

The lower half of the link options screen is shown in Figure 22-3.

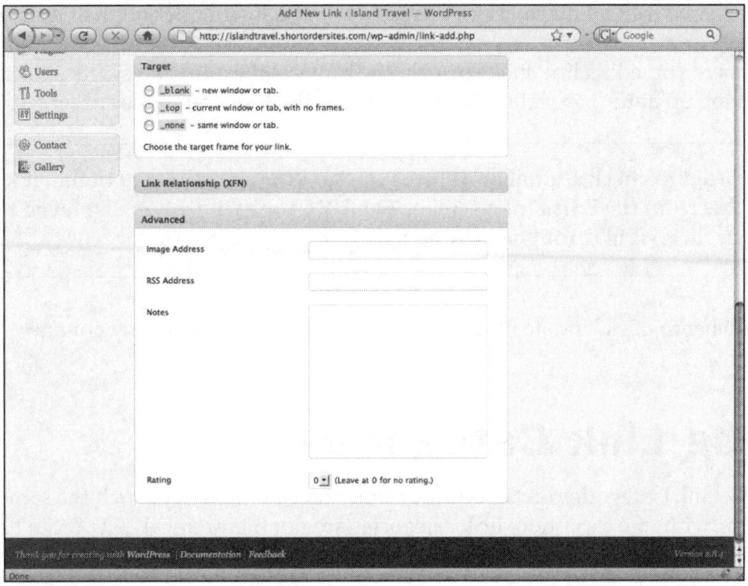

Figure 22-3

Target: This tells your browser where to open up the website when the link is clicked: either in a new window/tab or in the current window/tab. If you choose nothing, WordPress defaults to the current window/tab.

Link Relationship (XFN): (To fit everything onto the screen, this box is shown in collapsed mode.) The Xhtml Friends Network is a standard to show the social relationships between you and the people behind the sites you're linking to, such as family, business, or romantic relationships. For that purpose, clicking a relationship creates a special attribute in the HTML code for your link, which you can then use to designate unique styles using CSS (for example, you could give your "crushes" a different color than your "date" links or display an image to indicate a family member).

Advanced: One of the features you're most likely to use in this box is the Rating menu. You can sort links by their rating or display a link's rating. The other feature I want to mention is the Image field. You can associate an image with your link, using either a full URL (perhaps from the site you're linking to) or a path to your image directory (/images/mylink.jpg). You'll want the image to be fairly small, say 16 × 16 pixels, so it fits nicely next to your link.

Remember, if you find you rarely use sections like Link Relationship or Advanced, you can hide them altogether by going to the Screen Options button at the top right of the Add New Link screen and de-selecting them.

Save: There's a checkbox here to make the link Private, which means the link will be visible only from the administration area.

Once you've entered all the information, you just click the Add Link button at the top.

The screen where you edit a link looks exactly the same as the Add New Link screen, except you'll see a Visit Link button up at the top right. That lets you test the link and make sure it's still working.

> If you need to check a number of links to see if they're still functional, it's easiest to do this from the Edit Links screen. The URL for each link is displayed there and you can click right through to the site.

Always remember to click Update Link when you've finished making any changes.

Managing Link Categories

From Links ⇨ Link Categories on the admin menu you can do pretty much the same things you can for post categories, with one exception: link categories are not hierarchical — you can't have subcategories. Like posts, the Link Categories screen is divided into two sections, as shown in Figure 22-4.

On the left you add link categories and on the right you manage existing ones. Categories are displayed in alphabetical order.

To edit a link category you simply click its name or click Edit in the text menu that appears when you mouseover. You can also choose Quick Edit to change just the name or the slug.

This screen displays 20 links at a time and there is no option to change that, so if you have a lot of link categories, you'll need to page through them using the page links at the top and bottom of the list or you can do a search for a particular category.

You can delete link categories individually or in bulk, using the Bulk Actions menu. As with posts, if you delete a link category and there are links assigned to it, they will be reassigned automatically to the default category — the links are not deleted.

Just like posts, WordPress also has a permanent category for links that you cannot delete. That category is called Blogroll (you can edit the name) and it's set as the default category — if you forget to assign a link to at least one category, it automatically goes in the default category. You can choose a different default category under Settings ⇨ Writing.

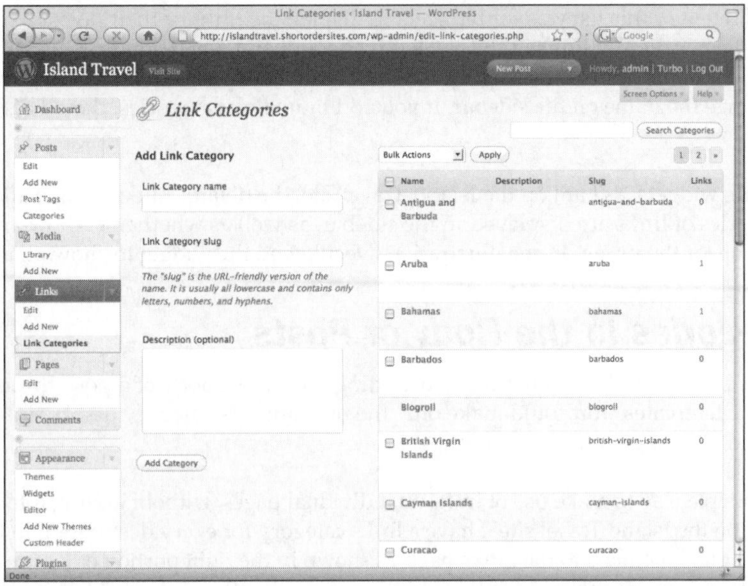

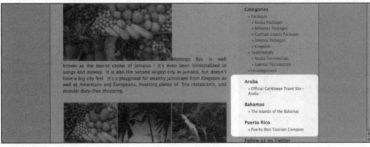

Figure 22-4

Displaying Links

WordPress makes it easy to display your links without much effort. Most themes include both a sidebar listing of your default link category and a links page template.

Sidebar Links

You've probably already noticed on the Island Travel site that there are links showing in the sidebar, as you can see on the left portion of Figure 22-5.

Figure 22-5

The original intent of this list was for bloggers to display the links of their favorite sites — often other blogs. Most themes display links in the sidebar by default and when you first install WordPress you'll see some links under the default category Blogroll. Of course, you're able to change the name, which will also change the name on the sidebar. If you add more link categories, they'll display in the sidebar as well.

If you're using widgets, as I am on the Island Travel site, the default Links widget allows you to choose which categories of links are displayed in the sidebar, as well as whether to show an image, the name, the description, or the rating. In the illustration I've allowed the widget to show all available categories.

Link Categories in the Body of Posts

You can also use your links in other ways, including within the body of a post, through customization of your theme templates. You could make only the relevant link category display in a post or in the sidebar, based the category of the current post.

However, a simple way to make use of links on individual pages, without getting into changing coding, is illustrated on the Island Travel site. I have a links category for every destination in the Caribbean, so I simply have a graphic linked to the Links page, as shown in the right portion of Figure 22-6. This reminds visitors that there are links relevant to the current page, rather than relying on them to choose the Links page from the main menu.

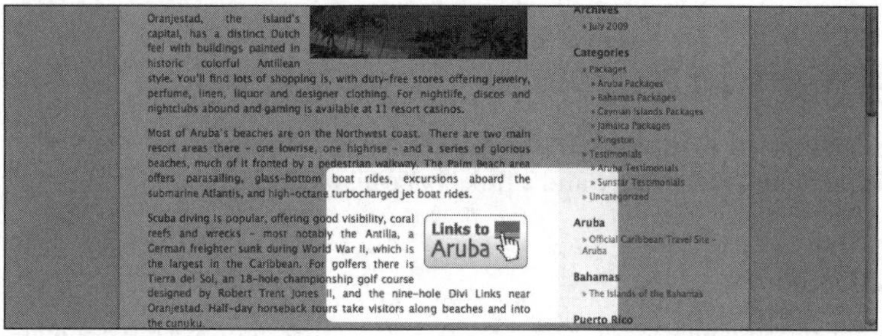

Figure 22-6

The Links Page

You'll probably only want to show the most general links in the sidebar, especially if you have a lot of them, as I do on the Island Travel site. The best way to display all your links is on a Links page. Most WordPress themes include a template for that exact purpose, which you'll find in the Template drop-down menu of the Add Page or Edit Page screens (see Lesson 10 on creating pages using templates).

What this template does is automatically display your links alphabetically and by category. Your theme will probably make the links look nice, but you can customize that look by editing your CSS style sheet.

Try It

In this lesson you practice adding a link.

Lesson Requirements

A website you want to link to.

Step-by-Step

Add a link to the WordPress links manager.

1. Go to Links ⇨ Add New.
2. Enter the Name you want to give this link.
3. Paste in the Web Address from your browser's address bar.
4. A Description is optional, but if entered will display when you mouseover the link.
5. Assign the link to one or more Categories.
6. Choose the Target where the browser will show the link's web site.
7. When finished, click the Add Link button.
8. On the live site check your Links page to see the new addition.

 To see some of the examples from this lesson, watch the video for Lesson 22 on the enclosed DVD.

Managing Comments

One of the hallmarks of blogging is the ability of visitors to leave comments on what's been written, and because WordPress was developed as blogging software it has an extensive comments system. In this lesson I show you how WordPress handles comments and some ways you can use them outside of a blogging context.

Allow Comments or Not?

When you're writing a blog, having people comment on your posts is an important part of the blog experience. You want to open up a dialogue with your visitors and even between your visitors. You might choose to close off comments after a certain period of time, but virtually no one with a blog would think about getting rid of comments altogether.

It's a different story when you're building a non-blog site with WordPress. There are far fewer places on the site where you would want people to comment. There's no particular need to allow visitors to comment on the About Us page of the Island Travel site, for example. On the other hand, I want people to comment on posts about a particular travel destination or a piece of news about the travel industry. That's where the individual comment control comes in handy, and I show you how to set that up in the next section.

The important point is that you need to consider the purposes of your website and how the WordPress comment function might fit in with those purposes. Every site will be different and every area on your site needs to be considered separately as well.

Admin Settings for Commenting

You can find the site-wide settings for commenting in the admin menu under Settings ➪ Discussion. By default, WordPress sets up the following parameters:

❑   The comment form and existing comments will appear on any post or page.

❑   To post a comment visitors must fill out their name and e-mail.

❑   The ability to comment is always open — there's no time limit on the comments for a particular post or page.

❑   All comments are held for approval unless the commenter has been approved before.

❑   The e-mail address listed in WordPress administration will be notified if any comments are posted or if any comments are held for moderation.

❑   Any comment is held for moderation if it contains more than two links.

❑   No words or web addresses are blacklisted.

❑   Avatars (small graphics or photos) are displayed with each comment and a default avatar is selected if the visitor doesn't provide one.

For a blog, these are pretty basic settings, and in many cases you won't need to make any changes. For a website, however, there's one setting in particular that you'll probably want to change and that's the ability to comment on every post and page, shown in Figure 23-1, under Default Article Settings.

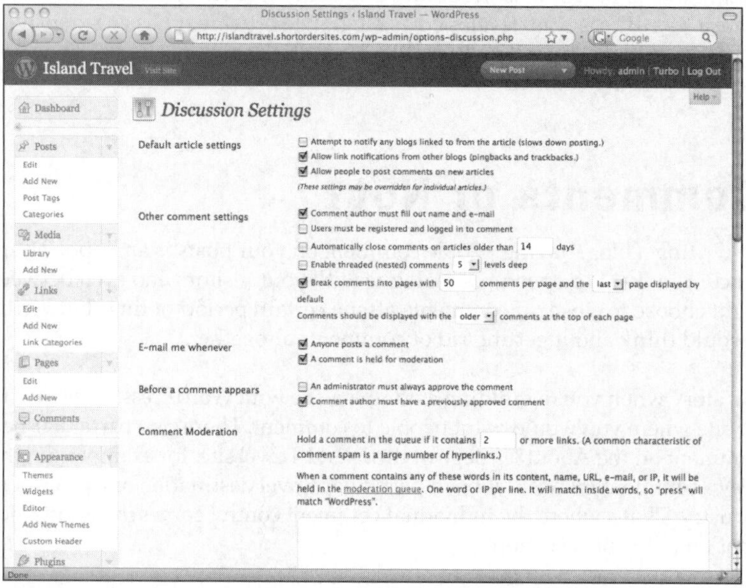

Figure 23-1

> **Don't be confused by the use of the term "article" in the Discussion Settings. Article just means posts or pages.**

If you turn off commenting for every post and page, you still have the ability to allow commenting on any particular post and page. WordPress reminds you of that when it says: *These settings may be overridden for individual articles.* To refresh your memory, that individual comment control is found near the bottom of the Add New or Edit Post screens under the Discussion heading. If you've turned off commenting, the checkbox for the post will be blank; if you've turned it on, the box will be checked.

If you've had site-wide commenting turned on and then turn it off, all posts up to that time will continue to show old comments, though no new comments can be made. For new posts, commenting will not be available unless you manually turn it on for a specific post.

Whichever default comments setting you choose, you'll still need to pay attention to the Discussion Settings when you're creating new posts.

One other useful option under Settings ➪ Discussion is the ability to automatically have comments close after a specified period of time, say, 60 days. Existing comments will continue to show, there just can't be any new comments. Some people use this feature if they're having trouble blocking spam comments, but they want to allow a bit of time for legitimate comments to be made. Others don't want to deal even with legitimate comments on old topics. With this feature you don't have to remember to manually turn off commenting after a post has been up for a while.

If you have commenting turned on, and you're seeing the comment box on posts but not pages, it's probably because the page templates for your theme do not have the code for commenting. The WordPress default theme is set up this way. The assumption is that people only want commenting for posts and not pages. If you do want the option to have people comment on pages, you could switch to another theme or add the code to your current templates.

Display Order of Comments

Traditionally, blogs have shown the oldest comments first. Part of the reason is that comments can often flow in the form of a discussion — you need to know what's been said earlier to follow what a later commenter is reacting to.

However, some people prefer to show the most recent comments first, one theory being that visitors who keep returning will want to first see what's new in the comments area, without having to scroll (sometimes a very long way) to the bottom.

WordPress recently made it possible to choose between the two. The default is still oldest comments first, but under Settings ➪ Discussion in the Other Comment Settings area you'll see a drop-down menu allowing you to select Older or Newer comments first.

Threaded Comments

No matter what order comments are displayed in, comments often don't flow in an orderly manner. If someone is commenting on a point made 15 comments earlier it can get difficult to keep track of the conversation. That's why WordPress offers the option of allowing threaded or nested comments. This displays a reply button beside each comment in addition to the comment box at the bottom of the post. If a visitor uses the reply button, then their comment shows up inside the comment they're replying to.

You can turn on this feature under Settings ➪ Discussion Settings. Look for *Enable threaded (nested) comments* and you can also allow the nesting to go up to 10 comments deep (default is 5). Be aware, though, that not all themes will properly display threaded comments. Even if yours doesn't, there are plugins to help you manage them or you can have your style sheet modified to do so.

Finding Comments

When I was showing you the WordPress Dashboard in Lesson 4, you saw the Comments area, which displays several of the most recent comments. From there you can link directly to the comments admin area.

The other point of entry is the Comments link on the admin menu (there are no submenu items for this), which takes you to the Edit Comments screen, shown in Figure 23-2.

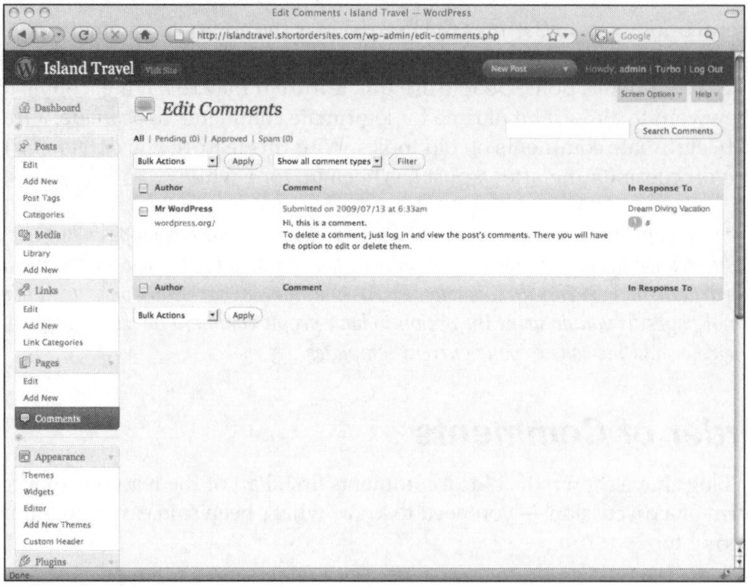

Figure 23-2

For each comment you're shown the author's name and a URL if the author entered one. Then you'll see the comment itself, along with the date and time it was submitted. Underneath the comment, if you mouseover the row, you'll see a menu with the following options:

- ❑ **Approve:** You can approve the comment (or Unapprove it depending on context).

- ❑ **Spam:** This marks the comment as spam so the information can be used by anti-spam plugins to learn what to block.

- ❑ **Delete:** This deletes the comment.

- ❑ **Edit:** Use this to edit the parameters of the comment, including the body, so you can remove bad language and so on.

- ❑ **Quick Edit:** This allows you to perform virtually all Edit tasks without going to a new screen.

- ❑ **Reply:** This lets you reply directly to the comment in the way described earlier when I talked about threaded comments. If your theme is set up to do so, your reply is shown with the comment it's in response to.

On the far right of the comments listing you see the title of the post that the comment was responding to, with a link to the posts's edit screen. The small hash symbol (#) provides a link to the post as it appears on your site.

You can filter the comments by Comments or Pings. I explain pings in more detail in Lesson 25, but basically these are links to your post as opposed to someone making a comment through your site.

You can also filter comments based on whether they're Pending (awaiting approval), Approved, or have been labeled as Spam.

Finally, you can search through the text of the comments by using the Search box at the top right of the screen.

Approving, Editing, or Deleting Comments

Assuming you've retained the default settings that require comments to be approved (at least the first time someone comments) and for the administrator to be e-mailed about it, you'll know there are comments waiting because you'll get an e-mail. The other way to know is if you log in to WordPress; there'll be a tiny orange icon beside Comments on the side menu, telling you how many are awaiting approval.

You can approve a comment by clicking Approve on the text menu that displays when you mouseover a comment on the Edit Comments screen. If you have a lot of comments to approve, just check the box for each, choose Approve from the Bulk Actions drop-down menu at the top or bottom, and click Apply.

Before or after you've approved a comment, you can edit the contents by clicking Edit on that text menu. You'll see a screen like the one in Figure 23-3.

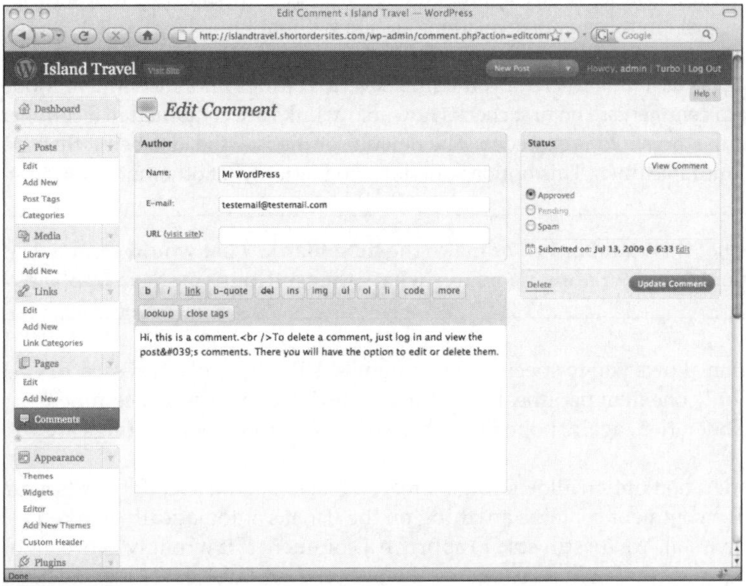

Figure 23-3

From this screen you can edit all the parameters, including the date and time it was submitted (see the Status box).

Notice that the comment Text Editor is available only in HTML mode and the buttons are the same as the ones whose functions are described in detail in Lesson 7. Visitors do not get any formatting buttons when entering comments, but there are plugins which offer all sorts of options in that regard.

As always, remember to click Update Comment when you're finished editing.

To delete a comment or comments, you again have the choice to delete individually or in bulk when you're in the Edit Comments listing screen. When you're editing an individual comment, you can delete it from the link in the Status box.

> If you set WordPress to email you whenever a comment is being held for modera-
> tion, the email will contain direct links for approving or deleting the link, or mark-
> ing it as spam.

Dealing with Spam Comments

Although spam comments are dealt with from the same menus as approving or deleting, I've left them for a separate section. WordPress comes with a number of methods for dealing with spam comments and dozens of plugins. I talk about the plugins in Lesson 37; here I want to mention some of the built-in tools.

The first line of defense with spam comments is to make sure you require all comments to be moderated (not counting those visitors you've approved once already — if you keep that setting in place). That way you don't have just anything appearing on your site without knowing about it.

On the Settings ➪ Discussion screen you'll find several settings under Comment Moderation that can help deal with spam comments. The first checks how many links are contained in a comment and holds it for moderation if the threshold is exceeded. The default setting is 2, the idea being that spam comments will often contain multiple links. This option functions no matter what other moderation settings you have.

> Never set this number to 0 or make the field blank. That would send every single
> comment to moderation, no matter what other settings you have in place.

The next option allows you to specify words, names, URLs, e-mail addresses, or even IP addresses — be sure to have only one item per line. If anything on this list appears in a comment, it will automatically be held for moderation, again, no matter what your other comments settings are.

The final moderation option allows you to create a blacklist. You specify words, names, and so on, but in this case, if a comment contains anything on the list, it's automatically marked as spam, not simply put into moderation. You're still able to approve a comment if it wrongly gets caught by this blacklist.

I keep using the term "mark as spam" and it means that not only will comments marked as spam not appear on your site, they'll stay in your database and can be used by plugins (see Lesson 37) to compare with future comments and help determine if they're spam too.

Try It

In this lesson you practice approving a comment.

Lesson Requirements

Have someone comment on one of your posts, or you can do it yourself as long as you log out of WordPress before doing so (if you're still logged in, you'll be commenting as an administrator and automatically be approved).

Step-by-Step

How to approve a comment.

1. Log in to WordPress.

2. On the Dashboard you should see the new comment in the Comments box and on the left side menu there should be at least one item in the orange icon beside Comments.

3. You could approve the comment right from the Dashboard if you mouseover the comment and use the Approve link on the menu that appears.

4. If you want to read the entire comment first, click Edit and when you're satisfied mark it as Approved in the Status box. Finally, click Update Comment.

5. From the Dashboard you can also click Pending in the Right Now box and you'll see a list of comments requiring approval.

 To see some of the examples from this lesson, watch the video for Lesson 23 on the enclosed DVD.

Connecting to Content on Other Sites

You can enhance the content of your site in many ways by tapping into content available on other sites and displaying it on your own. Just as your WordPress site can generate RSS feeds of your material, you can tap into the feeds generated by other sites. Some of this content may even be generated by you, as in the case of your postings on Facebook, Twitter, and other social media sites.

In this lesson, I show you how to integrate this content into your site and talk a bit about where to look for such content.

Connecting to Your Social Media Accounts

If you have social media accounts, such as Twitter or Facebook, the content you're generating on those sites could be useful on your WordPress site. If you don't have any social media accounts related to the topic of your site, you should get some! Then you can have your latest entries on those social media sites displayed automatically on your WordPress site.

I'll show you how it's done with Twitter, but the process is very similar for most other sites.

You'll need some code from Twitter first, and most social media sites make it very easy to get that, as you can see in Figure 24-1.

Many sites make it easy, as Twitter does here, to customize how the feed will look on your site, how many items it will display, and so on. When you're through customizing, you'll click something like Finish & Grab Code or Generate Code, and you're presented with the code, as in Figure 24-2.

Figure 24-1

Figure 24-2

Sometimes there will be a button to automatically copy the code for you, but in many cases you'll need to do it yourself, as is the case in Figure 24-2. Place your cursor in the text box and press Ctrl+A to select it all, then Ctrl+C to copy it. Now you're ready to paste the code into a widget on your site.

In WordPress, go to Appearance ⇨ Widgets and find the Text widget on the left-hand side. When you drag it over to the Sidebar 1 area on the right, it opens up and you can paste in your coding, as shown in Figure 24-3.

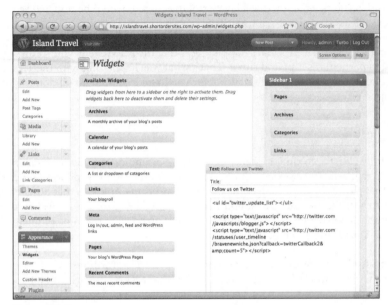

Figure 24-3

When you save the widget, you'll see on your site whatever style of feed you chose on your social media site.

Adding Content Feeds from Other Sites

You've probably seen websites that have news headlines or the latest weather forecast. Usually these are content feeds from other websites, and though there's much more out there than just headlines and forecasts, the idea is that these feeds provide constantly updated information. That information typically takes the form of a title and summary, with a link back to the original website where you get all the details.

The two most common methods for getting these feeds are JavaScript and RSS. You won't need to know anything technical to make use of these feeds — you see shortly how WordPress widgets make it a snap — but it's helpful to know a bit of background.

> **Always make sure you have permission to use a feed of any type. Generally sites are happy to have people using their feeds, but even then there may be some registration process required or even a small fee.**

JavaScript Feeds

JavaScript is a language that's used by web pages to make your browser take certain actions when you move your mouse, click things, leave a page, and so on. When you fill out a form and it tells you that your password isn't long enough, that's JavaScript in action. It would be unusual these days for a website not to use at least some JavaScript.

In the case of a JavaScript feed, what's happening is that the HTML tells your browser to go to another website, load a particular script and run it. That's what was happening with the Twitter coding that I just copied into Island Travel. There's nothing for you to maintain; that's all done by the website hosting the JavaScript.

RSS Feeds

RSS stands for, at least according to some, "really simple syndication." Some TV shows, newspaper columns, and radio shows are examples of syndicated content — the producers send out their shows to companies that pay to show or publish the content. The beauty of RSS is that other people just click a button on your website and they are subscribed (through an RSS reader, for example) to your content. When you publish new content, it automatically shows up on their machine or on another website, which is what I'm talking about in this section.

Accessing RSS feeds from other sites is pretty straightforward in WordPress. Go to Appearance ➪ Widgets and look for a widget called RSS. Drag it over to the Sidebar area on the right, and it opens up to display the window shown in Figure 24-4.

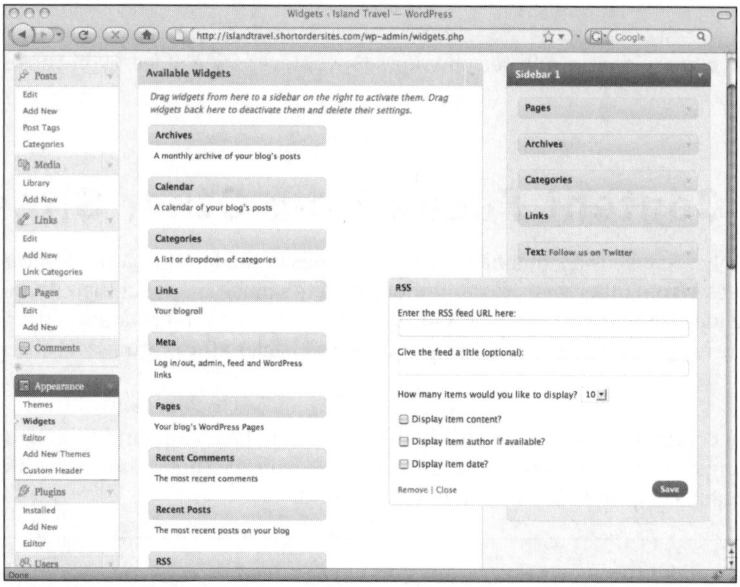

Figure 24-4

The first thing you're asked for is the URL for the RSS feed. This is the information you copy from the website providing the feed. When you're searching for RSS feeds, you'll be given a URL which, if you open it in a browser, produces a page like this one from www.aruba.com in Figure 24-5.

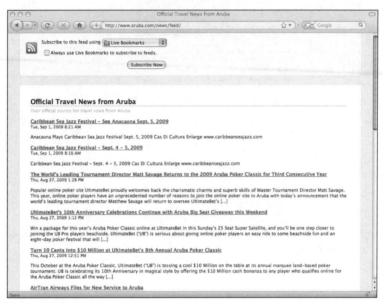

Figure 24-5

Copy the URL of this page from your browser's address bar, and then paste it into the WordPress widget where it says Enter the RSS feed URL here.

You can then give a title to what will appear in your sidebar, after which you have a choice of how many items to display from the feed (default is 5) along with which parts of the feed you would like to display: Content, Author, and Date.

Click Save and close the widget. When you refresh your live site, you'll see the RSS feed in your sidebar, like my Aruba feed on the Island Travel site in Figure 24-6.

You can find RSS feeds in two ways. If you find some content that could work well on your site, look for an RSS feed icon or link on that page — also look for permission to use the feed on your site. The other way is to search for RSS feeds in Google and you'll discover dozens of directories that let you search for RSS feeds by topic. You can also look for "widgets" — not the kind in WordPress — which are custom programs, often for free, that will use JavaScript, RSS, or other means to pull content onto your site.

For the sake of simplicity, I've shown you how to place content in your site's sidebar, using RSS feeds or JavaScript. You can also put this content into posts and pages, but you'll need a plugin for WordPress that will enable code to run within the main content area of your site. You could also customize your theme templates to allow RSS feeds to display in a particular place outside the sidebar.

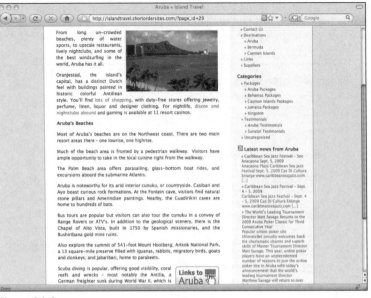

Figure 24-6

Try It

In this lesson you practice putting an RSS feed in your sidebar.

Lesson Requirements

Have the URL of a content feed that you would like to put in your sidebar. One simple way is to go to a friend's blog and get the URL for his or her feed.

Step-by-Step

Add an RSS feed to the sidebar.

1. Have the URL of the RSS feed available on your clipboard or in a text file somewhere.

2. Go to Appearance ➪ Widgets.

3. Locate the RSS feed widget in the Available box on the left side.

4. Drag the RSS feed over to the Sidebar area on the right.

5. Paste the URL into the field marked Enter the RSS Feed URL Here.

6. Give the feed a title if you like.

7. Check Display Item Content if you want more than just the title of each item.

8. Do the same for Author if you want that to display.

9. Do the same for Date.

10. Click Save.

11. Refresh your website and view the feed live.

12. If you're seeing nothing or you have an error, double-check the URL of the feed once more and try again.

 To see some of the examples from this lesson, watch the video for Lesson 24 on the enclosed DVD.

Helping Others
Connect to Your Site

In the preceding lesson I showed you how to bring in content from other sites; now it's time to look at ways WordPress can help others make use of your content. Whether it's through a link to your site, publishing an RSS (really simple syndication) feed of your site, or subscribing to your site through their RSS reader, having people connect to your site is an important part of your promotional plans and maintaining interaction with others on the Web.

RSS Feeds of Your Content

WordPress makes good on the "really simple" in really simple syndication (RSS) feeds because they aren't so simple. First of all, there are many syndication formats, of which RSS is only one. Add to that the fact there are several versions of RSS, let alone the question of how to output your content in each format, and you get a sense of how complex the world of web feeds can be. Thankfully, WordPress takes care of all of it for you, generating four separate feeds for a post's content: RSS 0.92, RSS 2.0, Atom and RDF/RSS 1.0.

Although WordPress automatically generates these different feeds, themes typically include only one or two (RSS2 is the most common). If you want help customizing your theme to include more feeds, go to `http://codex.wordpress.org/WordPress_Feeds`.

WordPress also makes it easy for your visitors to get RSS feeds for very specific content on your site. If you want them to subscribe to all posts for a particular category, just create a link like this: `http://www.yourdomain.com/categoryname/feed` (the format for this link will depend on your Permalink settings — see the final section of this lesson). On the Island Travel site, for example, it would be good to put a link on pages about Aruba that allows visitors to subscribe to the post category Aruba Packages. That way they can stay up to date on the latest vacation offerings. Similarly, you could have a feed for all posts tagged with the term "Kingston" or even have a feed for a specific page on the site.

Although WordPress automatically generates RSS feeds, you do have a couple of parameters you can set for how your feeds will be displayed, and you'll find them under Settings ➪ Reading, as shown in Figure 25-1.

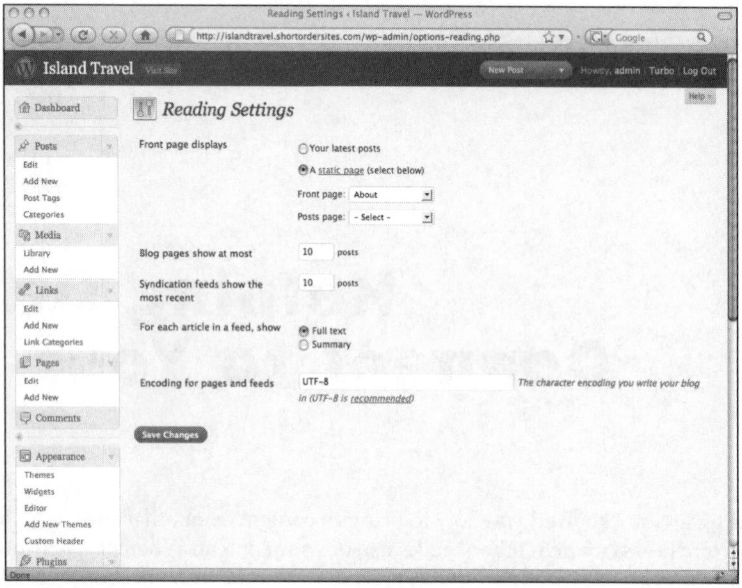

Figure 25-1

You can set the number of items to be shown in any syndication feed (the default is 10). The other option is whether to allow the full text to be shown in the feed or just a summary — the default is full text, but the choice is not cut and dried.

The theory behind allowing the full text is that subscribers might be more likely to read it because they don't have to click through to get the complete story. If your goal is primarily to get the content read, this option makes sense. If your goal is to drive traffic to your site, providing only a summary is a way of getting readers to click through to view the rest of the material. I leave you to ponder the pros and cons.

You can extend your RSS feed capabilities by using a third-party service, such as Feedburner, to manage your feeds (these services provide ways of tracking how many people are subscribing to you, what they're doing when on your site, and so on). A number of plugins for WordPress make it simple to integrate your site with these services, such as FD Feedburner.

Setting Pingbacks and Trackbacks

Pingbacks and trackbacks are types of notifications that someone has linked to your site, and these notifications show up in the comments on your posts. Pingbacks are the more important of the two, as trackbacks are really only used for linking to older blogging systems.

Creating a pingback to another site is easy — just link to that site in the body of your post. In order for the other site owner to be notified, they have to have pingbacks enabled on their site. Trackbacks to another site also require that site's owner to have them turned on; the difference is that you need to paste a special URL into the trackback notification box on your Add/Edit post screen, and you have to do that even if you linked to the site in the body of the post.

This means that in order to receive pingbacks to your own site, you simply have to have pingbacks and trackbacks turned on (you'll see how to do that in a moment). You can test that pingbacks are working by creating a link in one of your posts to another of your posts, and then watch for the pingback to show up in the comments. If you want people to be able to trackback to your site, you'll have to provide them with the trackback URL that they need to paste into their trackback box. Check if your theme displays the trackback URL — the default theme doesn't, for example. If not, you can add it by modifying the necessary template(s) in your theme.

So how do you make sure pingbacks and trackbacks are enabled on your WordPress site? Go to Settings ➪ Discussion and you'll see this under Default Article Settings (Figure 25-2).

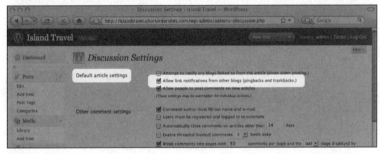

Figure 25-2

By default, WordPress allows trackbacks and pingbacks for all posts and pages. You can turn this off and you would still be able to activate them for individual posts or pages in the Discussion section of the Add or Edit screens, but it's simplest to leave this activated for everything. If you have WordPress set to allow comments to appear only after they've been approved, the same will be true for trackbacks and pingbacks. You can moderate the ones that appear in the Dashboard or click through to the Edit Comments area if you have more waiting.

Because trackbacks to your site can be created without the other site owner actually linking to you in the body of a post, some people don't feel they're reliable indicators that someone has linked to you. Others find they get a lot of spam through trackbacks. WordPress enables/disables pingbacks and trackbacks together, so they're either both on or both off. There are some plugins that allow you to deal with them separately.

Setting Permalinks

You want other sites to link to your content — it's one of the most important ways to build traffic to your site — but you want to make sure that, over time, those links don't end up pointing to the wrong page. On a blog, for example, posts only display on the front page until they're replaced with newer posts. On websites in general the title of a post may get changed or a post might be moved from one category to another. That's good for flexibility, but not so good for people linking to your content. It would be like moving to another city and not letting your friends and family know where you are. One way to solve the problem is to have a permanent address for each post on your site, and WordPress does that through what are called *permalinks*.

Every post, page, and category in WordPress has a fixed permalink. That's because they all have unique and permanent IDs — even if you delete something, its ID cannot be used again. An example of such a link would be `http://www.yourdomain.com/?p=45`. As long as someone knows that URL, they can always get to item #45.

You can see the permalink for a post or a page just below the Title area (it won't show until you've entered something for the title), as illustrated in Figure 25-3.

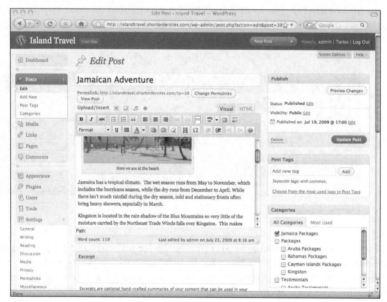

Figure 25-3

However, WordPress's default permalinks are not very memorable URLs and they don't give search engines much of a hint as to what the content is for a particular item (I talk more about permalinks and search engines in Lesson 31). That's why you can tell WordPress to show the world very different sorts of permalinks.

Under Settings ➪ Permalinks you can customize the look of these links as much as you'd like — the screen is shown in Figure 25-4.

The default setting is shown at the top, and then you see several suggested presets (I generally use the third one down — Month and Name). You can even create your own custom permalinks using the set of tags at the WordPress.org website — a link is provided at the top of the Permalinks page.

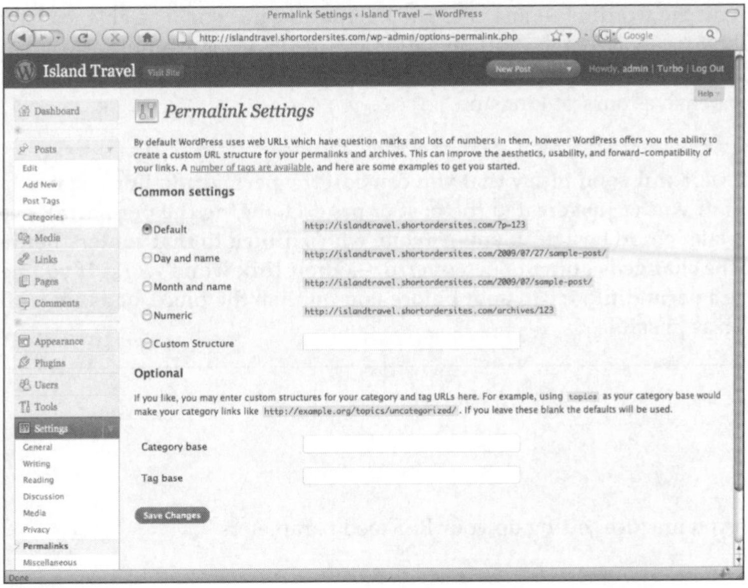

Figure 25-4

If you switch to one of these custom settings, you'll find that the permalinks option also changes below the titles of posts and pages, as shown in the upper half of Figure 25-5.

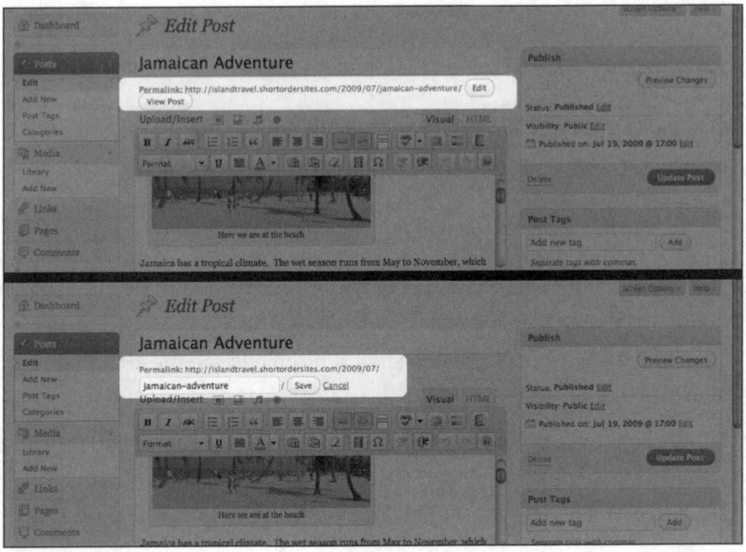

Figure 25-5

You can also edit the wording — just click the Edit button and you'll be able to change the last section of the permalink, as shown in the bottom half of Figure 25-5. For example, if you have a very long title such as "A great way to see Kingston on just $30 per day" you could go in and edit the permalink to say, perhaps, "inexpensive-tours-of-kingston."

It's all well and good to say that you can edit the permalink, but you need to be careful. If you've just created the post or page, changing the permalink even a day or two later could be a problem. Anyone who's linked to that content before you made the change is going to get an error — their link won't work. If you need to change a permalink, try to do it before you publish the piece, or as soon after you publish as possible.

Try It

In this lesson you practice setting up your RSS feed parameters.

Lesson Requirements

No special requirements.

Step-by-Step

How to set up an RSS feed.

1. Go to Settings ➪ Readings.

2. Set *Syndication feeds show the most recent* to 5 (default is 10).

3. Set *For each article in a feed, show* to Summary (default is full text).

4. Click Save Changes.

5. If you have an RSS reader, such as Google News Reader or Bloglines, try subscribing to your site. Simply go to your live site and click the Subscribe button on your reader — it should pick up your RSS feed.

6. Assuming you have some posts, you should be able to see those in the feed.

 To see some of the examples from this lesson, watch the video for Lesson 25 on the enclosed DVD.

Having Multiple Site Users

Even in a small company or organization, you may need more than one person working on your website. At the same time, you may not want each of those people to have the same access to the site, such as the ability to change the theme or delete pages. WordPress makes the management of these various levels of access quite easy through what are called *roles*.

The whole purpose of having different roles is to prevent people from making bad mistakes and doing something that affects the entire site. That's where careful thinking about a user's requirements is so crucial — you only want them to have permissions that allow them to do their particular work.

User Roles and Their Capabilities

There are five user roles in WordPress and in order of decreasing capabilities they are:

- ❑ Administrator
- ❑ Editor
- ❑ Author
- ❑ Contributor
- ❑ Subscriber

In the case of Island Travel, with its two offices, I could have a single Administrator to take care of technical aspects of the site, and a single Editor who oversees all site content. Each travel agent could be an Author managing their own posts, with a few non-agency people who act as Contributors. Customers and potential customers could be Subscribers who are able to view website content that the public can't see.

With these examples in mind, let's go through each of the five user roles in a bit more detail:

❑ **Administrator**: As the name suggests, an Administrator has access to every single administrative function in WordPress, including editing theme files, changing themes, adding plugins, user details, and so on. It's probably not a good idea to have more than a couple of Administrators or they could wind up overriding each other's work — the "too many cooks" syndrome.

❑ **Editor**: The Editor role allows the maximum amount of control over all the content of the website, without being able to change settings that control the site itself, such as themes or plugins. Editors can add or delete any content-related items in WordPress, including categories, posts, pages, and links. They have full access to the media library and full control over publishing content. Editors can also add and delete users, but they cannot edit user information.

❑ **Author**: Authors within WordPress are meant to be like columnists in a newspaper or magazine. They have full control over their own content — adding, editing, publishing, and deleting — but no one else's. Authors cannot add or delete post or link categories and they cannot use unfiltered HTML in their posts — code such as JavaScript or certain HTML tags or attributes pasted from a program like Dreamweaver.

❑ **Contributor**: Contributors can create, edit, or delete their own posts, but they cannot publish those posts (they can save drafts). They can't edit or delete even their own posts once those have been published by an Editor or Administrator. Contributors do, however, appear on the Post Author drop-down menu.

❑ **Subscriber:** The name of this user role shouldn't be confused with subscribing to a website or blog through an RSS feed. In this case, Subscriber is meant in the sense of a registered visitor — someone who can see content or take actions on a site that unregistered visitors can't. Basically the only permissions subscribers have in the admin section is the ability to change their profile (name, e-mail, interests, avatar, and so on).

For complete details on each role's capabilities, check out the WordPress site at `http://codex.wordpress .org/Roles_and_Capabilities`.

Adding a User

There are two ways to become a user on a WordPress site: being added manually by an Administrator or registering through a registration form. The automated form is meant for easily signing up subscribers so they can view special content on your site, and you would use the manual process for adding any of the other roles.

By default, the automated sign-up form is disabled. You activate it on the Settings ➪ General screen by checking off the Membership box. The word "membership" is a bit confusing because what you're setting here is the ability for people to register themselves as new users on the system. There is no user role called "member" and you may or may not think of the users who sign up as members. The wording on the drop-down menu just below is clearer: New User Default Role. This sets the role that users will be assigned when they register themselves, as well as the default role in the drop down menu when manually creating new users. By default, that role is Subscriber.

> Don't change the Default User Role unless you've really thought things through. Even allowing just anyone to become a Contributor opens up your system to people posting content (even if they can't publish) and being listed on the drop-down author menu for posts. And you certainly wouldn't want to allow just anyone to be an Editor, Author, or Administrator.

To manually add a new user to the system, click Users ➪ Add New on the main admin menu and you'll be greeted with the screen shown in Figure 26-1.

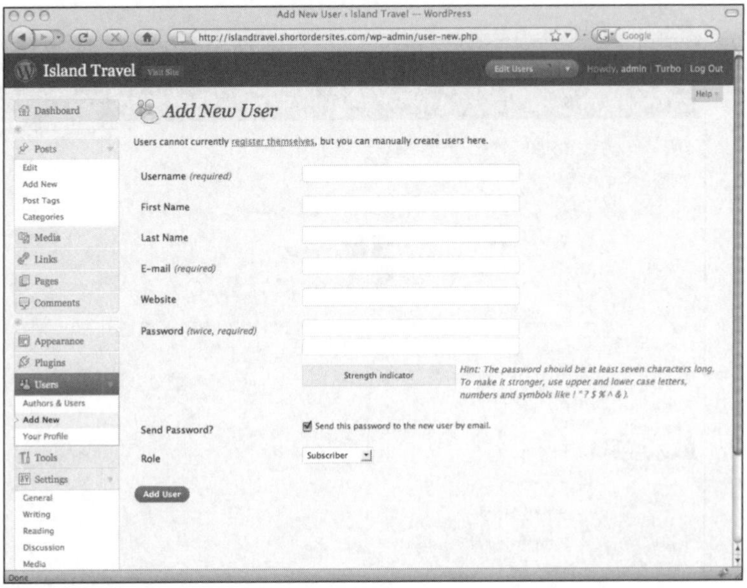

Figure 26-1

At the very top you'll see a notice, which in this case says "Users cannot currently register themselves." There's a link there and it takes you to the Settings ➪ General screen that I just talked about. If you change the default setting to allow visitors to register themselves as users, the notice would remind you that they can do so and provide the same link in case you want to switch back to the default.

You need only three things to create a new user: a username, an e-mail address, and a password. You'll also want confirm which role you're assigning to the user (the default is Subscriber). When you create a new user, login details are e-mailed to the user by default. If you don't want them e-mailed, uncheck the Send Password box. Once users have their login information, they can change or fill in any of the fields on the profile screen I showed you in Lesson 5 (except the username).

Usernames and e-mail addresses must be unique. WordPress warns you if either exists already in the system.

Changing a User's Capabilities

Need to promote a Contributor to Author status? Tired of one of the Administrators always switching themes and you want to bump them down to Subscriber? An Administrator can change a user's role by going to Users ➪ Authors & Users, finding the user on the list, and going into their personal profile by clicking Edit, which appears when your mouse moves over a listing. Figure 26-2 shows the top portion of the resulting personal profile screen.

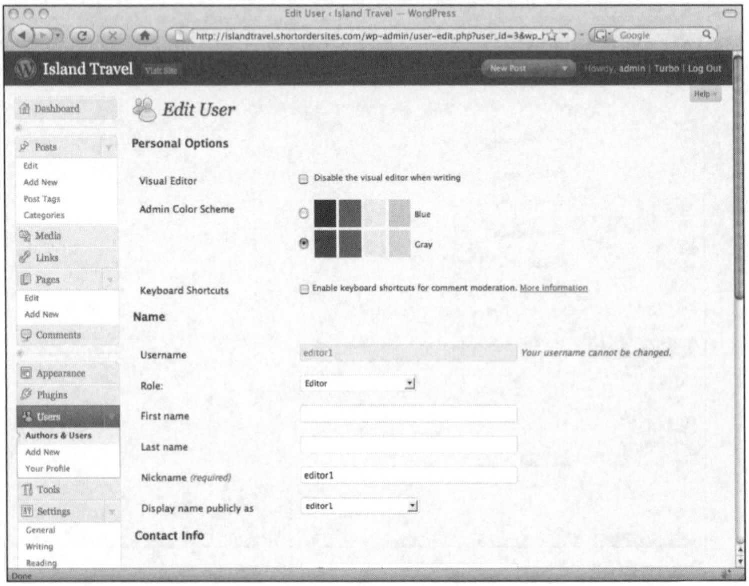

Figure 26-2

Just below the Username is the drop-down menu for their role. Select a role and click Update User.

If you need to change large numbers of users at once, go to Users ➪ Authors & Users and check off all the users you want to change. Then from the Change Role To drop-down menu at the top of the page, select the new role and click Change, as shown in Figure 26-3.

If all or most of the users have the same role, you can speed up the process by filtering the page by role using the menu just below the page title.

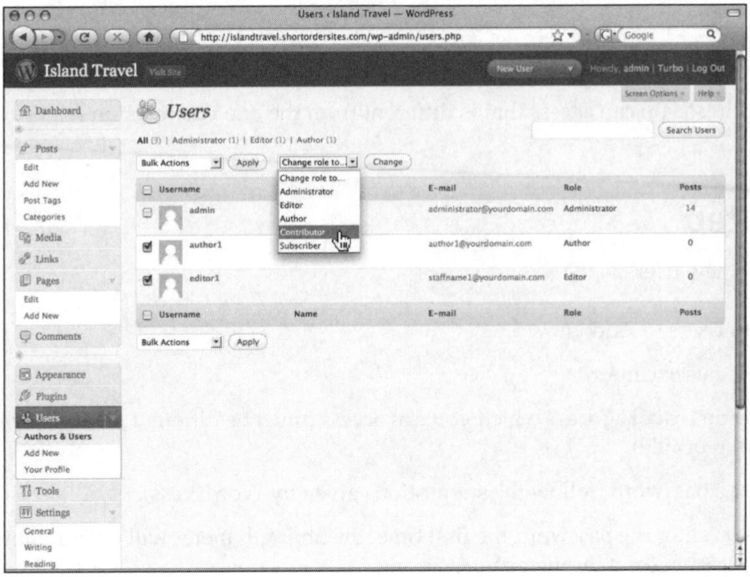

Figure 26-3

Users and Security

Following are three key points concerning users and security:

1. **Choose the lowest possible role:** Don't make someone an Editor when they really just need to be an Author. The higher the role, the more power you're entrusting to the user. And if you turn on the self-registration feature, don't allow users to sign up for anything more than Subscriber.

2. **Emphasize the importance of tough passwords:** You may give new users a diabolical password, but they can go in and change that later. Impress on them the need to not use natural language words, and to use upper- and lowercase, numbers, and so on. (WordPress has this reminder and a strength indicator that gives users an extra nudge.)

3. **Monitor your users:** In particular if you have more than a few users, it's important to check your list of users on a regular basis. The unexpected appearance of a new user with a high-end role could be the sign of a hacker.

Try It

In this lesson you practice adding a new user.

Lesson Requirements

An e-mail address you can access that is different from the one you're using for your WordPress administrator role.

Step-by-Step

How to add a new user.

1. Go to Users ➪ Add New.
2. Enter a username.
3. Enter an e-mail address which you can access (must be different from the email you use in your current profile).
4. Enter a password (follow the suggestions given by WordPress).
5. As you enter the password the first time, the Strength meter will tell you how good it is — at the very least make it Strong or Very Strong.
6. Enter the password a second time.
7. Make sure the Send Password box is checked off.
8. Select a role for this user (other than Administrator).
9. Click Add User.
10. Log out of WordPress as an Administrator.
11. Check your e-mail for your user information.
12. Try logging in with your username and password.
13. As long as the new user's role was not Administrator, you shouldn't see Settings on the side menu, and depending on the user level, you may not see other parts of the menu either.

 To see some of the examples from this lesson, watch the video for Lesson 26 on the enclosed DVD.

Part VII: Customizing the Look of Your Site

Customizing Your Header Content

Unless you have a WordPress theme custom-built for you, you'll usually need to make some adjustments to get your site looking the way you want it. This is particularly true if you're building a business website with WordPress, and the most important change to make is in the header portion of the theme — adding a company logo, for example. In this lesson I use the Island Travel site to show you some ways in which you can customize your header content.

> *Parts of this lesson are going to require some FTP work and some HTML. If you had someone install WordPress for you, you might want hire that person or a web designer to take care of this section for you.*

Built-in Header Customization

Some WordPress themes make it easy to change elements on your site, including the header, without getting into style sheets or uploading new graphics. The default theme is an example of this. If you go to Appearance ➪ Custom Header you're presented with a view of the header area of your site. You can make changes to the color scheme or you can revert to the original colors.

If you click Font Color, Upper Color, or Lower Color, a popup color picker appears and you choose from that palette. In Figure 27-1 you can see how I've changed the lower portion of the blue gradient as well as the color of the title, and now the color picker for the Upper area is visible.

Figure 27-1

When you click Update Header, the live site shows your changes. Not all themes offer this or other kinds of customization, but it might be a consideration when you're choosing a theme.

Using the Theme Editor

No matter which theme you have, WordPress makes it easy to alter the style sheet (and other files) using the Theme Editor. Go to Appearance ➪ Editor and, by default, you'll see your current theme's style sheet ready for editing. You're looking at the actual file on the server, so remember that when you save changes here, they're happening live on the site.

How do you know which CSS rules are controlling your theme's title? The simplest way to find out is to right mouse click and select View Source while browsing your site, and find the text for the title. Then make a note of the HTML tag for the title and any id or class attributes (remember to look at the HTML just before the title as well, because it may have a role in controlling the title).

In the case of the title, it's fairly easy because for most WordPress themes, it will be the only H1 tag on the entire site. Now you know what to look for as you scroll down the style sheet in the Editor, as shown in the upper half of Figure 27-2.

Suppose I want to change the look of the title of my site. I can see from the H1, H2, H3 rule that these headings have all been assigned the same font family. In this case I only want to change the font family for H1. I could create a new rule just for H1, but you can see that there already is a rule for that, so I simply add the new font family, as you can see in the lower portion of Figure 27-2. You can also see that I changed the font-size and alignment at the same time.

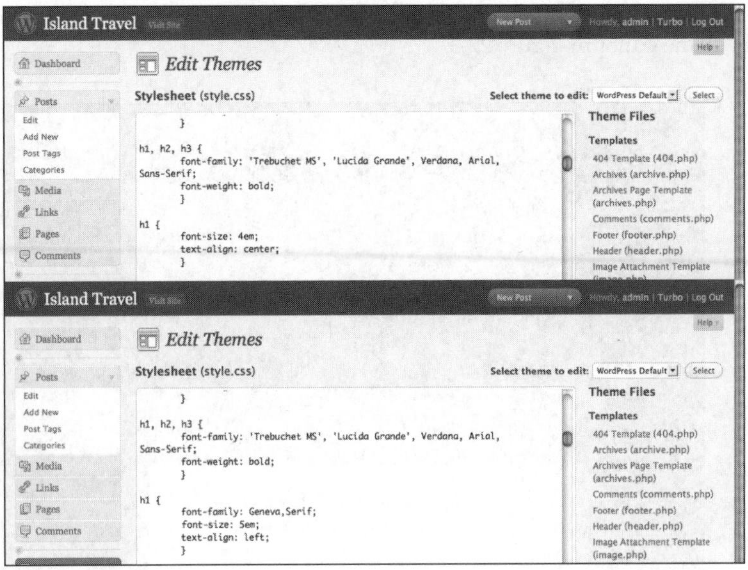

Figure 27-2

When the changes are done, click Update File and then you can refresh the live site and see what it looks like.

When you try to save changes in the theme editor, you may get a warning message that says "You may need to make this file writable…" This means that you do not have sufficient permission to change the file. You have a couple of options. You can either use an FTP program to download your theme's style sheet, make changes on your computer and upload it again, or try to get the permissions changed so that you can use the WordPress interface.

Adding a Logo

Having a logo or other branding graphics will be important for any site beyond a personal blog. In this section, I show you a couple of options for placing a logo in the header area of the site.

Logo Plus Existing Title Text

The first option is to keep the default title text and add a logo to the right or the left of it. This will involve editing the header file, the style sheet, and uploading the logo to your server. All of this could be accomplished in a number of ways, but there's only space enough to show you one.

The first step is to create a properly sized version of your logo in a .gif or .png format so its background can be transparent. To know the size, just look in your style sheet for the height given to the area containing the title and description for the site. In the case of the default theme, the CSS name for the area is `headerimg` and it's 192 pixels tall. I want my logo to fit easily within that, so I'm going with a height of 120 pixels.

Now take a look at the HTML code for the part of the header I'm going to be working with, as high-lighted in the theme editor in Figure 27-3.

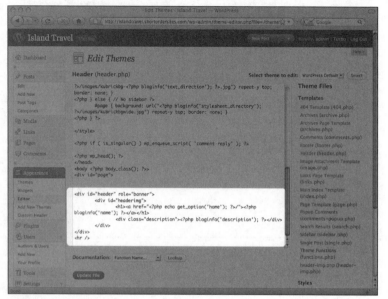

Figure 27-3

I can see that headerimg, containing my title and description, is a distinct division (div) inside a larger division called header. Because I want my logo to be on the left side of the title, it will need a CSS rule that says keep it to the left of headerimg. I'm also going to need HTML code to tell WordPress where to find my logo and it looks like this:

```
<img id="logo" src="<?php bloginfo('template_directory');?>/images/logo.gif" />
```

The bloginfo('template_directory') command is a WordPress template tag so that no matter which theme I'm using, it will look in the proper folder on the server. The id="logo" is a unique iden-tifier that I can use in my CSS style sheet to make the logo image do whatever I want.

I place this code for the logo into my header.php file just before the headerimg division, and click Update File to save changes to the header file. Using my FTP program, I upload the logo.gif file into the images folder of the default theme.

If I don't do anything with my CSS style sheet, the header will look like the top half of Figure 27-4 (I had to highlight the white title or it wouldn't have been visible).

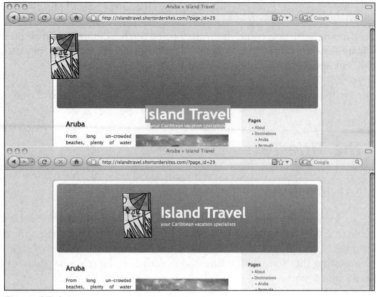

Figure 27-4

Clearly, that's not what I want. Using the theme editor, then, I'll update the CSS rules for the title and description. Currently they're both centered, so I need to change their text alignment so that they'll be flush left to the logo, like so:

```
h1 {
    font-size: 4em;
    text-align: left;
}
#headerimg .description {
    font-size: 1.2em;
    text-align: left;
}
```

I also need to add some rules to govern the logo itself; keep it to the left of the title and ensure it's not up at the top left of the header. The resulting CSS looks like this:

```
#logo {
    float: left;
    padding-top: 40px;
    padding-left: 200px;
    padding-right: 25px;
}
```

After saving the style sheet, you can see the changes in the lower half of Figure 27-4.

Of course there's much more you could do to customize the header area. Notice all the space over on the right. With adjustments to your header template file you could, for example, place a banner in that space announcing current specials, or whatever you like.

You can do more with branding by also changing the background image, and that's something I cover in Lesson 29.

Replacing the Title Text

If your logo contains the title of your site, you'll want to get rid of the header text and description altogether. I'll do that now for the Island Travel site.

As in the previous section, I'll create a transparent logo, this time with the company title and description in it, and I'll upload it to the images folder of the theme. I'll need exactly the same HTML code for the image, but this time, instead of putting it before the headerimg division, it will go inside headerimg and replace all of the coding that showed the title and description. Here's what that part of my header.php template file looks like now:

```
<div id="header" role="banner">
<div id="headerimg">
<img id="logo" src="http://islandtravel.shortordersites.com/
wp-content/themes/default/images/logo.gif" />
    </div>
</div>
```

I could have eliminated the headerimg division altogether, but I might want to put other content in the header at a later date and the headerimg division would be helpful for positioning that content.

> If you're not going to use the default title and description in your header, don't change or erase them in the admin settings. They're used for many purposes besides the header, the most important being in the title area of your browser (which is used by search engines to index your site).

Once I've updated the header template, I can adjust the positioning of the logo (if you're trying this after making the changes in the previous section, remember to get rid of the rules for #logo). In this case I want to center the logo in the header area and after a bit of trial and error I get the following:

```
#logo {
    padding-top: 40px;
    padding-left: 160px;
}
```

After updating my style sheet, I refresh the live site and the result is shown in Figure 27-5.

Figure 27-5

All of these examples are meant to show you the basics of making these kinds of changes to the header of your site. How you make the changes on your particular theme, how you position graphics, and so on, will be different in every case, but the idea is the same.

Try It

In this lesson you change the alignment of the title and description in the default theme.

Lesson Requirements

Make sure you're running the default WordPress theme.

Step-by-Step

How to change the alignment of the title and description

1. Go to Appearance ⇨ Editor.

2. Check that you're viewing the style sheet for the default WordPress theme — it will say Stylesheet at the top and the Theme Name will be at the top of the text area.

3. The title of your site is governed in the default theme by the HTML tag h1, so look for that in your style sheet. You want the rule that says `font-size: 4em` and `text-align: center`.

4. Change the text alignment to *left*.

5. The rule governing the description should be immediately after the h1 rule. It will be named `#headerimg .description`.

6. Change the text alignment to *left*.

7. Click Update File.

8. On the live site, refresh your browser and check that the change has been made.

9. Put the title and description back to the original setting if this was just an exercise.

 To see some of the examples from this lesson, watch the video for Lesson 27 on the enclosed DVD.

Customizing the Look of Posts

A good deal of the look of a website has to do with the look and layout of the text. Whether it's choosing fonts, choosing sizes, or choosing colors, the appearance of your text is important not only for a unified look, but for the site's readability. In Lesson 8 I talked about using the Text Editor to lay out individual posts. Now I want to look at using the style sheet to control the look of all posts.

Making Text Easy to Read

The following are four key elements to the readability of text on the Internet:

- ❑ The font
- ❑ The size of the text
- ❑ The spacing between lines of text
- ❑ The width of the text area

Most of these elements will be taken care of in a well-built theme, but you still may want to change them.

In the case of Island Travel, you've no doubt noticed that all the text is justified — the left and right margins are flush. And you may remember me saying that, for the most part, I don't like justified text. So I'm going to change my style sheet to get rid of the justification.

The first step is to find out what CSS rule is governing the justified text on the site. By looking at the source code for Island Travel I know that text within any division named "post" will be justified, so in my style sheet I look for the post rule that says `text-align: justify;` and I change it to `text-align: left;`. After saving my style sheet and refreshing my browser, the result can be seen in the left half of Figure 28-1.

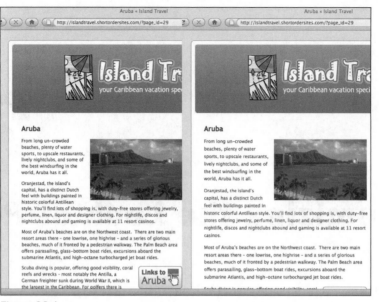

Figure 28-1

That's the text alignment I was looking for. But there's something else that's not quite right for my eye, and that's the spacing between lines. I like it more open so that the text does not feel as cramped. A search through my style sheet reveals that the line height (space between lines) is being controlled not by the post class, but the entry class (`.narrowcolumn .entry` and `.widecolumn .entry` to be precise), so I change that from 1.4 em to 1.6em. After saving and refreshing, my text now looks like the right half of Figure 28-1.

The font face and the size of the text are already good for what I want, so that completes my styling of text for readability. Now it's time to make text elements match my design.

Coloring Links and Headings

The color of text elements is important to maintaining a unified look throughout your site, so let's look at how CSS can control the colors of things like links, headers, and body text.

Link Colors

A couple of common approaches to the coloring of links exist: base it on a background color or use a contrasting color. In the case of Island Travel, for example, I could use a variation on brown that compliments the background or I could use green or blue — the highlight colors I've chosen for other elements in the graphics.

Turning to the CSS style sheet, the rules for links generally are found near the top of the style sheet or perhaps in a section called links or typography. At this point I'm looking for the general rules governing the HTML link tag <a>. The two most common rules will be for "a" and "a:hover," the latter being the state of the link when you mouseover it. There may be several rules for specific link types (such as the links in post metadata, category links, and so on) so you'll need to do some hunting. In the case of the default WordPress theme here's what I find:

```
a, h2 a:hover, h3 a:hover {
    color: #06c;
    text-decoration: none;
}
a:hover {
    color: #147;
    text-decoration: underline;
}
```

Typically, CSS style sheets will use a numeric code to represent colors; for example, a medium dark blue is represented by #1B1BB3 (hexadecimal) or RGB(27,27,179). In this case the style sheet is using the three-character short form of the hexadecimal code. In order to change the color of my links I'll need to find out the corresponding codes. You can get these codes from a graphics program or an online converter (my favorite is Color Scheme Designer at www.colorschemedesigner.com).

I'll try all three colors for my travel agency links and see what they look like. Unfortunately the differences don't show up in black and white illustrations, so I can't demonstrate them here but you'll be able to see them in the video for this lesson.

The brown does not stand out all that well in the body of the text, and the blue is being used for the links on the sidebar, so I think I'll go with the green as a nice link highlight.

Heading Colors and Styling

The other important color decision for site-wide text involves headings, such as for pages, posts, or sections of the sidebar. You want to make sure that these complement your color scheme. To find out what style sheet names are controlling your headings, check the source code of your site, but if the theme is built properly, headings should use tags that begin with H: h1, h2, h3, h4, and so on. The numbers are meant to correspond to the importance of the heading. The h1 tag is usually reserved for the title of the website, so you're typically concerned with h2 or h3 when looking for headings within the body or sidebar.

On the Island Travel site, I want to make all of my page and post headings blue. Those headings are governed by the h2 tag. When I check my style sheet, I see that h2 and h3 tags are colored by the same rule. I don't want to change the color of all h2 and h3 tags, only the ones at the tops of single pages or posts. Those h2 tags are always inside a division called "post" so I can create a new CSS rule just for them. Not only do I want the titles blue, but I want them a bit larger than they currently are and it would be nice to add a bit of decoration, so I'm putting a gray line just above the heading. The code I add to the end of my style sheet looks like this:

```
.post h2 { color: #21759B; padding-top: 5px; border-top: 2px solid #a6a6a6; }
```

The border property tells the browser to place a gray solid line that's 2 pixels thick on top of the letters, while the padding property tells the browser to leave a 5-pixel space between the letters and the gray line.

The result of this new CSS rule is shown in Figure 28-2.

Figure 28-2

Style sheets allow you to do so much with headings — you could create a colored bar across the page with the heading in white, or you could create a graphic that appears to the left of the heading; the possibilities are limited only by your imagination (and how easy it is for your visitors to read!).

Creating Special Text Areas with CSS

Sometimes it's useful to draw attention to certain text by creating a frame or box around which all the other text flows. You can do very basic boxes using some CSS.

To make this very easy to use, I'm going to create a CSS class, so the rule can be used over and over again on the site. I'll call this class "rightbox" because I'm making it float to the right of all the other text. I could then make a class called "leftbox" for when I want the frame to float to the left.

In my CSS rule for rightbox I do the following:

`float: right;` — All other text flows around it on the left

`width: 150px;` — Sets the width of the box, but it can't be so wide that it crowds the text flowing around it

`margin-left: 10px;` — Create some space between its border and the other text

`border: 1px solid #000000;` — Give the box a thin solid black border

`padding: 10px;` — Give some space between the border and the text inside the box

`background-color: #efefef;` — Give the box a light gray color

I save that new rule at the end of style.css and now it's time to create a text box in one of my posts.

I switch to the HTML mode of my Text Editor and find the place in my post where I want the text box to begin and place my cursor there. Then I type in `<div class="rightbox">`, enter my text, and type `</div>`. After saving the post, the result on the live site is shown in Figure 28-3.

Figure 28-3

If you switch to Visual mode while editing the post, you won't see the `<div>` tags and you won't see the box effect because Visual mode does not display posts using the theme's style sheet. However, you can verify that the text is being controlled by the new rule by checking the status bar at the bottom left of the Text Editor while your cursor is anywhere in that text. It should say "path: div.rightbox."

Try It

In this lesson you change the color of links on your site.

Lesson Requirements

Make sure you're using the default theme for WordPress.

Step-by-Step

How to change the color of links.

1. Go to Appearance ➪ Editor.

2. Check that by default you're viewing the style sheet for the default theme — it will say Stylesheet at the top and the Theme Name will be at the top of the text area.

3. Scroll down until you find the rule `a, h2 a:hover, h3 a:hover`

4. Write down the current color code — #06c; — and then replace it with the hexadecimal code for the color you want.

5. Click Update File.

6. On the live site, refresh your browser and check that the change has been made.

7. Put the link color back to the original if this was just an exercise.

 To see some of the examples from this lesson, watch the video for Lesson 28 on the enclosed DVD.

Customizing Design and Layout

I've shown you ways to incorporate your logo or other branding graphics into the header, but what else can be done to truly make the look of the site your own? In this lesson I show you how to change the background of the header and of the site, and I switch the sidebar location to match the original plans for Island Travel.

Changing the Background of the Header

The Island Travel logo looks okay in the default theme header, but it would be nice to have it looking exactly the way I'd like, and that means changing the background image. However, it's important to understand exactly what needs changing because web pages often have a structure that's different from what appears onscreen.

In the case of the WordPress default theme, it looks at first as if all I need to change is the rounded blue background behind the logo. But if I place my cursor over that region and right-click to View Background Image, I see the graphic in Figure 29-1 (this only works in Firefox; for Internet Explorer you Save or Copy Background and open it up to view it).

Notice that the blue region has a border and then a bit of gray that matches the overall background color of the site. This is how web designers achieve most of what you see on the Internet: visually separate elements may be a single graphic and visually uniform areas may be comprised of separate elements.

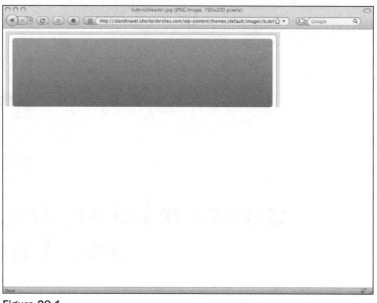

Figure 29-1

Because this graphic is more than just the blue area of the header, and I'm planning to change the background color of the site, I'll have to change the background on this image to match.

> To save a lot of time or money, be sure you've settled on a background for the site before making these changes. You'll need to add that same background to all the other site graphics as well, and if it's not right, there'll be a lot of changes to make.

I'll also need to ensure that the white border area and thin black border still match up with the background image behind the rest of the site. This is where you'll test your skills in a graphics program or else turn over this aspect of your site to a web designer.

Of course I don't have to keep the exact same visual structure (borders, height of the header area, and so on) that the default theme is using, but it's a useful exercise to show how to maintain that structure in case you have a theme that you really like but just want to change minor aspects of the look.

So, having made the changes — being sure to name the graphic exactly as it appears in the theme — Figure 29-2 shows what the new header background looks like on the live site after I've uploaded it to the images folder of the theme.

You can see how the background of the site no longer matches, but I'll fix that in the next section. The header, though, does much more to help brand Island Travel as a tropical vacation website.

Figure 29-2

Changing Theme Graphics

As you saw with the header background, the simplest way to make a theme look exactly the way you want is to keep the existing visual structure (presumably that's what you liked about the theme in the first place) and just change colors or textures. It's time to do that for the remainder of the Island Travel site.

First thing is to make an inventory of what needs to be changed. If you're familiar with HTML you could do that from the source code in your browser or from the CSS style sheet, but I like to work visually so I just do the View Background Image method for all areas of the site.

In the case of the default WordPress theme, just two additional background graphics control the overall look of the site, as you can see from Figure 29-3.

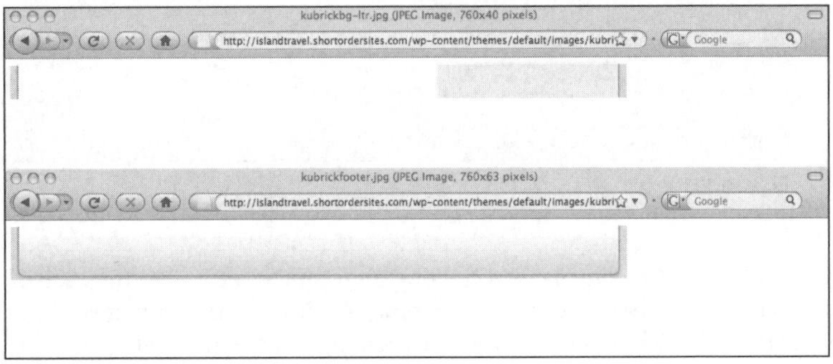

Figure 29-3

The top graphic is the background for the main body of the site — the white area of the content and the gray of the sidebar — while the lower graphic is for the footer area of the site., In both cases, of course, I'll need to replace the little strips of gray background color around the edges with the sandy color I've chosen my overall site background. I like the gradient toward the bottom of the footer bar, so I'll keep that, but I'll color it a very light blue.

The content area remains white, so no changes there. But the sidebar is a different matter. It might be a bit hard to see in Figure 29-3, but the sidebar has a light gray area behind it. However, I want the sidebar on the left of the screen, so this graphic is going to have to reflect that. The width is a good one, so I'll keep that, but I'll change the light gray to a light blue.

> Keep copies of all the work you do in your graphics program, or have your web designer hold on to copies for you. If you change your mind about something (now or six months down the road) it can easily be updated without having to do it from scratch again.

Remembering to keep the names of the files exactly as they were, and uploading them to the images folder of the theme (or whatever folder the theme uses), you can see what all these changes look like in Figure 29-4.

Figure 29-4

If the background of the entire site is created using a graphic — as it is in the case of the WordPress default theme — you're simply replacing the graphic as with the other images. If the background is generated entirely with CSS color codes, you'll need to change the style sheet.

Everything's looking good, except of course that the sidebar text is still over on the right and the colored area for the sidebar is over on the left; time for some style sheet work.

Moving the Sidebar

What you're about to see is a great demonstration of the power of using style sheets and templating the HTML. With just a few coding changes in a single file, the entire Island Travel structure will be transformed on every page of the site.

Basically, I'm just going to tell the sidebar region and the content region to switch the relationship that the current style sheet rules are giving them. In the default theme style sheet, these rules are far apart in the coding, so I've brought them together in the top half of Figure 29-5 and put the new coding below that for ease of comparison.

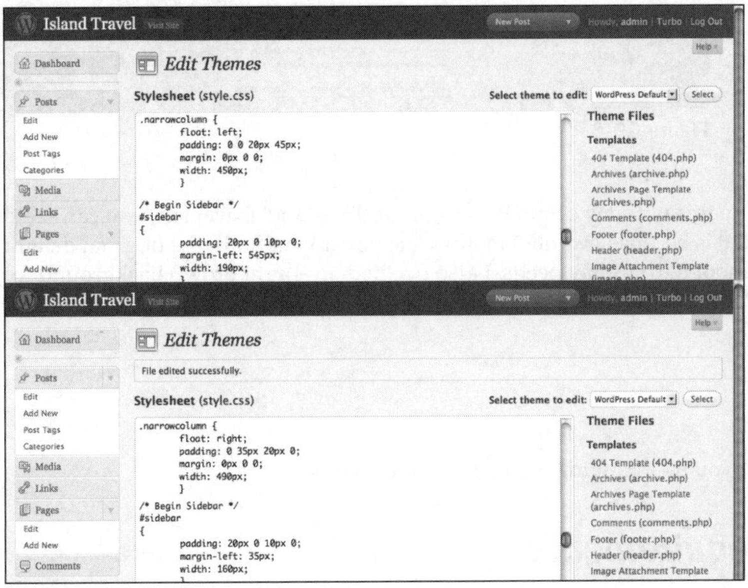

Figure 29-5

The original CSS at the top is telling the content area (`narrowcolumn`) to float to the left of the sidebar. I've switched the styling to make the content area do the opposite, as well as change padding to match the new relationship.

I've also taken the opportunity to make the content area a bit larger and the sidebar a bit smaller (I also adjusted the background image so that the light blue sidebar is narrower). You can see the results of the CSS changes on the live site in Figure 29-6.

Figure 29-6

If you compare this with my original concept for the Island Travel site, you can see that it's a bit different. Part of that is because I wanted to illustrate how to maintain the original default theme look while changing it enough to suit my needs. I also decided on a light brown background for the site instead of the green. When it came down to it I found the green too overpowering.

Try It

In this lesson you try changing a graphic in your theme.

Lesson Requirements

A graphics program, an FTP program, and access to your server files.

Step-by-Step

How to change a graphic in a theme.

1. In your FTP program navigate to the images folder of your theme.

2. Locate a graphic that's used in the structure of your theme, for example the graphic for the footer area.

3. Download it to a new folder called something like Theme Backup Graphic.

4. In your graphics program, open up the file you downloaded.

5. Save the graphic to a new folder called something like Theme Test Graphic.

6. Make some noticeable change to the graphic and click Save.

7. Upload the new version to the images folder of your theme.

8. Refresh your site and check that the new graphic is displaying.

9. If this was just an exercise, remember to upload the original graphic and make sure the site is looking as it should.

 To see some of the examples from this lesson, watch the video for Lesson 29 on the enclosed DVD.

Part VIII: Becoming Search Engine Friendly

30

Optimizing Your Content

The most common way for people to find a website is through search engines, but although searches return thousands, even millions of pages of results, few people go past even the third or fourth page. It's no surprise then that so much attention is paid to achieving high search engine rankings. Search engine optimization (SEO) is a complex and constantly changing topic, well beyond the scope of this book, but in this and the following lesson I show you some things you can do in WordPress to better your chances of good rankings.

I think the healthiest way to think about SEO is to keep in mind the goal of search engines: to deliver results in order of greatest relevance to the search terms entered. The faster their users can find the right information, the better, so search engines work very hard to try and make sure the sites they rank highest will be the most useful to their clients. If you work hard to make sure your site is useful to your visitors, the better your chance of being ranked well for the search terms most relevant to your site. In other words, think about your visitors' needs first.

Having said that, you can use some techniques to make sure that your great content conforms to the ways search engines read that content.

Writing Useful Titles

In this section I cover the importance of relevant titles for posts. There is another kind of title used in HTML coding for links and images, but I'm leaving those for their respective sections later in this lesson.

Having a good title for posts is crucial because of the number of ways that WordPress uses them, all of which are related to search engine ranking. Take a look at the highlighted coding in Figure 30-1.

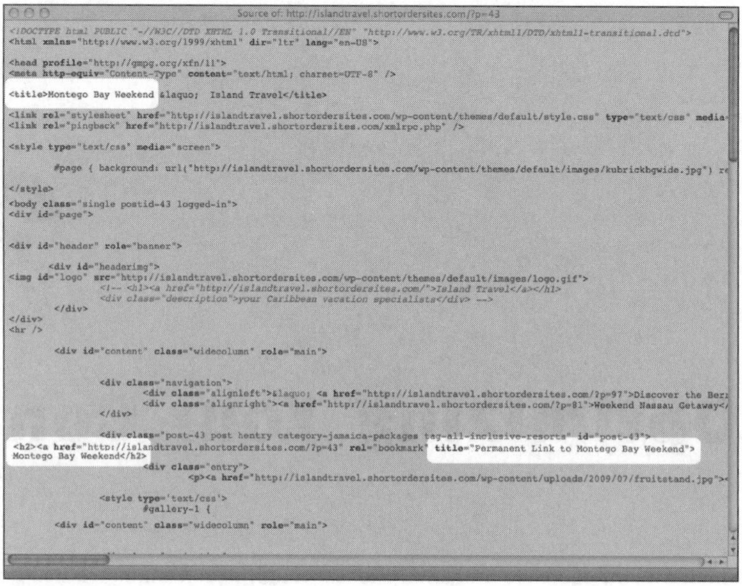

Figure 30-1

1. In most themes, the `<title>` tag of the post's HTML page uses the title of your website (set under Settings ➪ General) along with the title of the post.

2. When the title is linked, WordPress creates a title attribute for the link tag which says "Permanent link to (the title itself goes here)."

3. As the first H2 element in the HTML, a post's title ranks very high in the structural hierarchy.

These are all elements that search engines use in various ways when calculating the relevance of a page, and WordPress automatically makes sure your title is placed in each of them — it's up to you to make sure the title is relevant.

By relevant, I don't just mean relevant to the content of the post. A title also needs to match the wording visitors are likely to use when searching. You need to think of not only what information your audience wants, but the terms in which they want to be spoken to. Very likely, those same terms are ones they'll use when searching.

Though the details of what makes a relevant or useful title will always depend on the particular post, a few guidelines can be helpful from a search standpoint:

Be succinct: If you look at the titles of results in search engines you'll notice that they're truncated if they're too long (around 60 characters is the typical stopping point). It would nice for your entire title to show in the search results, but at the very least have the most important words first.

Use key search terms: Looking at search results again you'll see that search terms are highlighted everywhere, including the title for each result. If your title has that search term in it, you'll benefit from the highlighting. And following on what I said about succinct titles, put the key search terms as near the beginning of the title as you can.

Don't try to be fancy: If you can work a good turn of phrase into a title while keeping it clear and succinct, more power to you, but don't worry about being clever (unless that's important to your visitors).

If you're having trouble boiling down the content into a succinct title, it may be that you're biting off more than your visitors can chew in a single post. Would the material be better handled in smaller units? Looking at it from a search engine's point of view, if too much of the content is not directly related to the title, it seems to the search engine that relevance is lost and the ranking could go down. Your visitors may see the relevance, but search engine algorithms aren't as sophisticated.

You can help the search engines by breaking down a single page of material into several linked pages, each with its own information related to its own title (search engine experts disagree about how long pages ought to be, but they all talk about only a few hundred words as an ideal). Of course you need to balance this against making your visitors do too much clicking to get their information, but they also don't want to be scrolling through ten screens' worth of material.

Writing Useful Content

What you say on your web page is the key to visitor satisfaction and therefore to search engine ranking. If you have high quality, relevant content, visitors will be happy and so will the search engines. But as I said earlier, search engines aren't as sophisticated, so you need to structure your content in certain ways to ensure that they get the relevance.

In the eyes of search engines, the primary factor for the relevance of content is keywords. Starting with the words entered by a searcher, the search engines scan web page content to see how well it relates to those words — the keywords. The details of how search engines scan content for relevance varies between search engines and over time as well — their algorithms are constantly being tweaked to achieve better results. However, here are some basic tips concerning keywords, which, even if they somehow stopped being helpful with rankings are still helpful to visitors:

Be consistent: If your title says the post is about all-inclusive resorts, don't use the term full-service resorts in your content. Your visitor might understand that they're the same, but you can't take the chance that search engines will understand that.

Use keywords early on: If the term all-inclusive resorts is in your title and yet doesn't appear until your second or third paragraph, your visitors and the search engines may be excused for wondering if they're reading the right page. Visitors may well continue on, but search engines are less forgiving.

Don't hit people over the head: Visitors know from the title that the post is about all-inclusive resorts; it gets annoying to see the term in every single sentence. The search engine equivalent is to assume that the repetition is meant to trick it into seeing the page as relevant, and apart from lowering your ranking, such behavior, taken to an extreme, could get your page (or even your site) marked as spam.

As this last point suggests, relevant content is not simply about keywords. Search engine algorithms have become increasingly sophisticated over the years, and keyword density, as it's called, is one of only several factors for which content is analyzed.

As long as you're sticking to the topic, everything will be fine, though you should keep in mind the point I made earlier about breaking up huge pages into smaller ones, each with very focused content. This can be helpful not only to your visitors, but it means that search engines can judge each of those pages on different criteria rather than trying to analyze vast amounts of text that range over several topics (no matter how relevant those topics may be).

> **Never copy text from another site without quoting it and linking back to the site. Not only is it wrong, it's usually illegal to take content from elsewhere and claim it as your own (you'd be amazed at the number of people to whom this comes as a surprise). Always check the fair use and copyright laws for your country.**
>
> **Keep in mind too, that search engines are becoming more sophisticated at spotting duplicate content and this can affect the ranking of pages; if your site is nothing but duplicate content it could even be blacklisted.**
>
> **There are also services that site owners can use to check for plagiarism on the web.**

Linking Effectively

Search engines also determine the relevance of your site to someone's search by looking at links from two perspectives: inbound and outbound. Inbound links are ones on other sites that point to your site and though these are very important to search engine rankings, they're beyond the scope of this discussion. I'm concerned here with links in your posts that point to other sites. Search engines look in particular at two aspects of outbound links: relevance to the content of the post and the popularity of the site to which you're linking.

When you're creating links to other sites, always think of your visitors' needs and you're more likely to meet the standards of relevance. If the link promises to send me to a site with more information about great resorts in Jamaica and that site turns out to be a sales pitch for a time-share you're affiliated with, I will not be a happy visitor. What I read is what I want to get (if your link said I was going to find a great deal on a time-share, it would have been a relevant link).

> **In the popup link editor window of WordPress there's a Title field. It's good practice to enter a short description of what you're linking to, even if it's just the name of the site or the page. It's useful for your visitors and it's thought to have some role in search-engine ranking.**

Even when they're relevant, you can help improve the value of your outbound links — both to visitors and to search engines — by doing a bit of research. If there are two very good sites and one ranks higher in search results than the other, go with the higher-ranked site. Either site would be useful to your visitor, but the higher-ranked one may be given more weight by search engines. Of course you would put both sites in a links list, but I'm talking here about making choices within the text of a post — you don't want to crowd the body with too many links or it gets a bit overwhelming.

Quite often you'll also want to have links within posts that take visitors to other related material on your site. This is not only beneficial to visitors, but can be helpful with search rankings, though that seems to be the case only as your site gets more highly ranked.

Tagging Images

Search engines rely on two attributes of the HTML image tag to tell them something about the image. I've bolded those attributes in this sample code:

```
<img src="http://yourdomain.com/images/image.jpg" title="My New Car"
alt="Photo of my new Toyota Prius sitting in the driveway">
```

It's important that all your images have this descriptive text and in Lesson 13 I showed you the screens in WordPress where you can enter information for these attributes. Now look at these attributes with search engines in mind.

❑ **Title:** Titles should be very simple, leaving the details to the ALT attribute, and give the two or three keywords that describe the content of the image. Don't load up the title with keywords that aren't relevant to the immediate content. If the image is of a beach in Aruba, use "Beach in Aruba," not "Caribbean travel deals on beaches in Aruba." Your post may be about travel deals in the Caribbean, but that's not what the image is about. Stick to the facts. Also, keep in mind that WordPress automatically uses your file's name for the Title field. Sometimes people think you have to stay with that, but you need to change it to a proper title. WordPress is just trying to make sure there's something for the title.

> Speaking of filenames, search engines may give a bit of weight to names that contain keywords for what's in the image. So save the file as `aruba-beach.jpg` instead of what comes out of your camera, like `img39827.tif`. The dash is important; don't use an underscore because that can be misread by some search engines as no space at all: `arubabeach`.

❑ **Caption:** This is the name that WordPress gives to the content that's put in the ALT attribute. Though you can have a lot of detail in here, again, you need to stick to the facts. Avoid putting non-relevant material, and don't try to stuff the caption with keywords. For example, don't say "Picture of a beach in Aruba. Beaches in Aruba tend to be less crowded than other Caribbean destinations. Aruba has a lot of great beaches. This beach is located in Northern Aruba." Not only is it annoying to visitors, but you could get penalized by the search engines. However, do make sure you say Aruba if that's a keyword for your post.

Try It

In this lesson you optimize one of your important posts or pages.

Lesson Requirements

A post or page with three or four paragraphs of text, some links, and an image. If possible, make it one that's central to the theme of your website or blog.

Step-by-Step

How to optimize the content of a post.

1. Open your post in the Edit Post screen.

2. Read through the post and in another program or on a piece of paper write a short sentence describing what the post is about. Set aside this summary for the moment.

3. List two or three of the most important words or phrases in the post.

4. Ask yourself if these keywords are ones that people would use to search for the topic covered by your post.

5. Do some research by entering those keywords into a search engine and see what comes back — are these sites related to yours? Ask friends, co-workers, or customers to do a search related to your site and note what keywords they use. Check online keyword tools such as Google's (`http://adwords .google.com/select/KeywordToolExternal`) to get a sense of how people are using your keywords and what possible alternatives might be.

6. Revise your list of keywords as necessary.

7. Check the title of your post — does it use the most important of your keyword(s) and does it convey what that short sentence from step 2 conveyed?

8. Take the summary of your post that you wrote in step 2 and compare it with your opening paragraph. Does that paragraph clearly convey your summary? If not, rewrite it.

9. Check that your opening paragraph uses the keywords you've come up with. If not, rewrite it.

10. Check the rest of the post to make sure your keywords appear several times in the text in a natural way. Rewrite as necessary.

11. Check your links to make sure they're going to useful, high-ranking sites (check the search engines to make sure those sites are coming up on the first page for their keywords).

12. Check that any images in the post have clear and accurate titles and captions, and, where appropriate, they use the keywords chosen earlier.

13. Remember to update your post.

 To see some of the examples from this lesson, watch the video for Lesson 30 on the enclosed DVD.

Optimizing Your Site as a Whole

In the previous lesson I talked about optimizing your content in ways that help increase your rankings in the search engines. Now it's time to look at site-wide factors that affect how search engines rank you, and how to control them using WordPress.

Optimizing Admin Settings

The first setting you need to check is one I mentioned when installing WordPress, and that's the Blog Visibility setting, found under Settings ⇨ Privacy as shown in Figure 31-1.

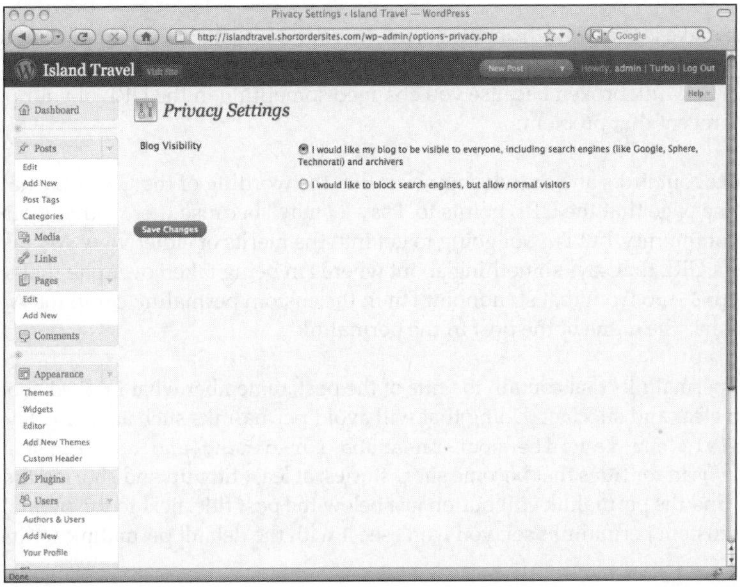

Figure 31-1

Right after installation, I suggested that Blog Visibility be turned off while you're building your site, but now that you're finished, you need to make sure it's turned on.

Blog Visibility determines whether WordPress notifies a list of updating services that you have new content. You can find this list of services under Settings ⇨ Writing. By default there is only service set up — Ping-O-Matic — but it covers over 20 of the major services for you, such as Technorati and Google Blog Search (for a full list visit `http://pingomatic.com`). You can add more services any time and this can be useful if there's a specialized updating service that targets the audience you're looking for.

Another Admin Setting that's very important is your Blog Title under Settings ⇨ General. If you decide to use a graphic for the title of your blog in the header area, be sure to keep the Blog Title in your admin settings because, as I mentioned in Lesson 30, it's used by WordPress when creating the title that appears at the top of your browser window, which in turn is used by search engines not only in calculating your ranking, but for display purposes in results pages. Make sure this title is the one people would use if they're looking up your name.

One final admin setting that's important is for comments, under Settings ⇨ Discussion. Where appropriate on your site, make sure you allow comments. You can either enable them for the whole site and turn them off for specific posts or pages, or you can leave them off and turn them on for specific posts or pages. Allowing comments is an important part of making your website part of a wider community and encourages linking back and forth between sites.

Customizing Permalinks

I left permalinks as a separate section even though it's an admin setting because it warrants a completely separate discussion of its own. In Lesson 25 I talked about setting permalinks through the Settings ⇨ Permalinks screen, as well as editing permalinks for individual posts. I was concerned in that lesson with how people link to your site, and now I want to discuss permalinks with respect to search engines.

The first point to make is that links from other sites (inbound links) are very important to search engines, as long as the link is from a quality, popular site. It would be shame to have a link from a trusted site and to suddenly have that link broken because you changed something in the URL of your page. Permalinks are designed to prevent that problem.

The second point about links and search engines is that the wording of the URL may have some effect on the ranking for the page that the URL points to. I say it "may" because there's an ongoing debate about this in the SEO community, but I'm not going to get into the merits of either view. My take on it is that, as a visitor, I prefer a URL that says something about where I'm being taken over one that tells me I'm going to `/index.php?p=45`. So from that standpoint I'm in the custom permalink camp for WordPress, choosing a setting that has the name of the post in the permalink.

If you do choose permalinks that contain the title of the post, remember what I talked about with respect to titles: keep them clear and succinct. Doing that will avoid permalinks such as `http://www.yourdomain .com/testimonials/our-favorite-spot-in-aruba-for-dining-and-dancing-all-night-long`. If you do find the need for titles that become short stories, at least tidy up and shorten the permalink by editing it. You'll find the permalink edit button just below the post title, next to the permalink itself (but only if you have custom permalinks set; you won't see it with the default permalink setting).

Naming Categories

Just as giving posts useful titles is important for search engines, so is proper naming of categories. The key here is to be as specific as you can: use Scuba Diving and not just Diving.

Remember how I named my Island Travel subcategories? Instead of Testimonials ➪ Aruba, I used Testimonials ➪ Aruba Testimonials so it wouldn't be confused with Destinations ➪ Aruba. Aruba Testimonials is more descriptive of my category anyway, so it helps with visitors and search engines knowing where they are and what to expect from the content.

You can of course change the wording that permalinks use for categories, by going to Posts ➪ Categories and editing the category slug. Again, be careful not to change things once the category has started being used or you run the risk of breaking any links that had been created in the meantime.

Using Meta and Title Tags

It used to be that everyone was worried about something called meta tags — if you don't have the right meta tags, the search engines won't index you properly. The meta tags for keywords and descriptions still play a role in search-engine ranking, but to a far lesser extent. Of the two, the description is more important because it often gets used in search results as the one or two lines you see under the link's title.

If you look at the source code or the header file for a new WordPress installation, you'll see that neither the meta description nor the meta keywords are included in the coding. You're best off installing a plugin to manage them so that you can have unique descriptions for individual posts (I talk about such plugins in Lesson 37). If you simply put a meta description in the `header.php` file, it will be the same for every post and that's not a good thing from a search engine standpoint because it looks like you have duplicate content.

In the previous lesson I talked about the importance of useful titles for posts and how most themes use the post title for the title tag of the HTML page. That title tag is used by search engines, not only for understanding what the page is about, but also as the lead line of a site's listing in search results.

If your theme only shows the title of your website in the title tag that's not good because to the search engines it will look like every page is about the same topic. At the very least you should replace the entire title tag in your header.php template file with this: `<title><?php wp_title(); ?> - <?php bloginfo('name'); ?></title>`. That way, the title of the particular post will be what search engines (and your visitors) see first. The best solution, though would be to install an SEO plugin that allows you to have title tags that are more descriptive than the actual titles of the posts.

Try It

In this lesson you check the names of your existing categories for their search engine friendliness.

Lesson Requirements

At least a few categories for your posts.

Step-by-Step

How to make your category names more search engine friendly.

1. Go to Posts ⇨ Categories.

2. Look over your categories with search engines in mind. Do the category names accurately identify the content you're putting into the categories? Even if a category name is accurate, is that the most likely term that people would use to search for that content? Could you separate a category into two or more categories (either at the same level or as subcategories) to better separate the content into topics that people might search for independently?

3. Before changing any category name, consider how long you've had your site, whether you have a lot of people linking to that category, and whether you have a permalink structure that uses category names, because changing the name will change the URL for that category.

4. If you do change a category's name, remember to change the name of the category slug as well (lowercase with dashes between words).

 To see some of the examples from this lesson, watch the video for Lesson 31 on the enclosed DVD.

Part IX: Housekeeping Chores

32

How Is Your Site Doing?

Knowing how many people are visiting your site, what they're doing while they're there, and who's linking to your site are all important for tracking the success of your site and knowing how to move forward with it. Some of this is done by WordPress and some of it you'll need outside help with — I cover both in this lesson.

Comments are obviously a very direct way of knowing how people are feeling about your site and you can use those comments to understand how to improve your site. If you get a lot of comments on a particular topic, that's a pretty sure sign that you should be talking about that topic regularly, and vice versa. No single piece of data is certain of course, but when you add them all up they can give you a pretty sophisticated picture of how you're doing and where you should be going in the future.

Monitoring Pingbacks and Incoming Links

On the WordPress Dashboard you'll find two quick ways to find out who's linking to your site: the Comments area showing pingbacks and trackbacks, and the Incoming Links box.

Pingbacks and Trackbacks

In Lesson 25 you learned how to enable pingbacks and trackbacks — two distinct ways of being notified that others are linking to your content. Now it's time to monitor them.

WordPress treats both as if they're comments. You can moderate pingbacks and trackbacks, including marking them as spam. In the case of trackbacks you can also edit the excerpt from the other website, just as you can edit the comments that people leave.

How valuable are trackbacks and pingbacks? Aside from the ones that are spam — that's why moderating is important — they each have their advantages for knowing how you're doing.

Trackbacks are good because they provide a short snippet of what the other site was saying when it linked to you. Although pingbacks don't show any content, they're considered a bit more reliable because they happen automatically when someone links (a person could create a trackback to your site without actually linking to you).

Incoming Links

If pingbacks and trackbacks tell you someone is linking to your site, what's the purpose of the Incoming Links box highlighted in Figure 32-1?

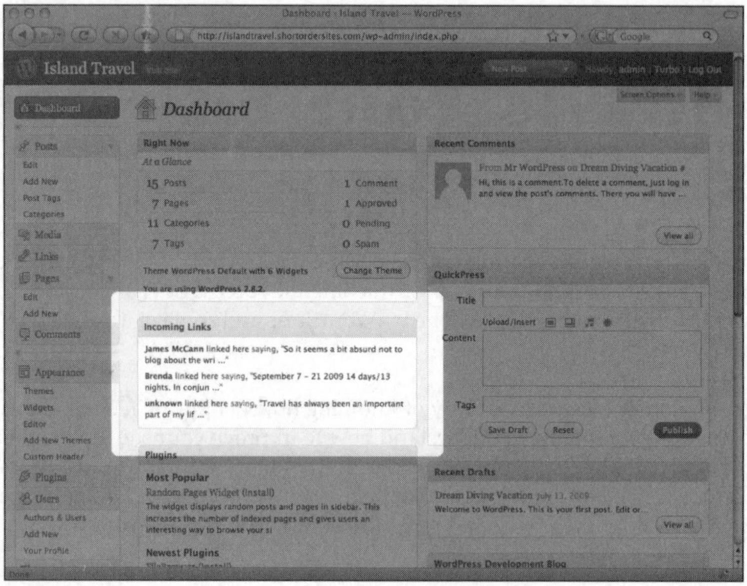

Figure 32-1

The answer is that pingbacks and trackbacks work only on individual posts, and only if you and the person linking to you both have the functions turned on. The value of Incoming Links is that it displays a list of who's linking to your site in general, a specific page, or an individual post — whether or not trackbacks and pingbacks are functioning.

By default, the Incoming Links box checks for your website's address on Google Blog Search, but you can change that if you'd prefer to monitor your site in another blog search engine such as Technorati. Mouseover the right-hand side of the Incoming Links title and you'll see a link called Configure, which creates the box highlighted in Figure 32-2.

You'll see the form asking you to enter the RSS feed URL. Just paste it in, choose how many items to display, and click Submit.

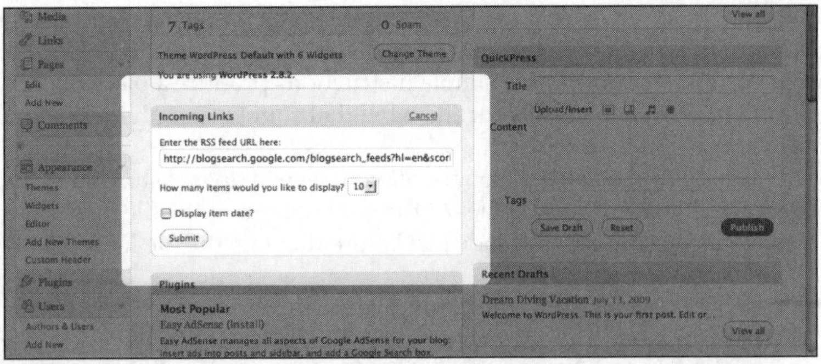

Figure 32-2

Don't be discouraged if nothing is showing in your Incoming Links box when you first set up a site. It will take some time to get people to link to you. This is also one way to monitor if your link-building program is working.

Monitoring Site Statistics

There is no built-in statistics system for WordPress, but you have a number of choices for finding out detailed information on who's visiting your site.

The simplest method is to use the statistics provided by your hosting company. It will have at least one package — such as Webalizer or AWstats — that will give you lots of details about your site visitors. Sometimes you can access these stats through a URL or you may need to go through your web hosting panel (like Plesk or cPanel). Check the host's knowledge base for instructions on accessing stats.

Another option is to use the statistics system at WordPress.com — the hosted version of WordPress. You can do this through a plugin called, not surprisingly, WordPress.com Stats. In the video for this lesson, I show you the statistics generated by this plugin, but to get this particular plugin to work, you'll need to sign up at WordPress.com — just to get an account; you don't need to create a blog.

With the WordPress.com username you can get a special code called the API Key, and then you just enter that into the WordPress.com Stats plugin.

> You'll also need this same WordPress API Key to activate the anti-spam plugin called Akismet (it comes preloaded on all WordPress installations).

Other statistics plugins for WordPress keep track of statistics using a database, and though some of them are very good, they're one more thing to maintain on your site. The WordPress.com statistics are all handled for you with no maintenance required.

Whichever of these options you use for statistics, it's a good idea to put Google Analytics on your site as well. This completely free and comprehensive service can be set up very quickly. Even if you don't already have a Google account, signing up for one is fast (at the top right corner of the Google home page click Sign In and look for the Don't Have An Account? link). Then you can create a Google Analytics section of your account, where simple instructions produce a piece of code that you then paste into the `footer.php` template of your theme. If that sounds complicated, it's not.

Assuming you've copied the code from Google, all you have to do is go to Appearance ➪ Editor and select the `footer.php` file from your theme. At the very bottom of the file, you'll see the closing body tag `</body>` and when you paste in the code just before that tag, the file looks like Figure 32-3.

Figure 32-3

Remember to click Update File. The code is now active on your site. You can double-check by refreshing your site in your browser and looking at the source code (right-click and choose View Source). You'll also need to check that Google is finding the code — simply follow Google Analytics' verification instructions, at which point the statistics will start flowing.

Try It

In this lesson you practice changing the blog search URL for Incoming Links.

Lesson Requirements

No special requirements, just some familiarity with using search engines.

Step-by-Step

How to change the RSS feed monitored in Incoming Links.

1. Go to the Dashboard in WordPress and find the Incoming Links box.

2. Mouseover the right-hand side of the Incoming Links header until you see the link appear.

3. Click Configure and you'll see the configuration form.

4. Go to your favorite blog search engine — such as search.technorati.com or www.icerocket.com.

5. Do a search for your domain name.

6. Look for the RSS feed link somewhere on the page (it often says Subscribe and shows the orange RSS icon).

7. Right-click the RSS link.

8. Choose Copy Link Location.

9. Back in WordPress, paste the link into the Incoming Links URL field of the Configure box.

10. Choose the number of results you want to show.

11. Decide whether you want to display the date.

12. Click Submit.

13. If you have people linking to your site, the Incoming Links box should now show the most recent ones.

 To see some of the examples from this lesson, watch the video for Lesson 32 on the enclosed DVD.

33

Keeping Up to Date

Like any software, WordPress is constantly being improved — more features, better speed, increased security, and so on — as are the themes and plugins. Fortunately, keeping them all up to date is pretty straightforward.

Why should you update? I've seen WordPress sites still happily running on Version 2.0. The only trouble is, some security holes have since been plugged and that's the number one reason for updating. Having access to new features and a better interface (there's no comparison between the admin screen of Version 2 and Version 2.8) are the other reasons for keeping up. Also, the longer you leave an update, the greater the chance of problems because over time the database structure can change significantly, and trying to make all those changes at one sitting may be impossible (at least with an automated update).

On the other hand, rushing to do a new update is not always advisable either. Despite vigorous testing, we all know that software can still come to market with minor or even major bugs that should be fixed. It isn't until they're released that these problems may present themselves, so it can be wise to wait a few weeks after a new update, unless of course the bug is so major that your site is at risk.

Updating WordPress

Even at its most difficult — a manual update — keeping WordPress current is a fairly simple task. Since Version 2.7, WordPress has featured a built-in automated update, and plugins that automate the process are available for earlier versions. I'll go through both options in a moment, but first a word about how you know when to update.

WordPress is very clear about the availability of updates. A warning message with a link to perform the update is displayed at the top of every admin screen until the update is completed. If you're logged in as any role other than Administrator, the message tells you to notify your administrator of the update. Also, an Update button appears on the Dashboard if there's an update available — it will be next to the name of the version you're running.

If you don't regularly make changes to your site's content, you may not see the update message for many weeks. In that case, it might be good to join the update notifications list at WordPress.org.

Automated Update

As of WordPress 2.7, the updating process became automated within the admin panel. If you have an earlier version, there's a good plugin called Wordpress [sic] Automated Upgrade and it functions from Version 1.5.2 and up.

The key with any update is to make sure you have your site backed up — as you see in the next lesson, you'll want to be doing this regularly anyway. Fortunately, WordPress reminds you to do the backup before proceeding with the automated update, as shown in Figure 33-1.

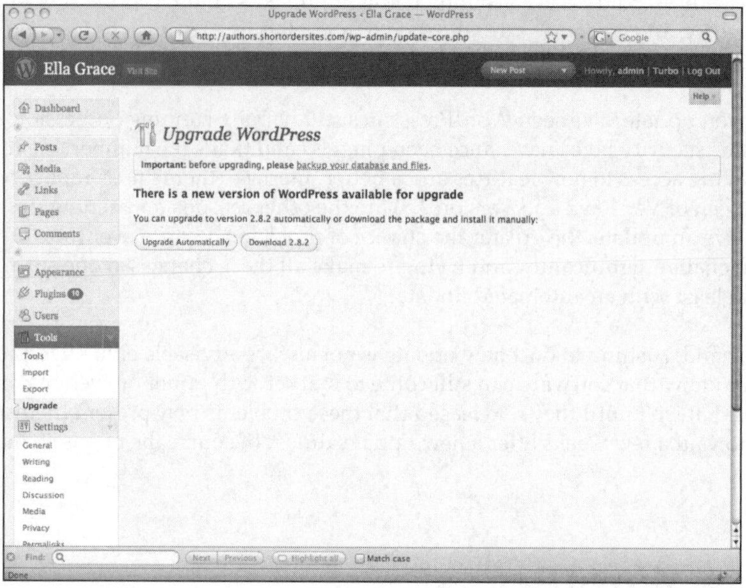

Figure 33-1

Once you click Upgrade Automatically, you'll see a list of tasks displayed one by one as WordPress performs them. At the conclusion, the screen will look like Figure 33-2.

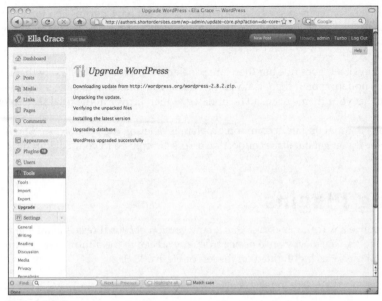

Figure 33-2

That last line tells you the update has worked.

Manual Update

If for some reason you want to manually update WordPress you certainly can.

There isn't enough room here to go into the details of a manual update because there are a lot of variables. WordPress.org has a handy three-step manual updating process — http://codex.wordpress.org/ Upgrading_WordPress — but even with that it warns you that you may need even more details on its extended upgrade instructions page — http://codex.wordpress.org/Upgrading_WordPress_Extended.

As with the automated update, it's important to do a backup of both the database and the entire set of WordPress files and folders on your server. The other crucial element of a manual update is to know which files you can't overwrite and which themselves may need to be manually changed, saved, and uploaded again. The WordPress site helps you with all of that.

Troubleshooting WordPress Updates

The two most common problems encountered in the automated update are that the server is not configured to allow the automated update and the plugins or themes are not compatible with the updated version of WordPress.

If you're getting error messages saying WordPress does not have permission to perform the automated upgrade, you'll either have to change permissions or get your hosting company to do that for you, or you'll need to do the manual upgrade.

If the installation itself goes fine but there are problems with the site, it's likely that one of the existing plugins needs updating or, if there is no update for it, you'll need to disable it for the time being. It's also possible that your theme needs to be updated, which I cover in the final section of this lesson.

In the case of a manual update, a common problem is deleting the `wp-config.php` file. You'll know it's no longer there if you get database connection errors. Simply go to your backup files and reload it.

Updating Plugins

Just as you receive a warning message that a new version of WordPress is available, you also receive notices for plugins. The most visible notice from any screen in the admin area is a tiny graphic displayed on your menu, as highlighted on the left of Figure 33-3.

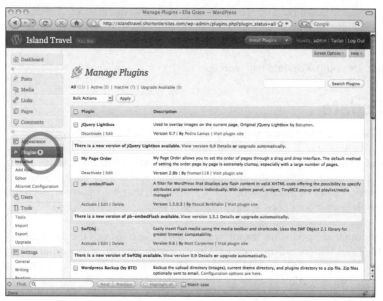

Figure 33-3

The number in the graphic tells you how many plugins need updating. Figure 33-3 shows the Manage Plugins screen and if you click the Upgrade Available filter at the top right you'll see just the plugins that need an update. The update information is clearly marked in the colored stripe, with links to the plugin details or to automatically upgrade.

When you automatically upgrade a plugin, you'll see a screen very similar to the WordPress upgrade, with each item in the process appearing as it's completed. What you want to see at the bottom of the list is the phrase *Plugin reactivated successfully*. Then you're done.

If you're experiencing problems after a WordPress update, but none of your plugins shows an update available, you may need to troubleshoot by deactivating plugins until you find the one causing the trouble. Once you know which it is, you can click through to the plugin's homepage and see if there's an update that got missed. You may find that the plugin author is still working on an update or is no longer supporting the plugin. In either case, you'll need to deactivate the plugin. You can always update and reactivate later if the author makes a new version.

Updating or Installing New Themes

Like plugins, themes may need updating for various reasons. It could be that they have a special functionality that relied on something in WordPress that has now changed. Or the new version of the theme takes advantage of new features in WordPress. In either case, you'll need to perform an update.

With some themes, the update happens automatically when you update WordPress. For others you'll need to go to the theme's homepage (there's a link in the theme library listing) and see if there's a new version available. If there is, you download the folder and then upload it to your themes directory of wp-content.

Installing a New Theme

There may come a time when you'd like to change to a new theme. If you haven't customized the current theme at all, the switch is pretty easy. You just go to Appearance ⇨ Add New Themes and you can browse through the WordPress directory of free themes. The nice part is you can filter the search with a wide variety of parameters, such as number of columns, color schemes, features like custom header, and so on. Select the themes you want and they'll appear in your library of available themes under Appearance ⇨ Themes.

If you decide that one of these new themes should replace your current theme, you simply activate it from the Manage Themes screen. There's a thumbnail screenshot to remind you of what the theme looks like, but you can also preview what your site will look like in the theme by clicking Preview. When you're ready, click Activate and the new theme instantly replaces the old.

Remember, if you had any customizations in your original theme, such as page templates, they won't be there in the new theme unless you explicitly added them to the new theme's folder.

If you're buying a theme or getting a customized one, you'll need to manually upload its folder to the theme folder of your wp-content folder. Then go to Appearance ⇨ Themes and you should see the new theme in the listings, ready for preview or activation.

Keep in mind that all themes are different. Even if you didn't customize your old theme, it may have been able to do things that your new theme can't, and vice versa. Watch that parts of your site aren't relying on something that's no longer available.

Try It

It's difficult to practice an update unless your WordPress installation actually needs updating, so in this lesson you learn how to find and install a new theme (you won't actually be changing your theme).

Lesson Requirements

No special requirements.

Step-by-Step

How to find and install a new theme.

1.   Go to Appearance ⇨ Add New Theme.

2.   Use the Feature Filter section to choose themes that match whatever criteria you want — number of columns, colors, and so on. You'll see a thumbnail for each of the results of your search.

3.   Click Preview to see a sample blog using the theme.

4.   When you're finished with the preview, click the X at the top left of the popup screen.

5.   Once you're sure you like that theme, click Install. A popup window appears with the thumbnail of the theme.

6.   Click Install Now.

7.   You'll see an Installing Theme screen with a list of the tasks being performed and the final message should be *Successfully installed the theme THEME NAME*.

8.   Click Appearance ⇨ Themes to double-check that the new theme is listed in your theme library. Remember that installing a theme only puts it in your theme library, it does not activate the theme and make it live on your site.

 To see some of the examples from this lesson, watch the video for Lesson 33 on the enclosed DVD.

34

Backing Up Your Site

There's nothing more devastating in the world of computing than not having a backup of your data when something goes wrong, and the same is true on the Web. Hard drives die on web servers and even the most sophisticated server backup systems are vulnerable to human error or acts of nature.

> **Your hosting company may offer automated backups, but double-check exactly what that means. If it's just your WordPress database, it's only half a backup. If all necessary WordPress files are getting backed up, be sure that you can get access to those backups and download them to your computer for additional safety.**

A Backup Routine

Here's one simple routine for backing up your WordPress site. In the folder on your hard drive where you have anything relating to your site, create a new folder called My Site Back-ups. Then pick a time each month (more frequently if you're constantly adding new content) when you're going to stop for a moment and back up your site.

Each time you do the backup, create a new folder in My Site Back-ups using a dating system such as 20090617 (year-month-day). Usually you'll just want the most recent backup and this naming system makes it easy to find, but also if you need to restore the site from an earlier time.

Backing up WordPress is a two-step process, so in this 20090617 folder you're going to have two subfolders: one for the database backup and one for the web server files. The following sections look at how you get the material for each of these.

Backing Up Your Web Server Files

When you FTP into your web server, what you'll see will vary to some extent depending on what exactly you have on your website. If it's entirely contained within WordPress, you're going to see a file structure much like that shown in Figure 34-1.

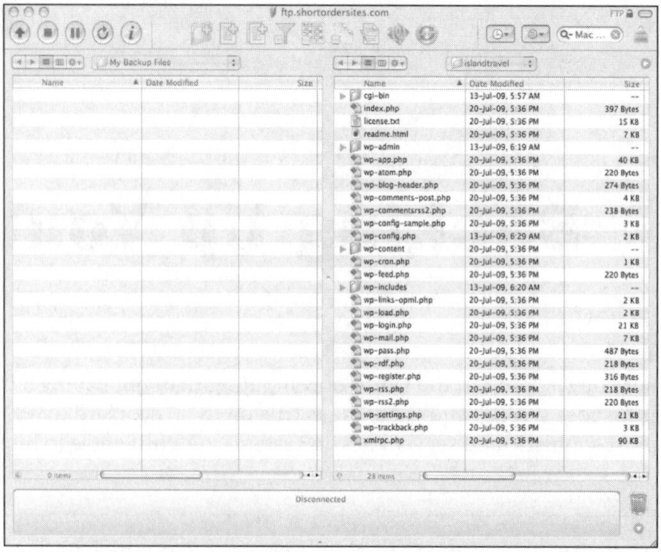

Figure 34-1

The simplest routine is to download everything you see in this root directory. Some will argue that you really only need to do this once (unless you upgrade your WordPress, in which case you'd need to do another download) and then on your regular backup routine, all you need to back up is the folder called `wp-content`. The reason they say this is because it's the `wp-content` folder that contains everything unique to your installation of WordPress: themes, plugins, and media files. WordPress files outside of `wp-content` don't change (the `wp-config.php` file could change if you switch databases or something).

Here's my argument in favor of backing up the entire root directory of your website:

1. It doesn't take up much time or space to download all the files.

2. A full backup keeps all files together rather than having `wp-content` backups in one place and the core WordPress files elsewhere.

3. If you have to move to a new server, it's just simpler to upload everything at once without having to think about anything (except making sure your `wp-config.php` file is accessing the new database with the right passwords, and so on).

It's up to you, but *at the very minimum you must back up the* `wp-content` *folder* in your backup routine.

Backing Up Your Database

The other half of your backup routine involves the database where WordPress stores your written content and the settings that control, among other things, the relationships between your content (categories and so on). WordPress uses a MySQL database so you can use any method that backs up a database of that type. The most common interface provided by hosting companies is called phpMyAdmin and it provides a pretty user-friendly interface for managing databases, including doing backups.

I won't go into the details of the process here — you can find lots of good resources online if you look up "phpmyadmin backup." Always make sure you're reading instructions for your version of phpMyAdmin. Using the Export function, the most important points are to ensure that you're backing up all the database tables, that you choose SQL as the output format, and that you use Save As File. You would save that file to the database folder in the backup folder I talked earlier about creating.

If your hosting company has an automated database backup feature, you can use that too, again making sure it's backed up in the right way. Have the company e-mail the backup to you, or it may be available on its site for you to download or placed in folder on your site and you can download it from there. Again, you want to have a copy on your computer.

> *Under Tools ➪ Export you'll find a feature of WordPress that appears to do what a database backup does, but it's quite different. This feature extracts all the content from your database and preserves elements of the structure in a language called XML, but it is not a full database backup. The file generated is meant to be imported back into a WordPress installation, and as long as the version of WordPress is the same as the one from which you exported, things go pretty smoothly. Still, I wouldn't recommend this as your primary backup, especially not when plugins are available to make full backups very simple.*

Some Database Backup Plugins

Simplicity and automation are two advantages to using plugins to manage your WordPress database backups. It's that latter one I find particularly helpful. As easy as the routine is that I just showed you, it's just as easy to forget to do it. Plugins can help by doing the backup at a specified time, over and over again. However, not all plugins perform the same tasks, so you'll want to check out the options. I have a couple of plugin suggestions here, but new ones are always being added at www.wordpress.org/extend/plugins.

WP-DBManager is a very powerful database management plugin that has a number of the features you find in phpMyAdmin, and backing up is just one of them. However the backup function is much simpler and it not only keeps a copy on the server, but it allows you to e-mail any or all of the backups to yourself or some other location. It also has automatic scheduling of backups, e-mailed wherever you want. Another useful feature is the ability to easily restore a backup copy of your database.

WP-DB-Backup is a very straightforward plugin whose only job is to back up your database. By default, the plugin backs up only the core WordPress database tables, but you can choose to include any other tables (it gives you a list) that are used by plugins. There is also a scheduling feature.

If you're not comfortable working with an FTP program, there are also plugins that automate the backing up of your wp-content files, such as *Wordpress* [sic] *Backup*.

Try It

Because many options for database backup exist, in this lesson you focus on practicing backing up your WordPress files.

Lesson Requirements

FTP program and access to your hosting account.

Step-by-Step

How to backup your WordPress files.

1. Open your FTP program.

2. Log in to your server.

3. In the window showing your computer, find or create your Backups folder and then create a folder with today's date, for example, 20090703, and in that folder create another folder called WordPress Files.

4. In the server-side window, navigate until you find the wp- files (these may be in your root web directory — www or public_html, for example — or they may be in a subdirectory that you created specially for WordPress).

5. Select all the files in the directory that has the WordPress files (it doesn't matter if some of them aren't part of WordPress — they're part of your site).

6. Click Download (or the down arrow).

7. All the files on the right should now also be in the window at the left (your WordPress Files folder).

8. Disconnect from your server and shut down your FTP program.

 To see some of the examples from this lesson, watch the video for Lesson 34 on the enclosed DVD.

Part X: Extending WordPress

Installing and
Activating Plugins

There are a lot of things that WordPress doesn't do, and that's a good thing. The simpler the base, the more secure, the more bug-free, and the more efficient it can be. It's also easier to update a simple structure. But you'll probably want WordPress to do more, and that's where plugins fit in, so to speak.

In this lesson you learn about finding, installing, and activating plugins. Lesson 37 provides a quick guide to help you sort through the more than 6,500 plugins available — in the few days I was working on this chapter, more than 150 plugins were added to the directory!

What Is a Plugin?

Plugins are scripts that provide additional functionality to WordPress by using a combination of built-in WordPress code and new code. Plugins vary in complexity from a half page of script to folders with dozens of scripts and database tables.

Most plugins are open-source and available at no charge from thousands of individuals who often develop a feature for their own site and then share it with the WordPress community. Most plugin authors accept donations or have wish lists, and I strongly encourage everyone to send even a few dollars their way to help compensate for the incredible amount of time and talent they devote.

One of the best things about plugins is that you can unplug them. That's important because it helps protect the base of your website, by keeping the plugins separate from the core WordPress files. If something goes wrong with a plugin, either because of a conflict with other plugins or when you update WordPress, all you have to do is deactivate it.

Finding Plugins

The best place to go for plugins is Plugins ⇨ Add New. That's because WordPress has a built-in search function that imports data directly from the WordPress.org plugins directory. The handy thing about this directory is that it tells you how many people have downloaded a plugin and users are given a chance to rate the plugin. Plugin authors are also good about updating this directory with the latest versions of their offering.

The search screen on the Install Plugins page offers a whole range of options for finding plugins, as you can see in Figure 35-1.

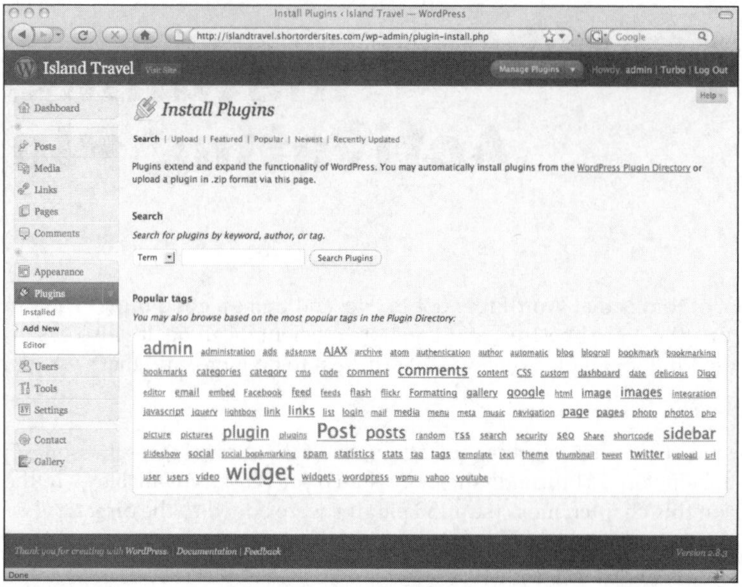

Figure 35-1

The menu at the top not only allows you to see a list of Featured, Popular, Newest, or Recently Updated plugins, but you can also Upload a plugin you may have previously downloaded to your hard drive.

The search function below that menu enables you to use keywords, author names, or tags to find plugins, and the Popular Tags cloud at the bottom of the screen gives a quick overview of what tags plugin authors have used to describe their contribution.

I'll do a search for "backup" and you can see the results in Figure 35-2.

All the data you're seeing is exactly what you would get if you went to WordPress.org and did that search, but one advantage is that you're shown a longer description here.

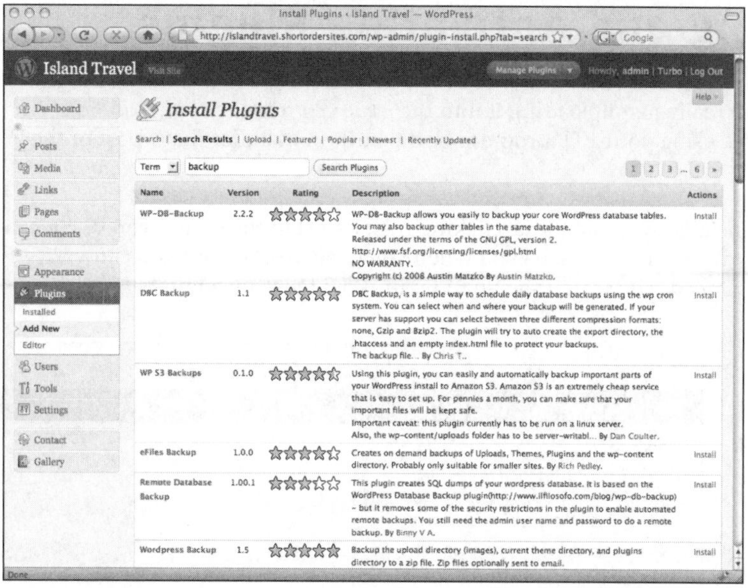

Figure 35-2

One thing that's missing from the search function here or at the WordPress site is the ability to sort the results. You can't display according to the number of downloads or the number of people who've rated the plugin. It's also important to try a few different keywords to make sure you've found all possible plugins for a topic. It depends how the author wrote the description, and sometimes I find that even the most basic keyword is missing, so I need to hunt around using variations.

In terms of what to look for in the search results, I use three criteria for judging multiple plugins that meet my feature requirements: the number of downloads, how many people have voted for it, and how recently it's been updated. You'll get a feel for weighing these three criteria. For instance, a plugin that has 40,000 downloads, 150 votes, and has been around for 5 years is likely going to be trumped by a plugin that only has 5,000 downloads, but just came out a month ago and already has 80 votes. The fact that the newer plugin has received half as many votes in a very short time suggests it will be better, plus being more recent, it may take advantage of current developments in WordPress, not to mention JavaScript and PHP.

You can learn more about a plugin by seeing what others are saying about it in the WordPress forums. If you click on the name of the plugin you'll be taken to the plugin's page on WordPress.org and over on the right-hand side you'll see the most recent forum references, if there are any. Some plugins have their own user forums, and you can find those by going to a plugin's home page — if one exists it will be on the right-hand side of the plugin's page in the WordPress directory. Finally, WordPress users around the Web also love to share lists and reviews of their favorite plugins, so you can pick up lots of tips from those sites as well.

Installing and Activating Plugins

Like any software, there's a difference between installing and activating plugins. When you install a plugin you're really just uploading it into the `plugins` folder of your `wp-content` folder. You can do that manually using your FTP program or the built-in installer that's part of the WordPress admin functions.

Automated installs are as simple as clicking Install next to the plugin you've chosen from the search list. The WordPress installer tells you when you're successful and you can verify that by going to Plugins ➪ Installed. The screen shown in Figure 35-3 tells you a number of things at a glance.

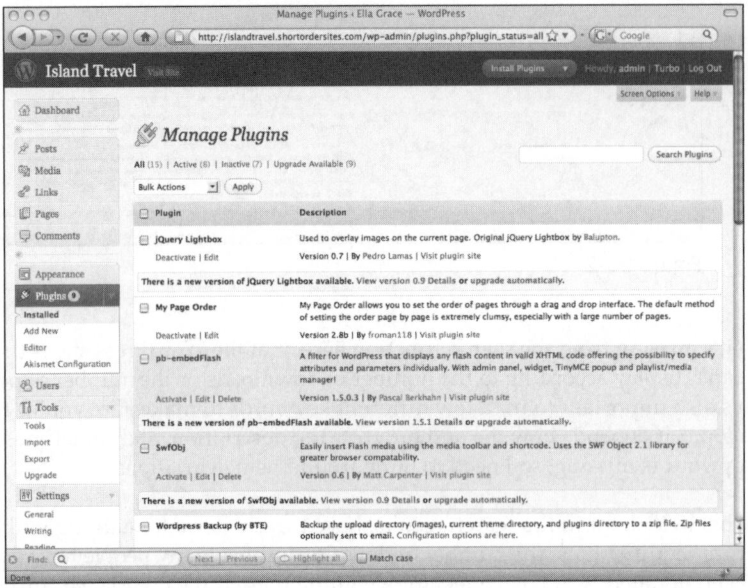

Figure 35-3

White rows are the active plugins, gray are installed but not active, and the colored bar on a row reminds you visually and textually that there's an update available for that plugin, with a link to do the update automatically.

You can also filter what you see on this Manage Plugins screen by using the menu at the top left. You can see All, Active, Recently Active, Inactive, or Upgrade Available (options display only if there are plugins that meet their criteria).

> Because I work with WordPress a lot, I like to download commonly used plugins from the WordPress site and keep copies on my computer so they're easy to find.

If you need an earlier version of a plugin, you can find them archived in the WordPress.org Plugin Directory. Go to the plugin's page and at the top right, under the current version number you'll find a link to Other Versions. On one occasion, after updating WordPress and all the plugins, I found that one of the plugins wasn't working. Re-installing an earlier version got it working again.

Troubleshooting Plugins

As I mentioned before, the two most common reasons for having trouble with plugins are conflicts between plugins or conflicts between an updated version of WordPress and an older plugin.

The great thing is that finding the problem plugin(s) and halting the problems on your live site is made fairly easy by the nature of plugins — you just start deactivating them one at time.

If your problem started with the activation of a new plugin, systematically deactivate each of the other plugins starting with the most recently activated.

If your problem began right after updating WordPress, first of all, make sure that you've updated every plugin. One of the reasons for not updating WordPress immediately upon release is that you want to give plugin authors a bit of time to come out with their updates (they're usually pretty good about bringing those out at the same time). With a major update of WordPress, you should see a lot of plugin update notices.

Once all the updates are done, if the problem still persists check the homepages for any plugins that did not have an update. There may be a notice there saying there's a delay or the plugin is no longer supported, or there may be notices about conflicts with other plugins.

Resolving the problem can be as simple as updating one or more plugins, but it may also be that there is no current fix and you either have to pay someone to fix the bugs on one or more plugins or, at the very least, do without that functionality until the problem can be solved.

Try It

In this lesson you learn to find a plugin, install it, and activate it.

Lesson Requirements

No special requirements.

Step-by-Step

In the next lesson, one of the plugins I show you in some detail is Contact Form 7, so let's find, install, and activate it.

1.   Go to Plugins ➪ Add New.

2.   Do a search for Contact Form 7. It should come up as the second result or at least somewhere near the top. Look for the author Takayuki Miyoshi at the end of the description.

3.   Click Install over on the right side.

4.   In the resulting popup window, click Install Now.

5.   In the Installing Plugin screen, if things are successful, you'll see a link at the bottom to Activate Plugin; click that.

6.   You'll be taken to the Manage Plugins screen and you should see Contact Form 7 as a white row indicating that it's active. Also, on the admin menu you should see the heading "Contact" near the very bottom of the menu.

7.   If you don't want this plugin, you can delete it later, but keep it for the next lesson at least so that you can try out some of the functionality.

 To see some of the examples from this lesson, watch the video for Lesson 35 on the enclosed DVD.

36

Example Plugins

Although every WordPress plugin performs different functions and operates differently, you can get a general sense of how they all operate by seeing a couple in action, and that's what this lesson is about.

I've installed two plugins on the Island Travel site that I think would be useful: NextGEN Gallery to manage photos and Contact Form 7 to help me easily create contact forms. In the next lesson I cover ten more uses for plugins and give some recommendations for those as well.

Photo Gallery Plugin — NextGEN Gallery

The most popular (more than one million downloads) and the most powerful photo management plugin is called NextGEN Gallery. Developed by Alex Rabe, this highly configurable plugin goes well beyond the image gallery function built into WordPress. I'll barely be able to scratch the surface of its capabilities, but you'll have a good sense what's possible.

When you activate NextGEN a special section is created on the admin menu, as you can see at the lower left of Figure 36-1 (immediately above it is a menu section created by the second sample plugin, Contact Form 7, which you will have seen already if you installed that plugin as part of the previous lesson's Try It section).

You can also see from this opening screen of NextGEN that it has its own kind of Dashboard showing you how many images you have, how many galleries and albums (I explain them in a moment), as well as a lot of technical details about your server settings and server graphics capabilities. You don't need to concern yourself with these details, but they're handy if a technical issue arises and someone on the WordPress forums asks you what your PHP Max Post Size is!

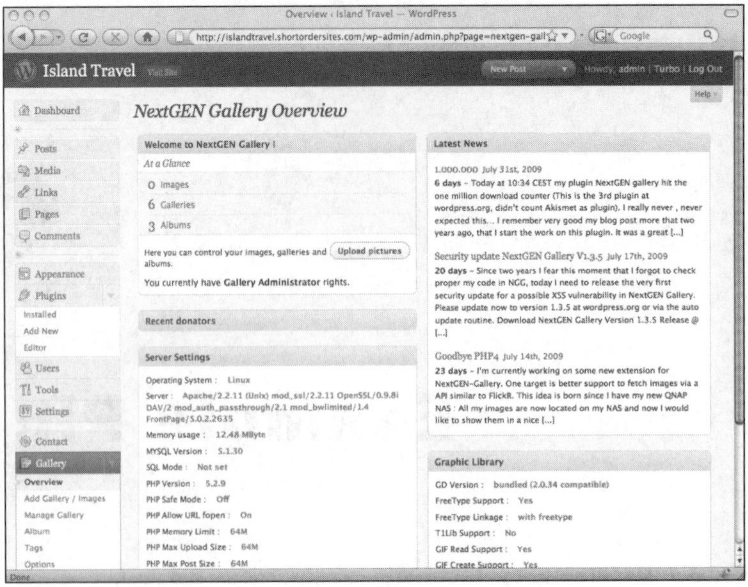

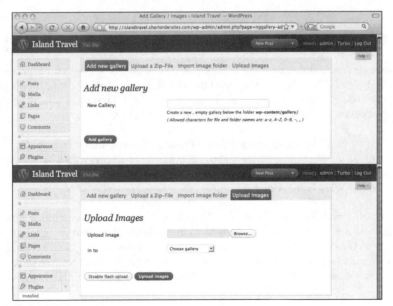

Figure 36-1

In the top-left box of the NextGEN Gallery Overview you'll see a button that says Upload Pictures. The name is a little misleading because clicking it takes you to the screen shown in the top half of Figure 36-2.

Figure 36-2

Instead of uploading images it's asking you to Add New Gallery. But if you look at the menu at the top, you'll see Upload Images over on the right — clicking that gives you the screen shown on the bottom half of Figure 36-2.

Notice that you're asked to upload an image into a gallery. All images have to be in at least one gallery, so before uploading your first image, you'll need to have created at least one gallery. I'll do that now for a gallery featuring beaches in Jamaica. I enter the name in the New Gallery field and click Add Gallery. I get a success message, as shown in Figure 36-3:

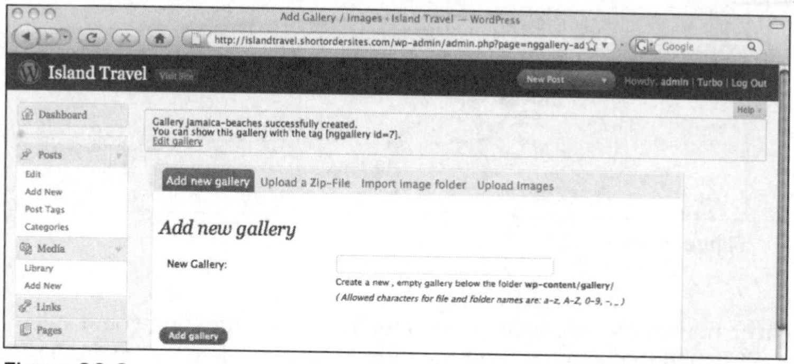

Figure 36-3

Now that I have a gallery, I can upload some pictures. NextGEN allows you to choose multiple files to upload a time (or entire folders through a separate upload window). Figure 36-4 shows that I've selected three images to upload, and I have a choice of removing them individually before clicking Upload Images. If you forget to choose a gallery from the drop down menu, a warning message pops up and you'll have to select all the images again.

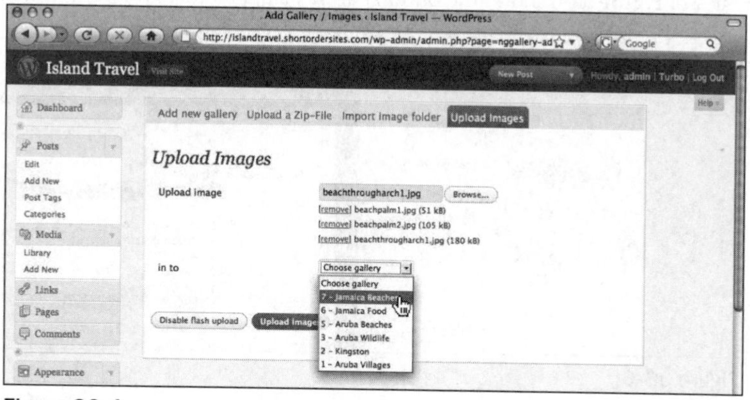

Figure 36-4

As each image uploads, there's a progress bar across the top of the screen and when everything is done you'll get a success message stating how many images were uploaded.

Once the images are uploaded to the gallery, there are powerful tools for managing them. I've combined a couple of screenshots in Figure 36-5 to show you as many of the features as possible at one time.

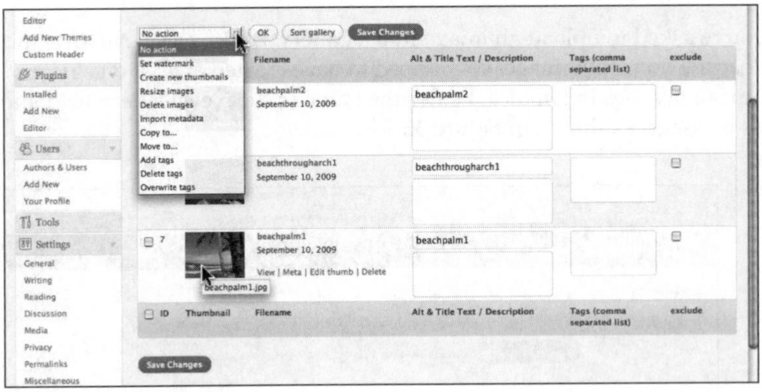

Figure 36-5

If you mouseover an image's thumbnail, a text menu appears, allowing you to View the full image, read any metadata contained in the image, Edit the thumbnail, or Delete the image. There are text fields for you to give the image a title and description as well as any tags. There's a checkbox to exclude an image, which means that it won't show when you display the gallery as a whole.

The drop-down menu near the top of the screen shows you the wide range of actions that can be applied to one or many images all at one time. You could copy them to another gallery, give them a watermark, add tags, and much more.

With a gallery created and some images uploaded, here's how to get materials from NextGEN into your posts. The left side of Figure 36-6 shows the button bar in Visual mode of the Text Editor, with the NextGEN button highlighted.

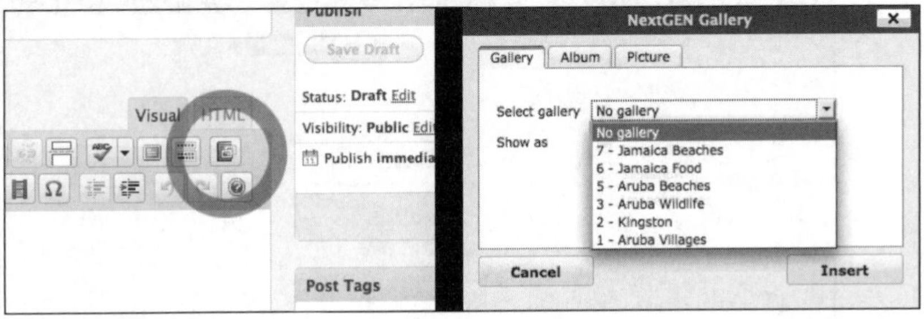

Figure 36-6

When you click on that button, you get a popup window, as shown on the right side of Figure 36-6. From there you can choose to insert any image, gallery or album from NextGEN.

How exactly do galleries and albums differ in NextGen? Galleries are the smallest groups of images, whereas albums are ways of grouping several galleries or a mix of galleries and other albums.

So in the case of Island Travel, I might set up a series of galleries — Kingston, Jamaica Beaches, Jamaica Food — then group them together under an album called Jamaica. I then group the album Jamaica with the album Aruba, and so on, under a single album called Caribbean. Or I could group all beach galleries under a single album called Caribbean Beaches.

The drag-and-drop interface for moving galleries and albums is very intuitive, as you can see in Figure 36-7.

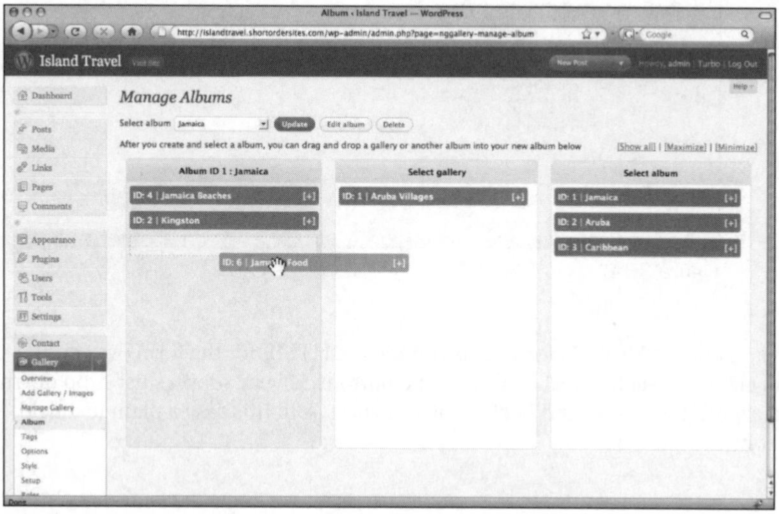

Figure 36-7

This powerful organizational capability, coupled with the ability to do things like automatically match up your images with WordPress tags or categories, allow different access to NextGEN functions based on WordPress user roles (Admin, Editor, and so on), and the ease with which you get fancy JavaScript or Flash slideshows makes NextGEN a must-have plugin for any image-intensive WordPress site.

Form Creation Plugin — Contact Form 7

WordPress does not have a form creation tool built-in, so a number of developers have made plugins that do the job very nicely. One of the best, I think, is Contact Form 7 by Takayuki Miyoshi. It's not as WYSIWYG as, say, cForms (another popular contact form plugin) but it's not as complicated either.

You access the plugin from a section of the side admin menu that appears after activation. You can see from Figure 36-8 that it's an extremely simple menu — a single Edit link.

In fact, the entire plugin runs on a single page. If you have more than one form, you'll see them all listed in the menu at the top of the page, where you can also add new forms.

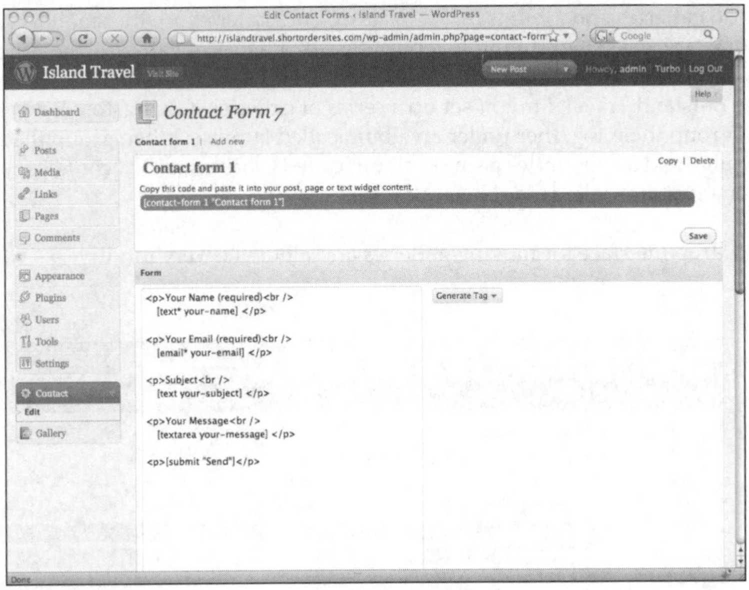

Figure 36-8

As I said, this is not a WYSIWYG format, so you see the HTML for the form over on the left. However, generating form elements, such as text fields or radio buttons, is very simple. Just drop down the Generate Tag menu on the right, choose the kind of element you want — in this case a plain text field — and you get a box like the one in Figure 36-9.

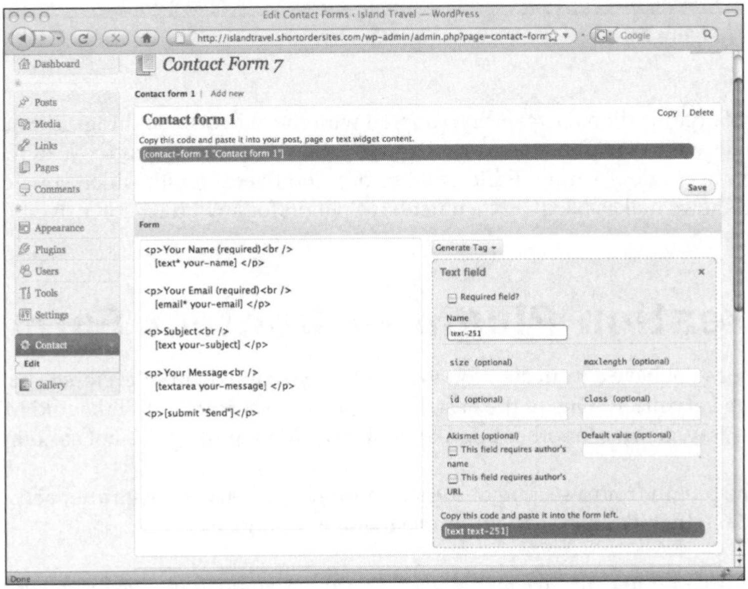

Figure 36-9

You have lots of options and when you're done, the brown bar at the bottom displays the code you copy and paste into the form HTML on the left.

The bottom half of the Contact Form 7 screen lets you set the e-mail where the form is sent (by default it uses your main WordPress e-mail). You can then format the e-mail that's sent, as you can see in Figure 36-10.

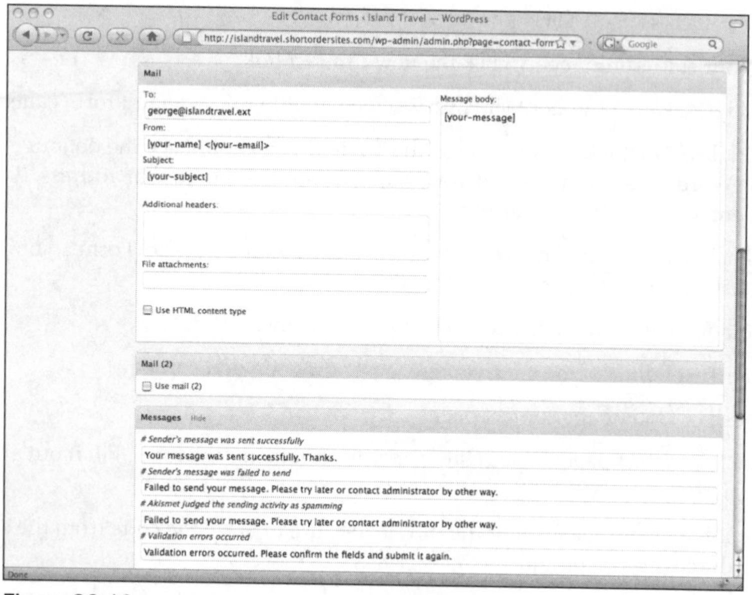

Figure 36-10

Again, you're going to need to do your own copying and pasting, but it's still very straightforward. The items in the square brackets are simply the names of the fields you set up in the top half of the screen. Contact Form 7 has created the most common items for you; you just need to fill in any other customizations you need. For a newsletter signup form, for example, I might want the e-mail to display certain fields that I created for that form. I just copy and paste the correct field names into the message body.

Try It

In this lesson you walk through a quick creation of a contact form using Contact Form 7.

Lesson Requirements

No special requirements.

Step-by-Step

How to create a simple contact form.

1. Go to Plugins ⇨ Add New. You can skip to step 6 if you installed the Contact Form 7 plugin during the Try It portion of the previous lesson.

2. Search for Contact Form 7.

3. Click Install.

4. In the resulting popup window, click Install Now.

5. On the success page, click Activate.

6. On your side admin menu, click the new Contact link.

7. You'll be taken to the Contact Form 7 screen and there's a default form called Contact Form 1.

8. Scroll down to the Mail area and in the To field you should see the default e-mail address from your WordPress installation. If you want the form to mail to that address, don't do anything, or else enter a new e-mail address.

9. Go back to the top of the screen and just below the title Contact Form 1 you'll see a dark brown bar with some code in it — copy that code.

10. If you don't already have a contact page, create one.

11. In the Text Editor of the contact page, paste the code you copied.

12. Publish or Update the contact page.

13. View the contact page on your site and you should see the form. Fill it out and e-mail yourself a message.

14. If you don't want the form or the plugin, be sure to erase the code from the contact page and then deactivate the plugin.

 To see some of the examples from this lesson, watch the video for Lesson 36 on the enclosed DVD.

37

Ten Other Common Uses
for Plugins

So far in this book, I've talked briefly about plugins that help back up your WordPress site, plugins for photo galleries, plugins for contact forms, and plugins for statistics.

This lesson looks at ten additional plugin categories to help you expand your site and briefly outlines a few specific plugins for each. I include the specific plugin names to make it easier when you're searching on the Plugins ⇨ Add New page.

Social Networking

Connecting WordPress to other social media is one of the hottest areas of plugin development these days and it's hard to keep up with new offerings. In Lesson 24 I talked about how easy it is to display your latest Tweets on your WordPress site and plugins are available that can help make it even easier.

Here, I want to talk about two other functions that plugins can provide with respect to social networking:

❑   Letting visitors easily use social media to let others know about your site

❑   Letting you easily repurpose your WordPress content on your social networking accounts

Visitors can share what they've found on your WordPress site if you install one of several multi-function plugins. Through a single button visitors can share your content by instant message, e-mail, social bookmark, or posting to Facebook or Twitter. Three of the simplest plugins that do this are *Add to Any*, *ShareThis*, and *Add This*. Some plugins target specific social networking tools. Twitter is hot right now and more and more plugins like the *TweetMeme Button* are becoming available. What's nice about this plugin is that it sits at the top of each post encouraging people to Tweet about the post, with a bubble showing how many people have already done that.

The other group of social networking plugins aims to make life easier for website owners who want the same information they just posted to their site to appear on their social networking account. Plugins such as *Twitter Tools* integrate your posts with your Twitter account, and plugins like *Wordbook* do the same for Facebook.

Mobile

Looking good on platforms like iPhone is becoming increasingly important, and there's a growing number of WordPress plugins to make a clean mobile view of your site as painless as possible.

WordPress Mobile Edition is a plugin and a theme — the plugin detects if someone is viewing your site on a mobile device and switches them to the special theme that is designed for mobile viewing. You can update the list of devices detected.

If you need to administer your WordPress site through a mobile device, *WPhone* can help by giving you the choice at login of viewing the admin screens in a special format.

Another group of mobile plugins, such as *WordPress Mobile Pack*, offers a combination of viewer and admin interfaces, plus automated features like cached image scaling, splitting posts into multiple pages, and special widgets aimed at mobile users.

Ad Managers

Ad management plugins for WordPress roughly fall into two categories: those that manage ads delivered through networks and those that manage both network ads and ones from your own advertisers.

If you're only interested in running ads from a single network, such as Google Adsense, then search for plugins using the name of the network. If you wan to run ads from multiple networks, then a plugin like *Advertising Manager* is the way to go. Affiliate marketing also fits into this category as well. If you're an affiliate with, say, Amazon, then do a search on the name to find plugins that help you manage your offerings.

If you're looking to manage both network ads and your own advertisers, plugins are available that help you upload the files, and then keep track of impressions and clickthroughs, such as *Ad-minister* or *Random/Rotating Ads V2*. However, free hosted services like *OpenX.org* also exist. These companies offer powerful ad delivery and tracking functions, and OpenX in particular has a great WordPress integration. All the software and ad delivery is done from its servers so you don't have to bother with the technical end of things.

Search Engine Optimization

In Lessons 30 and 31 I touched briefly on the complex issue of optimizing your website to increase its chances of a high ranking in search engine results. There are many plugins that can help you with this task, and the granddaddy of them all is *All in One SEO Pack* (in fact it's the most downloaded plugin of all).

Among the many features is the ability to not only automatically generate meta tags for individual pages, but to optimize titles automatically. Of course you can override these any time and do your own tweaking.

Some SEO plugins focus on particular tasks, such as *SEO Title Tag*, which let's you create search-engine friendly HTML title tags (your page may be titled About, but the title tag needs more detail). If you want to have easy control over how search engines index your site, *Robots Meta* is a very powerful plugin. If you've just installed WordPress you might consider the *SEO Automatic WP_CORE_TWEAKS* plugin which helps you take care of lots of little things, like switching the default post category from Uncategorized, getting rid of the Hello World post, and other little details.

Podcasting and Videos

If you're going to be working with more than the occasional video on your site, it's well worth installing a plugin to help display and manage them. One of the most powerful for managing videos is *wordTube* because it creates its own library from which you can create various playlists. It also handles audio files and lets you upload your videos as well as pasting URLs from third-party video sites like YouTube. Another very popular plugin that handles both audio and video is *podPress*, although at the time of writing it hadn't been updated in quite some time.

If you want a very simple way to manage links to videos on third-party sites, *Viper's Video Quicktags* is a popular plugin for that. It creates buttons on your Text Editor for a number of popular video sites, such as YouTube and Vimeo, while giving you lots of customization options for the display of the videos.

> *Many video plugins for WordPress rely on the JW Player (www.longtailvideo.com) to display video files. Although this player is available for free, that's only for non-commercial use. If your site is commercial (check the JW Player terms), you'll need to purchase a license. If you have multiple commercial sites, there are generous discounts for multi-site licenses.*

Google Maps

Plenty of plugins are available for putting Google Maps in your posts and pages, but many, such as the popular *XML Google Maps*, require the use of XML or other files to control the look of the map, positioning of markers, and so on — easy if you're the programmer type, not so much for the rest of us. *MapPress Easy Google Maps* makes the creation of maps very simple, yet still offers powerful features. In fact, you can edit maps right in your posts, drag markers wherever you want, control the look of the markers and the popup windows with your HTML editor, add photos to the popups, and much more.

> **Most WordPress mapping plugins are for Google Maps, which means you'll need a Google Maps API Key to run any of them. Not a problem, it's easy to get the key, but as of the writing of this book, you can only use that key on a single domain and you only get one key. Not so bad if you're running a single site, but for everyone else, you'll need to choose wisely before using up your precious key.**

E-commerce

 There are not a lot of choices for WordPress shopping cart or catalog plugins, but fortunately they're good choices *WP e-Commerce* is a very nice plugin and though it isn't free, it's very reasonable, even if you go for the add-on modules (and most people will want to). There's also a very active community of users for this plugin so you can get lots of help there, although the documentation is very good and setup is straightforward.

eShop takes a very different approach to integrating with WordPress. Instead of adding database tables to store catalog data, this plugin utilizes posts and pages for entering product information. It integrates with PayPal and a few other gateways, and it can handle downloadable products.

Of course, so many excellent open source shopping programs are available that it can be difficult to justify all the work needed to create WordPress plugins that will match their power and sophistication. On the other hand, with WordPress becoming more and more of a general content management system, the demand for having a single administration interface and not having to maintain two separate programs may lead to more e-commerce plugins.

Random Content

Displaying random content in the sidebar has long been a mainstay of blogging, so lots of WordPress plugins are available to help you randomize content such as posts, comments, and so on: *Random Posts* or *Random Posts Widget* or *Most Popular Posts*.

Plugins are also available that allow you to add content to your site that's outside of the WordPress post/page structure and randomly display it. Typically these are thought of as random quote generators, but the more sophisticated versions, such as *Stray Random Quotes*, can be used as mini content management systems, because they allow you to categorize content and then have detailed control of its display. So, for example, on the Island Travel site, I could have interesting facts about Aruba as a category, and then display only those facts, at random, on the pages about Aruba.

Comment Enhancement

For blogs in particular, comments are an important part of the interactivity and sense of community that you're trying to create. One of the ways to keep your visitors connected to your site is to use a plugin like *Subscribe to Comments*. This popular plugin allows commenters to receive email notification when a new comment is made about the post. They can unsubscribe from individual posts, update their email address and much more. To make the editing and management of comments easier, a plugin like *WP Ajax Edit Comments* is very helpful. It even allows comments not placed into moderation to be edited by the commenter for a limited time.

Some plugins will display a list of the most recent comments, for example the very popular *Get Recent Comments*, while others, like *Most Commented*, list the top posts based on how many comments they have.

Housekeeping

There are lots of housekeeping issues that can be addressed by plugins. Here are a few of the most important:

Spam

By default, WordPress comes with an anti-spam plugin called *Akismet* for which you'll need an API Key from WordPress.com, as I explained in Lesson 32. It's by far the most popular way of reducing the amount of comment spam, but many other plugins are available as well, such as *Bad Behaviour*, which takes the approach of stopping the spammers before they can leave a comment, by looking at their delivery system and other factors as they try to access your site. *WP-SpamFree Anti-Spam* also operates without an API Key or any sort of CAPTCHA challenges (those deliberately hard to read letters you see all the time). If you do want a visual CAPTCHA system there are lots of plugins to do that, but you're best off with one like *SI CAPTCHA for WordPress*, which includes audio for those who can't easily see the images. Other plugins, like *CryptX*, can be used to hide e-mail addresses in your posts so they can't be harvested by spammers.

Revisions

I mentioned earlier in the book about potential issues with WordPress's revision system — having databases bloated with records for every single revision. Searching on the word "revisions" will produce a long list of plugins to help you deal with this the way you want. Some, like *Revision Control*, allow you to keep revisions but deal with them globally or on a per-post basis, as well as delete specific revisions. Others, like *No Revisions*, simply make it easy to turn off revisions completely (instead of having to mess with the code in your config file).

Security

In addition to having tough passwords, proper file permissions, and updating WordPress and plugins, lots of other little things can add to security. Plugins like *WP Security Scan* or *Secure WordPress* will automatically perform tasks such as: keep tabs on file permissions, database security, hide your WordPress version information, or even place `index.html` files into folders that don't have one.

Try It

My best recommendation for trying something in this lesson is to search the WordPress.org plugins directory and get a feel for the variety of functions they can perform.

 To see a walkthrough of the plugin directory, watch the video for Lesson 37 on the enclosed DVD.

38

Extending WordPress Even Further

The goal of this book was to get you up and running with WordPress and show you how to use the software to build websites. I also introduced you to the possibilities of extending the functionality of WordPress through plugins. Now I want to say a little about the customization of theme templates, which is the next stage for making WordPress serve your needs.

Taking apart the coding of theme templates, reworking them, or creating new templates is not for the faint of heart, and the topic is certainly beyond the scope of this book. My aim is to give you some ideas about what customization can do for you, which, in turn, gives you a good starting point either for learning more yourself or for talking about customization with someone who knows how to work with WordPress themes.

One of the strengths of WordPress is that it's built from the ground up to be customized, and central to this design is the concept of theme templates. They contain the instructions for WordPress to retrieve information from the database — your posts, pages, and media files — and present it in the form of HTML pages. The most basic way that theme templates enable customization is the ability to change the look of your WordPress site in an instant by changing themes, but that's only the tip of the iceberg.

Template Hierarchy

Did you know that WordPress really only needs a single PHP file in a theme? No theme builder would choose that option because it would be both limiting and complicated to code, but because of a concept called *template hierarchy*, WordPress could, if need be, function with just an index.php file (along with a stylesheet).

When WordPress goes looking for instructions on how to assemble a particular HTML page, it has several lists of template files to look for. If it doesn't find one, it looks for the next one on the list, and so on. In the end, if none of the files are on the list, it looks for index.php. If it doesn't find that, then you're in trouble.

The beauty of this design is that in order to take advantage of the hierarchy, you just need to drop a properly named template file into your theme folder and WordPress will automatically start using it instead of the next file down the list. For example, if I want all posts in category 6 to display a certain amount of information with a certain look, I just create a template file called category-6.php and WordPress will follow the instructions in that file whenever it's displaying category 6.

When creating a new page, if you select something other than the default page template, you're making use of the template hierarchy. If you choose the Link template, what you're telling WordPress is to put links.php at the top of its list of template files to look for when displaying that page. Suppose links.php accidentally got erased — no problem, WordPress would simply look for page.php. If that didn't exist, WordPress would look for index.php. Aside from being a tool for customization, the template hierarchy is also a kind of fail-safe system that keeps your site displaying in one form or another.

> Remember that any amount of customization you do to a theme's templates means that you can't simply switch themes without replicating the customizations in the new theme.
>
> If you make a lot of customizations, your best strategy for switching to a new theme is to duplicate your customized theme to a newly named folder and then make changes to the files that control the look of the site. You'll also have to make some changes in the style .css file so that WordPress understands it's a different theme — you can find all the details of creating a new theme at http://codex.wordpress.org/Theme_Development.

The Power of Custom Fields

Now what you do inside template files is up to you and one of the most powerful tools for customizing template files is through the use of *custom fields*. As you may recall from earlier lessons, these are special fields in the WordPress database that you can create yourself by giving them a name (which can be then shared by all other posts or pages) and assigning a value for the particular post.

On the Island Travel site, for example, I could create a set of custom fields for use on destination pages: capital city, population, average hours of sunshine. Then I would code the template used by those pages to look for values in the three fields. If a value is found, the template would print out the information in whatever format I chose, for example, in a box just below the page title.

Custom fields are also great for setting up conditional situations that can actually produce a different layout of information. Suppose on all travel package posts for Island Travel I have a custom field called special-offer. I can code the template so that if the field says Yes, display the information in a certain order with a certain look, but if not, display it the regular way.

Keeping Things User-Friendly and Flexible

Whatever customizations you have done to your theme — by yourself or someone else — always remember to make them user-friendly. That reduces the need for calling someone in again at a later date. That really means thinking ahead when making modifications and asking if they could be used in other contexts, though maybe not right away.

As a result, you might want to make certain elements into variables that are easily controlled by WordPress users, such as through custom fields or even with a custom screen in the admin section. The key is to keep everything as flexible as possible.

For instance, if you create a new page template that's hard-coded in some respect to a particular category, why not make that category a variable that can be changed by the user in the custom fields area. Then the template could be used for a variety of purposes. Or instead of changing the coding in page.php to create a conditional situation, why not create a separate page template that could be used in a variety of situations. Even if you never used it again, the possibility is there and you also didn't need to fiddle with the base page.php file.

Some Final Thoughts

I hope this book has been and will continue to be a valuable resource for you and your WordPress site. My aim has been not simply to show you how to do things, but to explain some of the why's and help you to think about new ways to make your WordPress site work for you.

My clients always get very excited about their websites after I've built them in or converted them over to WordPress. They tell me they feel empowered and, as a result, they're more interested in maintaining and expanding their sites, which is exactly what a content management system ought to do.

So have fun with your new website and don't forget about the tremendous community of WordPress users out there. You'll never want for inspiration or help, and hopefully you can do the same for others as your experience grows.

Troubleshooting WordPress

I've tried throughout the book to include small troubleshooting tips with the lesson to which they relate. In this lesson the goal is help you think through the troubleshooting process.

Consider the variables involved in viewing a web page: what computer you're using, what web browser and what version, what Internet service provider you're using, what type of server the website is on, what version of WordPress you're running, what versions are being run for the dozens of software packages required to run a web server, and so on. No wonder then, that you might have a problem and virtually no one else has exactly the same one.

Addressing particular problems is next to impossible in a few pages, but what I can do is offer some strategies for trying to solve problems, as well as provide some ideas for getting more information online.

Troubleshooting an Installation

Although WordPress installations are straightforward, sometimes there are issues. Here are some suggestions for a few of the most common.

1. **Error connecting to the database**: Check that you correctly entered the database name, username, and password, and that you don't have any stray spaces before or after each variable (that can happen in particular when you're copying and pasting). Re-enter the information and try again.

2. **"Headers already sent" error messages:** This is usually caused by the presence of characters or whitespace before a file's opening `<?php` tag or after the closing `?>` tag. You can tell which file is causing the problem by looking for the part of the error message that begins `(output started at /path/` and the php file at the end of that path is the culprit.

It will also tell you the line number where the problem is occurring. Using a text editor — not Word or any word processor — check that there's nothing before the opening `<?php` tag or after the closing `?>` tag. Delete any characters or spaces, save the file, and upload again.

3. **500 Internal Server Error**: If you have access to your server logs (through hosting control panels like cPanel or Parallels for example) you should check there for specific information on the cause of the error. It may be a problem with an .htaccess file or from files not having the right permissions, but you really need the log report to point you in the right direction. If you don't have access to the log files you'll need to contact your hosting company.

Troubleshooting After Installation

Once WordPress is up and running, potential problems can be divided into three general categories:

❑ The entire site is down

❑ A particular function (usually a plugin) stops working

❑ Specific content is not appearing

Each category would lead you to look in a very different place for answers. If the site is down completely, there will often be an error message to guide you: no database connection, internal server error, and so on. If a plugin is not working, the answer is likely to do with the set of plugins you have activated (I give some hints about troubleshooting plugins in Lesson 35).

Whatever category of problem you're having, it's usually helpful to remember or find out if anything has changed recently:

❑ You added a new plugin

❑ You made some change in the admin settings

❑ You just upgraded WordPress or there was an upgrade and you haven't done it yet

❑ There was some problem or change with your hosting provider (it may have upgraded its version of PHP, for example)

Armed with this kind of information, you can narrow down the problem and get closer to an answer.

> One way to tell if there's been some web-wide problem is to check the WordPress forums and see if others have suddenly started reporting a similar issue.

If specific content is not appearing on your site, check that you properly saved the material or that you haven't deleted a category (in which case all posts from the category will have been moved automatically to the default category). It could be that you accidentally unpublished the item. Remember, unless you physically delete something from WordPress, it will still be in the system, even if it doesn't show on the live site.

Finding Help Online

Because problems with WordPress are often very specific to your particular circumstances, searching online for someone who's had the same problem is going to be your best bet. Fortunately, there's a huge community of WordPress users who share their experiences in a variety of ways, and here are some suggestions for finding them.

The WordPress.org Site

The number one place to start is the Forum section of the WordPress.org website. You'll find a wealth of information about real-world applications of WordPress and helpful solutions, as well as ideas on making WordPress do exactly what you need it to do. I know I've found a lot of inspiration there for customizations I'd never thought of. Although you don't need to register to use the forum, it's well worth it so that you can post problems for which you haven't found a solution.

> When you think you haven't found an answer to your problem, your first action should be: *search again*. If you still haven't found the answer, *search again*! Of course I mean use different wording for each search, follow suggested threads in the results you do find, and try to approach the search from different angles. *Be a detective*. You'll save yourself (and other people in the forum) a lot of time and trouble, and you won't clog the forum with repeat questions.
>
> I would almost guarantee that your problem has at least been voiced by someone, even if it hasn't been resolved, and you're better off joining that thread than starting a new one.

On the WordPress.org site you'll also find a very helpful set of frequently asked questions: `http://codex.wordpress.org/FAQ` as well as whole page of tips on how to find help: `http://codex.wordpress.org/Finding_WordPress_Help`.

Using Search Engines

When it comes to searching for help online the best tip is to be as specific as you can in your search terms. Simply typing *website is broken* or *page crashes* is far too general, but even if you type *menu not showing properly* that's still less specific than *the sidebar menu is not showing all my categories*. Once you're more specific, be sure to try other wording as well, such as *displaying* instead of *showing* — not everyone uses the same terminology.

Another aspect of being specific is to remember to narrow the search to your specific software. If the issue is with WordPress, be sure to include *+wordpress* (you may have to use Advanced Search to force a term to be in the search) along with whatever other terms you're searching for. Or if it's a problem with PHP, use *+php* to make sure you're focused on the right scripting language.

It's also important to put quotes around phrases: *sidebar widget* is a very different search from *"sidebar widget"* because the first will look for each word separately, whereas the second tells the search engine to find them together as a phrase.

If you're getting an error message, enclose the entire message (or if it's very long, choose what looks like the most relevant part) in quotation marks and do your search on that. Including your operating system in the search, along with your browser, can also get you to your answer faster.

Finding Professional Help

If you can't find an answer online or the answer is difficult to implement, it may be time to hire someone to troubleshoot for you. You can search for phrases like *wordpress expert*. You can also post your needs on sites like WordPress Jobs (`http://jobs.wordpress.net`) or on the WP-Pro mailing list (`http://lists.automattic.com/mailman/listinfo/wp-pro`).

B

Glossary

Activate a plugin   The next step after installing a plugin. WordPress displays a list of plugins you've installed, but you need to activate them before they function on your site. You can de-activate a plugin but that still leaves it installed.

Administrator   The highest level of WordPress users. Administrators have full access to all administrative functions, as opposed to, say, Editors, who cannot change the theme of a site or do anything with plugins.

Attachment   Any file that has been uploaded to a post or page and as a result is listed in the gallery for that post or page. Though the file can be used anywhere on the site, that uploading process created a unique relationship to the post or page and in that sense the file has been attached to it.

Avatar   A small graphic or image used in WordPress comments to represent the person making the comment.

Backup   Saving and storing a copy of any information. Backing up WordPress is a two-step process: backing up the database, and backing up the theme and uploaded files.

Blogroll   A list of links. The name comes from that fact that it was originally intended to display favorite blogs or other sites you regularly visit.

Bookmarklet   A button on a browser's bookmark bar that allows the user to perform a function quickly and easily. WordPress has a Press It bookmarklet that allows users to instantly blog about something they're viewing in their browser.

Capability   A task that a user is able to perform in the WordPress administrative area. Different users have varying degrees of capabilities, with administrators having all capabilities.

Category   Categories are used to group related content. WordPress has two types of categories: post categories and link categories. Pages cannot be categorized.

Class   An attribute in HTML that allows a CSS style to be applied to any part of a web page that has that class. Example: `<p class="importantparagraph">`.

CMS Content Management System. A CMS is software that allows users to easily store, organize, and update information, usually for display on the Web.

Comments Responses to your content that are submitted using a form and, if approved, are displayed for other visitors to read. You can choose whether to allow the comment form to appear on all, some, or none of your WordPress content.

cPanel A popular online tool that allows people to easily manage their web-hosting accounts (adding e-mail accounts, setting up databases, and so on).

CSS Cascading Style Sheets. A style sheet language used to control the look, formatting, and layout of a web page written in HTML. The cascading part refers to the ways in which style rules get applied.

Dashboard The homepage of the WordPress administrative interface.

Database Software that stores data in various types and enables relationships to be established between the data. WordPress uses a MySQL database.

Deprecated Functions or template tags in WordPress that are no longer supported and eventually will be obsolete.

Draft A post or page that has been saved but not yet published; also the state of a previously published page that has been unpublished.

Excerpt A short summary of a post that is entered separately in the excerpt field or is auto-generated using the first 55 words of the post.

Feed A data format used to provide users with frequently updated content. WordPress creates many different feeds of your site's content in a variety of feed types, such as RSS.

FTP File Transfer Protocol. An FTP program is used to transfer files back and forth to your server.

Gallery A list of all files associated with a particular post or page. Also, a display within the body of a post or page showing thumbnails of all image files belonging to a post or page.

Hosting Provider Anyone who runs a server connected to the Internet and provides accounts for people to run their websites and/or e-mail.

HTML Hypertext Markup Language. This is the basic language used to generate pages on the Internet. For example:

```
<p><em>Emphasized text</em> has certain tags around it, while all the text in this
paragraph is surrounded by the opening and closing paragraph tags</p>
```

ID An attribute in HTML that allows a CSS style to be applied to a unique area on a web page. In other words, an id name can only be used once per page. Example: `<p id="best paragraph">`.

Install a plugin In order to use plugins—add-on software that extends the functions of WordPress—you must first install them, which means that the file or files for the plugin have been uploaded to a special plugins folder on the server, using either a file transfer program (FTP) or the automated install process in WordPress.

JavaScript   One of the most popular client-side scripting languages for use on web pages. Client-side means that it runs in the visitor's browser, which allows JavaScript to react to clicks, mouse movements, and so on, producing effects such as menus changing color when you place your mouse over them. Not to be confused with the programming language Java.

The Loop   A section of WordPress template files that automatically runs through all possible pieces of content that meet a certain criteria and displays them according to the coding for that loop. For example, WordPress might loop through all posts in Category 6 and display the date, title, and body of each.

Meta   Typically used when talking about meta tags, which provide information about a web page, particularly to search engines, such as a description or a list of keywords relating to the page. In WordPress, the term is also used in relation to posts—post metadata—for such information as the date, categories, tags, and other details about the post.

MySQL   One of the most popular open-source databases. SQL stands for Structured Query Language. MySQL is the database used by WordPress.

Page   A WordPress page is often said to be for "static" content. This is meant to be a contrast with posts, which typically are organized by date and time. The history of a company would be material for a page, while a press release would be material for a post. WordPress pages can be organized into hierarchies of parent and child pages, but unlike posts cannot be categorized or tagged.

Permalink   This is short for "permanent link." The idea of a permanent link is to provide a way for others on the Internet to always find a page on your website, even if you change something that could affect that link, such as a post title.

Permissions   Attributes of a file or directory (folder) on a web server that determine what action a particular user may take with respect to that file or directory (reading, writing, or executing the content).

PHP   This scripting language is one of the most widely used for generating dynamic content on web pages. PHP is a server-side language, which means that it works before reaching the user's browser, as opposed to a language like JavaScript, which functions in the browser. WordPress is written using PHP. Virtually all hosting providers offer PHP, whether on a Windows, Unix/Linux, or Mac platform.

phpMyAdmin   A popular open-source interface for managing MySQL databases.

Pingback   One type of notification you receive in WordPress to tell you that someone has linked to content on your site. For this to happen, your site must be pingback-enabled, which is set in the admin section.

Plesk/Parallels   A popular online tool that makes it easy for people to manage their web hosting accounts (creating e-mail accounts, setting up databases, and so on).

Plugin   A file or set of files that provide additional functionality for WordPress, such as suggesting related content to visitors or displaying maps. Plugins must first be installed in WordPress and in order to work, must be activated.

Post   A type of content in WordPress that can be categorized. The order of displaying posts in a category can be controlled according to several parameters such as date published, title, and so on.

Post Status   Tells you whether a post or page is published, unpublished, in draft mode, or pending review.

Publish   Publishing a post or a page tells WordPress to display it on your site. You can always save them as drafts until you're ready to publish. You can also tell WordPress to automatically publish posts or pages in the future.

RSS   Really Simple Syndication. This is a type of feed format (see Feed).

Scheduling   By default, publishing a post or page in WordPress — making it live on your site — happens immediately, but you can also schedule them to publish at a future date and time.

Sidebar   The area of a website on the left or ride side of the page, where items such as navigation, advertising, and small chunks of content are displayed.

Slug   A word or series of words in lower-case lettering and containing no spaces. There are slugs for posts, pages, categories, tags, and authors, and they're used by WordPress to make URLs more descriptive.

Style Sheet   A file that contains the CSS used to create the look, formatting, and layout of a web page.

Tag   A keyword you assign to posts and which can be shared by other posts. Posts can have multiple tags. Tags are much like categories, but are not meant to be as broad in scope as categories.

Teaser   The portion of a post prior to the point where you've added a More tag to the post.

Template   A file in WordPress themes that provides instructions for assembling HTML pages. Templates may use other templates in the assembly process.

Text Editor   In WordPress this refers to the field on post or page editing screens where the content is edited. Also refers to a program on your computer that you should always use when editing WordPress theme files. Text editors (sometimes called plain text editors) do not introduce the extra information that word processors use, and which can cause problems for files on the Internet.

Theme   The set of files that controls the layout, look, and certain aspects of the content on the HTML pages generated by WordPress. A theme consists of at least one style sheet and at least one template file.

Trackback   One type of notification you receive in WordPress to tell you that someone has linked to content on your site.

Update   To replace the current version of WordPress, a plugin, or a theme, with a newer one.

Update (button)   When you see this word on a button, it means you must click it in order to save any changes you've made. It's very important to get in the habit of clicking this before you leave a screen, even if you don't remember changing anything.

URL or URI   Uniform Resource Locator or Uniform Resource Identifier. Although a URL is a subtype of URIs, the two are commonly treated as the same. A URI is any string of characters that identifies a resource on the Internet, but is most commonly used to refer to the address of a website or web page, such as www.wordpress.org.

User   Someone who is a registered user on a WordPress site. There are five levels of users with varying degrees of capabilities: Administrator, Editor, Author, Contributor, and Subscriber.

Widget   A piece of code that allows you to place chunks of content (for example, a list of categories, recent posts) on your website (typically in the sidebar) using a drag-and-drop interface.

WYSIWYG   Stands for What You See Is What You Get. In the WordPress Text Editor, there is a Visual mode, which displays posts in a partly WYSIWYG format (to see them exactly as they will appear on the web, you need to use Preview), as opposed to HTML mode, which displays the post with all the code used by the browser to display it.

C

What's on the DVD?

You've read about how WordPress can make creating and maintaining a website much easier — time to see it in action. I love working with my clients online or in person to help train them in the use of WordPress, and that's how I've approached this DVD: to be your virtual coach. So let's get started.

This appendix provides you with information on the contents of the DVD that accompanies this book. For the most up-to-date information, please refer to the ReadMe file located at the root of the DVD. Here is what you will find in this appendix:

- ❑ System Requirements
- ❑ Using the DVD
- ❑ What's on the DVD
- ❑ Troubleshooting

System Requirements

Make sure that your computer meets the minimum system requirements listed in this section. If your computer doesn't match up to most of these requirements, you may have a problem using the contents of the DVD.

- ❑ PC running Windows XP or later, or Mac running OSX
- ❑ A DVD-ROM drive
- ❑ Adobe Flash Player 9 or later (free download from Adobe.com)

Helpful, but not absolutely necessary:

- ❏　Internet connection
- ❏　Installed version of WordPress (or a blog with WordPress.com)

Using the DVD on a PC

To access the content from the DVD, follow these steps.

1.　Insert the DVD into your computer's DVD-ROM drive. The license agreement appears

The interface won't launch if you have autorun disabled. In that case, click Start ⇨ Run (For Windows Vista, Start ⇨ All Programs ⇨ Accessories ⇨ Run). In the dialog box that appears, type D:\Start.exe. (Replace D with the proper letter if your DVD drive uses a different letter. If you don't know the letter, see how your CD drive is listed under My Computer.) Click OK.

2.　Read through the license agreement, and then click the Accept button if you want to use the DVD.

The DVD interface appears. Simply select the lesson video you want to view.

Using the DVD on a Mac

To install the items from the DVD to your hard drive, follow these steps:

1.　Insert the DVD into your computer's DVD-ROM drive.

2.　The DVD icon will appear on your desktop; double-click to open.

3.　Double-click the Start button.

4.　Read the license agreement and click the Accept button to use the DVD.

5.　The DVD interface will appear. Here you can install the programs and run the demos.

What's on the DVD

Nothing beats watching how something is done and that's why I've provided several hours worth of video about how you can use WordPress. Most lessons in the book have an accompanying video, which not only illustrates several of the examples in the lesson, but goes well beyond what can be covered in print. You'll also gain more insight into the creation of the sample website discussed in the book: Island Travel.

If you have an existing WordPress site — a self-hosted version or a blog on WordPress.com — I encourage you to work along in the admin screen. If you don't have a site, you could install WordPress if you have a web hosting account (see Lesson 3) or you could open an account with WordPress.com. The main thing is that you be able to practice what's covered in the book and on these videos.

Troubleshooting

If you have difficulty installing or using any of the materials on the companion DVD, try the following solutions:

- ❑ **Turn off any anti-virus software that you may have running:** Installers sometimes mimic virus activity and can make your computer incorrectly believe that it is being infected by a virus. (Be sure to turn the anti-virus software back on later.)

- ❑ **Close all running programs:** The more programs you're running, the less memory is available to other programs. Installers also typically update files and programs; if you keep other programs running, installation may not work properly.

- ❑ **Reference the ReadMe:** Please refer to the ReadMe file located at the root of the DVD-ROM for the latest product information at the time of publication.

- ❑ **Reboot if necessary:** If all else fails, rebooting your machine can often clear any conflicts in the system.

Customer Care

If you have trouble with the DVD-ROM, please call the Wiley Product Technical Support phone number at (800) 762-2974. Outside the United States, call 1(317) 572-3994. You can also contact Wiley Product Technical Support at `http://support.wiley.com`. John Wiley & Sons will provide technical support only for installation and other general quality control items. For technical support on the applications themselves, consult the program's vendor or author.

To place additional orders or to request information about other Wiley products, please call (877) 762-2974.

Index